ANNUAL REPORT

OF THE

PRESIDENT

OF THE

Maryland Historical Society,

AND OF ITS

COMMITTEE ON THE GALLERY OF FINE ARTS.

1850.

BALTIMORE:
PRINTED BY JOHN D. TOY,
Corner of Market and St. Paul-sts.

List of Officers.

President.

J. SPEAR SMITH.

Vice-President.

JOHN P. KENNEDY.

Corresponding Secretary.

J. MORRISON HARRIS.

Recording Secretary.

S. F. STREETER.

Treasurer.

JOHN HANAN.

Librarian.

J. LOUIS SMITH.

Assistant Librarian.

F. B. MAYER.

Library Committee.

BRANTZ MAYER, GEORGE WM. BROWN, M. COURTNEY JENKINS.

Committee on the Gallery.

J. H. B. LATROBE, B. C. WARD, DR. THOMAS EDMONDSON.

Council of Government of Athenæum.

ROBERT LESLIE, JOHN BARNEY.

Trustees of Athenæum.

O. C. TIFFANY, SAMUEL W. SMITH, JOHNS HOPKINS.

Committee on Honorary Membership.

WILLIAM A. TALBOTT, JOHN I. DONALDSON, ALEXANDER FISHER.

REPORT OF THE PRESIDENT

OF THE

MARYLAND HISTORICAL SOCIETY,

AT THE

ANNUAL MEETING IN FEBRUARY, 1850.

GENTLEMEN:

SINCE the last Annual Report, considerable additions have been made to the books, maps, pamphlets and public documents of the Society. These acquisitions are fully equal to those of any preceding year, except perhaps the first, after our organization. They nearly all comport with the purposes of the institution, being of strictly historical character, or connected with the geography, statistics and proceedings of the Federal or State Governments. The Societies with which we are in correspondence have shown a gratifying attention, in regularly transmitting to us their various publications. Nor have we failed to communicate to them such essays as we have from time to time, had printed. Our representatives in Congress and in the General Assembly have, with commendable zeal, favored us with such of the State papers, surveys and maps, as it is so desirable for us to possess. To them, and to the individuals who have so generously recognised our claims, and honored us with many valuable donations during the year, our acknowledgments are eminently due.

The papers read before the Society since our last anniversary, though fewer in number than was hoped for, were in every way, creditable to the institution. The first of these, was an impressive paper, read by Dr. J. R. W. DUNBAR, a member of the Society, on the importance of an intimate and thorough acquaintance with the physiological laws, governing the human system. In this very instructive discourse, the influences and effects of a healthful or morbid condition of individuals, on their acts, were ably enforced, by various apt historical illustrations.

We are indebted to the Corresponding Secretary, J. M. Harris, Esq., for a sketch of the history and resources of California. In this eloquent composition we are presented with a graphic delineation of the topography and boundless riches of this new and vast addition to the territory of the Republic.

The very able annual address on "American Colonial History," by our associate, Thomas Donaldson, Esq., is admirably suited to guide the inquirer in the investigation of those salient points which mark our career as a nation. Nor can we fail to unite with him in his earnest appeal for a thorough instruction of our youth, in the history of America, as well as in that of Greece and Rome. No country, ancient or modern, can unfold such stainless pages of its annals as the States composing this Confederation. Indeed, if we impartially collate them with the records of other nations, we find that whilst the former are beaming with morality, humanity, and all the enjoyments of liberty, the latter are darkened by vice, cruelty, and the sufferings incident to arbitrary rule.

The deeply interesting and beautiful essay of the Recording Secretary, S. F. Streeter, Esq., on the fall of the Susquehanock Indians, was of a class of papers peculiarly adapted to the designs of the Society. The aboriginal inhabitants of this great continent are fast yielding to the more powerful race, now peopling their ancient domain. The time indeed, is not distant when few will remain to instruct us in their customs, arts and polity. The greater then the necessity for now rescuing from oblivion every memorial of a people so soon to be extinguished, or blended with those who are so superior to them in numbers if not in intellectual endowment. It is gratifying, then, to be able to inform you that the attention of Mr. Streeter is drawn to the history of the Maryland Indians, and we may entertain the hope of being favored, at no late day, with the results of his investigations.

I would again most earnestly invite you to the preparation of essays on topics appropriate to the intents of the Society, and tending to enlarge the scope of its benefits. Such productions are due not only to its own fame, but to a community from which it has received much respect and enduring patronage. You will readily concede that they enhance to a degree, which all must have appreciated, the charm and interest of our monthly meetings. The utility of such papers no one can doubt, even if there be no claim on the leisure and talent of those members who can, without much inconvenience, devote a few brief hours to so meritorious a task.

Whilst on this important matter, I will, with your indulgence, suggest a few themes which would very properly come within the range of our pursuits. Among them might be a memoir on the Benevolent Institutions of the State. This is especially an Anglo-Saxon province, for, of all the races of man, no other has done so much, or is nowdoing so much as is this, towards ameliorating the condition of his fellows.—Another topic, and a truly acceptable one, at this period, would be an historical sketch of the Colleges, Academies and Common Schools of Maryland. And here, as on the other subjects, the writer will find very useful materials among our collections. Our financial history is not only of great interest, but is signalized by many curious and remarkable incidents. The same may be said of our great works of internal improvement, which indeed, may justly be termed gigantic, when we compare our boundaries and population with those of most of our sister States. To discourses on these heads might well be added a treatise on the rich mineral resources of the State, with many others which will readily occur to you. I propose, myself, to deposite among the collection of the Society, during the year, the original records and correspondence relating to the defence of Baltimore in the war of 1812, with a brief memoir of that event.

The second Exhibition of Paintings in our Gallery has proved in no respect inferior to the first. It has, at the same time, been hailed with equal public approbation. Indeed, in such favor are they held that the probability is that a continuance of them, for many years in advance, will not only be successful, but will be demanded by the general sentiment. The net proceeds being specifically devoted to the purchase of paintings, by the best masters, will, in time, form a collection which, whilst it graces the city, will be honorable to this institution. The realization of this desirable result, has already begun, and it is nearly certain that in the next exhibition there will be several fine paintings, purchased by your committee and belonging to the Society. Thus will the redemption of our pledge to the community have made its first step towards the design, so early entertained, and so repeatedly announced. These annual exhibitions have already led to a closer study of the fine arts, and have attracted to them a more vivid attention than seems to have previously existed. This is as general as it is active, and will be promotive of an improvement in taste, and of a refined and disciplined judgment. Whilst American genius is taking the highest rank, whether in painting or sculpture, among the artists of Europe, it is but right that a just discrimination here should enable us to award that meed to which exalted merit is so richly entitled, and which it may so fairly claim. The task of the Committee on the Gallery is no enviable one. It is attended with infinite labor, as well in the preparation as in the management of the exhibitions. Yet, I am happy to add that all the various duties have been cheerfully discharged, and with exemplary patience and assiduity. To the gentlemen of that committee the thanks of the Sociey are largely due, for the taste they have shown in the selection of pictures, their skilful arrangement of them, and the signal success which has crowned their labors.

All the stipulations contained in the programme of 1845, for building an Athenæum, have been faithfully executed. In that address, we solicited "a free gift," in remuneration of which generous aid no return was proffered, other than "the genial influences over the public mind" of the institutions for which it was designed. The free gift was conferred in the disinterested spirit in which it was asked, and we must hope that the genial influences will, with each returning year, be more and more sensibly felt. The Athenæum was to be unincumbered by debt, and was to accommodate the Library Company, the Mercantile Library Association, and this Society. These promises have been fulfilled, and the three institutions are now enjoying every convenience, requisite to their safety and comfort. A Reading Room and a Gallery of Fine Arts were to form essential features in the comprehensive projet, and both are now in a state of auspicious advancement. I think, then, I may now say that the Athenæum has accomplished the very purposes to which it was destined, and that all the pledges on which the enterprise was based, have been faithfully redeemed. It stands the third, in the list of noble monuments, which adorn our city. Grateful to our own feelings and tastes, and admired by strangers, it affords an agreeable resort to both. No one who visits Baltimore and has leisure to view her many attractions, but comes here to enjoy the architectural symmetry of the edifice, its appropriate furnishing, and the varied means it contains for intellectual occupation and improvement. I believe, then, it is not too much to say, that its generous founders have been amply rewarded, for this munificent act of an exalted public spirit. The Societies, too, through whose instrumentality their bounty has been so well applied, may at the close of each year of their labors exchange congratulations on the good thus far achieved, and excite each other to continued exertions in their respective spheres.

7th February, 1850.

EXTRACTS FROM THE

FIRST ANNUAL REPORT

OF THE

COMMITTEE ON THE GALLERY,

READ TO THE SOCIETY, 1849.

THE undersigned, committee on the Gallery, have, as the Society are aware, reported, verbally, at each stated meeting, in regard to the matters with which they are charged; and, at the last meeting of the Society, announced the close of the first Annual Exhibition in the Gallery,—the return of the pictures to their respective owners,—and the general pecuniary results. [The committee now present to the Society as a part of this report, the accompanying statement—showing in detail, the monies that have been received and disbursed by them.]

It is proper to say here, that the committee, in what may be called, the getting up of the Exhibition, determined in the outset, that, inasmuch as one of the objects to be accomplished, was the improvement of the taste of the public in regard to Art, as well as the occupation and amusement of its idle hours,—they would admit no picture into the Exhibition, merely because it was a painted canvass properly framed; but would require, at least *some* merit, as a passport to the Gallery, in all the works of Art that were presented. The enforcement of this rule was not always an agreeable task: but the result of it was, that few, if any, Exhibitions ever held in our country, have surpassed in general value and excellence, that which has just been closed. The committee mention this now, particularly, in the hope, that the importance of the rule may be properly appreciated by the Society, and that its existence may become generally known. If it is adhered to, the result may be, that a place on the walls of the Gallery may become an object to be sought with eagerness by the artists of our country; and art may grow to be estimated in our community by a gradually improving standard, and appreciated by a more and more refined and exacting taste.

The mere opening of the Gallery for the Exhibition of every thing that might be offered, would, in the opinion of the committee, defeat the object of the Society, tend to deteriorate, rather than improve the public judgment in regard to works of art, and reduce the Society's rooms to the level of the auction mart, and its committee to the grade of salesmen. Unless the Annual Exhibitions can be kept up by good pictures, the committee trust they may be abandoned. That they can thus be kept up, however, the committee have much reason to believe. The stock of good pictures in Baltimore, is very far from being exhausted, and several years' supplies may be drawn at increased, but still justifiable, expense, from other cities. Perhaps, in this way, the Annual Exhibitions may be kept up, until their receipts shall have given to the Society the means of collecting a gallery of their own.

The committee are glad to believe, that the disposition made by them of the pictures on the walls, known generally as "the hanging," was in nearly all instances, satisfactory to the parties interested. In this, they were aided by the admirable construction of the Gallery, in every part of which there was sufficient light, even on the gloomiest days of the fall: and the committee are especially called upon to acknowledge the kindness and good humor, with which the owners of pictures submitted to a judgment, which had necessarily to be despotic in its character, in this particular. The labors of the committee, which otherwise would have been uncomfortable, were made in this way, most agreeable and satisfactory to themselves. The committee mention this particularly, because, this being the first Exhibition of the kind in Baltimore, it would not have been surprising, had the result been different.

The committee might here close their report, did they not deem it proper to place upon paper, the suggestions made by them, verbally, to the Society at its last meeting, in regard to the manner in which the nett proceeds of the Exhibition just closed, as well as of future Exhibitions would be appropriated, were the matter left in the hands of the committee.

The subject was one, on which differences of opinion might fairly exist, and which was not without its difficulties. The committee finally determined, however, that the best appropriation, which could be made of the funds, would be to obtain a good copy of the best work of each of the great masters, so that the Gallery of the Historical Society, should ultimately present to the eye, a history of painting, while the shelves of its library contained the written history of past and passing events. True, after all, it will be but a gallery of copies, that will have been collected; and there may be some, who may think, that copies must necessarily be valueless, because they are not originals. But a gallery of the originals of the pictures referred to, is now among the impossibilities of the world : and when it is recollected how artists, even, quarrel upon the point of originality, it may be admitted, that a gallery of copies may be most valuable and instructive. Nine out of ten of those who are attracted to an Exhibition, perhaps ninety-nine out of an hundred, would not be able to distinguish a good copy from the original, if they hung in adjoining rooms: and as the merit of the copies would be an especial object with the committee, all the purposes of a gallery of originals would be practically attained, so far as the public generally was concerned. Copies are perfectly competent to give to the observer, the style of drawing, composition and coloring of an artist. What there is the greatest danger of their failing in, is the expression of the picture. Yet this is very often obtained to the extent almost of perfect deception. But even if it is lost by the copyist, it is something, nay, it is a great deal, to be acquainted with three of the items going to produce the characteristic excellence of the master; and we may well be satisfied with these when it is impracticable to obtain the whole of his merits combined. It will be pleasant for all to be able, when they read of Titian, or Raphael, or Guercino, to see what may be considered as a fair representation of their works in the Gallery of the Athenæum. The Gallery will have an attraction in this respect, when the collection shall be completed, which will be peculiar. The committee are not aware that a similar design has elsewhere been carried out; not because it is not a good design, as they believe, but because of the natural grasping at originals, and the willingness of all connoisseurs to be imposed upon by the countless getters up of originals to be found all over Europe, and to some extent, and latterly, in this country also.

The committee, besides the reasons here given, have others, and more practical ones, perhaps, for the course they have determined on. The experience of the late Exhibition shewed the importance of the class of pictures, termed gallery pictures;—that is pictures of large size and striking subjects, that could, without detriment, be placed high on the walls, leaving room for cabinet pictures below them. The copies to be obtained by the committee would embrace such pictures as were thus found to be wanting:—and the committee take leave to assure the Society, that without such pictures, Annual Exhibitions will be impracticable. This reason for their plan, the committee beg it to be understood, is offered rather to reconcile any who may desire other appropriations of the proceeds of the Exhibitions, than because the committee themselves rely on it, or deem it worthy of art. Still it shews that what is in itself right operates in this, as in most other cases, usefully and profitably in more ways than one.

It only remains to add, in this connection, that should the Society's pictures ever cover the walls of the gallery, they could be removed to make room for others at the Annual Exhibitions.

The committee would not have it understood that they intend to be exclusive in the appropriation of the funds, at their control, to the end in view. They speak only of a general design—a plan, which must yield, when proper, to circumstances. It is no part of it to reject all modern pictures:—to make no purchases from living artists. When it will be proper to do this, the occasion will speak for itself, and the committee will hold themselves at liberty to avail of it.

The mode which the committee propose to pursue in obtaining copies is to fix, in the first place, upon the picture they desire to have copied, and then to ascertain, by correspondence, the terms on which a copy can be procured. There is a fellowship in art, all over the world, which will facilitate the enquiries of the committee; and art is so gracious in itself, and all its influences, that those even to whom nature has given no peculiar susceptibility to it, are ever found ready to contribute to its advancement. If any thing was necessary to prove this, reference need only be made to the sixteen thousand subscribers to the American Art Union of New York.

There remains yet a matter which the committee think it proper to mention in their report, with a view of ascertaining the wishes of the Society in regard to it. It is the disposition of the rooms of the Gallery in the intervals between the Annual Exhibitions—whether they are to remain in charge of the committee, or revert, at once, as soon as the Exhibition closes, to the general purposes of the Historical Society.

The Society are aware that there are already several pictures which have been deposited with the Society, and which may, perhaps, remain permanently upon the walls; and the committee have reason to believe that others will be, from time to time, loaned in this manner to the

Gallery. The experience of other places shews, that a gradual accumulation may possibly take place, in this way, in Baltimore. Again, there are many purposes connected with art, which it may be difficult to particularize in anticipation, that may make the rooms of the Gallery most useful.

Under these circumstances, the committee have thought that the control of the rooms should belong to them, if it was expected by the Society, that they should, in the intervals between the Exhibitions, exercise any functions in regard to art, or make any preparations either for a permanent gallery, or a new Exhibition. The matter is suggested now, that the action of the Society may be had in regard to it. If the control is given to the committee, it is proper to say, that the rooms will be limited to the Society's uses;—and not hired or rented for what, in theatrical language, may be called occasional performances, to strangers. The building is the free gift of the people of Baltimore. It is not necessary that it should be rented to pay tax or fee of any kind; and the committee would regret to see it placed on a footing with other rooms of the City, where dances and sermons and shows are made to alternate, with a view to pecuniary profit. It will be the desire of the committee to make the room attractive, as a gallery of paintings and statues, as soon as practicable; and to have it opened to the Society whenever a collection or a picture of interest shall be placed there.

Another view of this part of the subject of their report has been mentioned to the committee by members of the Society, which they deem it proper to repeat here, and which is certainly not without its force in connection with the proposal to place the rooms of the Gallery exclusively in charge of the committee.

The functions of the Society, in regard to art, are, as it may be said, rather accidental than otherwise: and it is desirable that the Gallery should be kept in its subordinate relations: that it should not swallow up the Historical Society: that the interest of it should not detract from the interest of the Library: that the members of the Society should not be drawn from their seats, at the stated meetings, to lounge among the pictures of the adjacent room. Say what we will, it is pleasant to look at the works of art, even when the memories of the past are calling us away from them, as eloquence and research offer them for our consideration:—and there is, at all events, some little danger that, if not guarded against, the Historical Society may be swallowed up in the Gallery, if one suite of rooms, in constant and free connection, receive the members,—who may, naturally enough, attend, under such circumstances, quite as much to see "how the pictures come on," as to hear addresses or essays, or enter into historical disquisitions.

Should this be so, the Gallery will have been a misfortune;—and the founders of the Society will have reason to regret its existence. Such a result, the committee think, can best be averted by keeping the Gallery in its subordinate position,—looking upon it as wholly collateral; placing it in the hands, exclusively, of a committee, the creation of the Society,—and keeping in view, prominently, the fact that the Historical Society belongs to the class of those institutions, whose noble usefulness has been illustrated by the labors of Gallatin, Prescott, Bancroft, Wheaton and others, of the distinguished men of our country.

Respectfully submitted,

JOHN H. B. LATROBE,
B. C. WARD,
WILLIAM McKIM, } *Committee.*

SECOND GENERAL REPORT

OF THE

COMMITTEE ON THE GALLERY.

The verbal reports made to the Society at its stated meetings, have kept it informed of the proceedings of the committee. They now present herewith, an account in detail of the receipts and expenses of the second Annual Exhibition of paintings, which closed on the 1st of December last; and they propose to state what they have done and propose to do, in carrying out the plan set forth in their first general report, and which then received the sanction of the Society.

Before entering on this, however, it may be proper for the committee to state, that the anticipations of their first report were more than realized in the late Exhibition. There were but few of the pictures of the previous year upon the walls; and these few were pictures of value, which had been cleaned and repaired in the interval, and thus were made equivalent to novelties. As a whole, the committee are of opinion that the second Exhibition was, to say the very least of it, equal to the first. In some respects it was superior. The average of merit, within certain degrees, was higher:—and although some striking pictures were missed, yet their places were very fairly supplied, and the general impression was independent of them. The committee adhered to the rule of excluding all pictures which had not *some* merit to entitle them to a place in the Gallery. And they are confirmed in the opinion, formerly expressed, that this is the only mode by which art can be fostered, the public taste improved, and the succeeding Exhibitions made at all times attractive.

The committee are of opinion that the third Exhibition may be gotten up without more repetitions than occurred in the second. Many pictures have been purchased in Baltimore during the last two years, and the Gallery will experience most beneficially the effects of a taste which it will have aided most materially in creating.

In carrying out the plan intimated in their first general report, the committee attempted to obtain the copies in the Baltimore Museum of the Madonna of St. Sixtus, of Raphael,—and the nativity, known as the "Notte," of Correggio. These copies are excellent. They were most carefully made from the originals in the Dresden Gallery, and brought to this country by a Mr. Arnold, who exhibited them with much success in N. York and Philadelphia. He held them at $10,000, and refused a large offer from a northern institution. Subsequently he took them to Canada, where becoming embarrassed he induced a Mr. James Jackson to take them in charge. Mr. Jackson brought them to Baltimore in 1836, and exhibited them in the Museum. Mr. De Selding, the then proprietor, bought the Madonna on the 21st November, 1836, for $1,140—the other picture was pledged to him for $500—the pledge to be a sale if the loan was not returned by a given day. This not being done, Mr. De Selding obtained the two pictures for $1,640—to which adding the cost of the frames, paid by Mr. De Selding, and the pictures stood him in about $1,756. [These facts have been but recently obtained, and not until after the pictures had been purchased for the Gallery.] Mr. De Selding leaving Baltimore, the pictures along with the collection in the Museum, became the property ultimately, through several mesne assignments, of Mr. P. T. Barnum of the American Museum, New York, who sold his interest to Messrs. Silsbee and Ham, subject to a lien for the purchase money; and the present proprietor of the Baltimore Museum, Mr. J. E. Owens, having succeeded to the rights of Messrs. S. & H., the ownership of the pictures finally rested with him and Mr. Barnum.

The committee offered, soon after their first general report, $1,000, to the then proprietors for the pictures. This they did without knowing their history, and acting on their own judgment alone. They considered this a fair price to be offered and received. The market for pictures of this size was a very limited one. Their value as an attraction to the Museum was but small, if any thing—looking to the character of the establishment—and the probability of a purchaser at a higher price was but a slight one.

The offer was refused however,—and as the committee could not advance on it, it only remained for them to appropriate their funds otherwise.

The next picture of interest that suggested itself was the Marriage of Cana, of Paul Veronese, in the Gallery of Louvre; and the correspondence which they entered into with Mr. Walsh, then the U. S. Consul at Paris, resulted in an agreement with William H. Powell, Esquire, to make a copy of the painting 12 feet in length for $800—of which sum $300 was to be paid to him at once,—the work to be finished in one year—say by the 1st of September, 1850. In this agreement the committee consider they have been fortunate. Mr. Powell is the artist employed to fill the remaining pannel in the Rotunda at Washington—and his reputation ensures a copy of the first class.

After the late exhibition, the committee, before appropriating the funds accruing from it, renewed their offer of the previous year to Mr. Owens for the Madonna and the Notte. This time it was accepted, and Mr. Barnum's consent being obtained, the money was paid, and the pictures are now in the Society's possession. They are in excellent condition, and the time that has elapsed since they were copied, has taken from them the rawness of recent works,—and to that extent much improved them.

At the commencement of the next Exhibition, therefore, the committee will have so far executed the plan of the Society as to have in the Gallery good copies of three of what may be called the great pictures of the world,—the Madonna—the Notte—and the Marriage of Cana,—the *chef d'ouvres*, respectively, of Raphael, Correggio and Paul Veronese.

The committee have already made a partial arrangement, through the kindness of Mr. Crawford, the sculptor, for a copy of the Communion of St. Jerome, of Domenichino, which is in the Vatican,—Mr. Crawford, whose studio is in Rome, having consented to engage the copyist, and superintend the execution of the work. This is another of the pictures of a world-wide reputation.

The pictures which the committee have next in view are the Peter Martyr, of Titian, in the Church of St. Giovanni E. Paolo, at Venice, and the Miracle of the Slave, of Tintoretto, now in the Gallery of the Louvre.

They might suggest others—such as the Descent from the Cross, of Rubens, in the Cathedral, at Antwerp,—but this would be running far a-head of their immediate means: and the committee, therefore, leave their list at present incomplete. It has occurred to them, however, that, perhaps, subscriptions might be obtained which would enable them, at once, to take measures to procure the above mentioned pictures, and indeed to complete their design without waiting for the slow receipts of the Annual Exhibitions.

In their last report the committee suggested the possibility of pictures being deposited in the Gallery; and to some extent this has been done. There are several excellent pictures now on deposit,—and there is little doubt that their number will increase from year to year.

In conclusion, the committee have to congratulate the Society upon the success thus far of the scheme which was adopted at the close of the first Exhibition; and to express the conviction that a great good has been done to art by the efforts of the Society, and a great improvement thereby effected in the public taste.

JOHN H. B. LATROBE,
B. C. WARD,
T. EDMONDSON, Jr.

LIST OF MEMBERS.

T. P. Andrews, U. S. A.
Geo. W. Andrews,
Wm. S. Appleton,
J. J. Atkinson,
G. R. W. Alnutt,
James M. Buchanan,
Wm. Geo. Baker,
Hugh Birkhead,
George Brown,
Geo. Wm. Brown,
F. W. Brune,
John C. Brune,
Wm. H. Brune,
F. W. Brune, Jr.,
Dr. John Buckler,
Dr. Thos. Buckler,
Robert P. Brown,
Robert D. Brown,
Arthur Burns,
Charles Bradenbaugh,
Wm. Bose,
N. C. Brooks,
John Barney,
Rev. R. H. Ball,
Rev. J. C. Backus,
Dr. Wm. J. Barry,
James L. Bartol,
Thos. E. Bond, Jr.
J. Mason Campbell,
Charles R. Carroll,
S. Sterett Carroll,
Geo. B. Coale,
E. S. Courtney,
Jas. C. Coale,
Cyrenius O. Cone, M. D.
B. U. Campbell,
Dabney S. Carr,
Charles Carroll,
Dr. J. Paul Cockey,
John Cole,
Geo. W. Dobbin,
John I. Donaldson,
Samuel I. Donaldson,
Thos. Donaldson,
Samuel C. Donaldson,
Robert A. Dobbin,
Dr. J. R. W. Dunbar,
Jacob R. Drege,
E. B. Dallam,
J. M. Edgar,
Geo. Earnest,
Dr. Thos. Edmondson,
Daniel Egbert, M. D., U. S. N.
Basil T. Elder,
W. Frederick Frick,
Alex. Fisher,
Walter Farnandis, Jr.
John H. Falconar,
Wm. H. Gatchell,
R. W. Gill,

Levin Gale,
Ed. M. Greenway, Jr.
John M. Gordon,
Dr. J. T. Graves,
Edward Gray,
Alex. B. Gordon,
John Glenn,
Charles J. M. Gwinn,
Sam'l K. George,
Geo. M. Gill,
Geo. Gibson, M. D.
J. Morrison Harris,
Dr. Jas. Hall,
Wm. Hamilton, Jr.
Henry R. Hazlehurst,
Henry Hardesty,
Dr. Jas. Hamilton, U. S. N.
Lewis Howell,
Sam'l Hurbut,
John B. Howell,
Johns Hopkins,
Robert Hull,
Wm. G. Harrison,
Dr. Chapin A. Harris,
Robert S. Hollins,
John Hanan,
Charles R. Howard, of Cowpens,
Austin Jenkins,
Mark Jenkins,
M. Courtney Jenkins,
Reverdy Johnson,
Reverdy Johnson, Jr.
W. H. Keighler,
John P. Kennedy,
J. T. Keys,
Edward Kurtz,
Robert R. Kirkland,
John H. B. Latrobe,
Benjamin H. Latrobe,
Z. Collins Lee,
Robert Leslie,
Aaron R. Levering,
Martin Lewis,
Edward M. Laroque,
John J. Lloyd,
F. Lucas, Jr.
Wm. P. Lemmon,
Randolph B. Latimer,
Brantz Mayer,
Charles F. Mayer,
Jas. H. McHenry,
Ramsey McHenry,
Wm. McKim,
Haslett McKim,
Dr. Leonard Mackall,
Wm. E. Mayhew, Jr.
Joseph C. Manning,
Joseph Merefield,
Dr. G. W. Miltenberger,
Geo. H. Miles,
Charles T. Maddox,
Dr. Sam. K. Martin,
Robert M. McLane,
J. V. L. McMahon,
John B. Morris,
John Murphy,
Thos. Murphy,
Wm. E. Mayhew,
Jonathan Meredith,
Wm. D. Miller,
Gen. Henry Mankin,
John B. Morris, Jr.
Robert Mickle,
Isaac Munroe,
Wm. M. Medcalfe,
Geo. Neilson,
J. Spear Nicholas,
M. E. Noyes,
Jno. H. Naff,
H. H. Perry,
Wm. P. Preston,
John G. Proud,
John Pickell,
James R. Patridge,
Rev. Wm. S. Plumer,
Chas. H. Pitts,

R. Purviance, Jr.
R. Purviance,
Enoch Pratt,
Wm. A. Poor,
Wm. B. Perine,
Dr. Wm. Power,
Lloyd N. Rogers,
Dr. A. C. Robinson,
Joseph Reynolds,
Joseph Robinson,
Wm. Robinson, Jr.
Andrew S. Ridgely,
Wm. Reynolds,
A. Schumacher,
Wm. Schley,
John Spear Smith,
Sam. W. Smith,
Thos. W. Smith,
Otis Spear,
Carroll Spence,
Thos. Swann,
James Swan,
Wm. Prescott Smith,
S. F. Streeter,
Geo. H. Steuart,
John S. Sumner,
B. R. Spalding,
Moses Sheppard,
J. H. Stickney,
Robert M. Smith,
Jno. Louis Smith,
Wm. C. Shaw,
C. A. Schaeffer,
J. J. Speed,
Joseph Smith, Jr.
Wm. A. Talbott,
S. T. Thompson,
Henry Tiffany,
Osmond Tiffany, Jr.
John S. Tyson,
Isaac Tyson, Jr.
Wm. R. Travers,
Wm. H. Travers,
St. Geo. W. Teackle,
J. Hanson Thomas,
O. C. Tiffany,
O. W. Treadwell,
John D. Toy,
Lawrence Thomsen,
Henry A. Thompson,
Alexander Turnbull,
Wm. G. Thomas,
Sam'l Epes Turner,
J. Frederick Von Kapff,
Libertus Van Bokkelin,
S. Teakle Wallis,
B. C. Ward,
Geo. H. Williams,
Joseph B. Williams,
Geo. Waesche,
Sam'l G. Wyman,
David S. Wilson,
J. Carroll Walsh,
James Welsh,
Henry M. Warfield,
Henry Webster,
Rev. C. J. White,
James Winchester,
John Campbell White, Jr.
Jas. S. Waters,
Wm. F. Worthington,
Wm. Woodville,
Thos. Wilson,
Dr. James Wynne,
Ambrose A. White,
Dr. Wm. Thos. Wilson,
Coleman Yellott.

HONORARY MEMBERS, IN 1850.

Jas. M. Wayne, ...	*Savannah, Ga.*
J. K. Tefft, ...	" "
Thomas Corwin, ...	*Ohio.*
James H. McDowell, ...	*Virginia.*
Alexander H. H. Stewart, ...	"
Henry Clay, ...	*Kentucky.*
Thos. H. Benton, ...	*Missouri.*
Geo. Folsom, ...	*New York.*
J. R. Bartlett, ...	"
Jas. Renwick, ...	"
J. L. Stephens, ...	"
Gulian C. Verplanck, ...	"
Capt. Wilkes, ...	*Washington City.*
David Ridgely, ...	"
Peter Force, ...	"
Rev. Dr. Ryder, ...	*Georgetown, D. C.*
Prof'r Joseph Henry, ...	*Washington, D. C.*
Geo. Bancroft, ...	" "
James M. Gilliss, U. S. N.	" "
W. H. Prescott, ...	*Boston, Mass.*
Edward Everett, ...	*Cambridge, Mass.*
Jared Sparks, ...	" "
Daniel Webster, ...	*Mass.*
Robert C. Winthrop, ...	"
George Ticknor, ...	"
B. Silliman, ...	*New Haven, Connecticut.*
D. Hoffman, ...	*London, England.*
Sir Henry Lytton Bulwer, ...	*England.*
Professor Rafn, ...	*Copenhagen.*
G. S. Hilliard, ...	*Boston.*
Baron Fred'k Von Raumer, . . .	*Berlin, Prussia.*
Lewis Cass, ...	*Detroit, Michigan.*
Washington Irving, ...	*New York.*
Rob't Walsh, ...	*Paris.*
J. R. Poinsett, ...	*Charleston, S. C.*
J. McP. Berrien, ...	*Savannah, Georgia.*
W. Gilmore Simms, ...	*Medway, S. C.*
J. Fennimore Cooper, ...	*Cooperstown, N. Y.*
M. Champollon Figeac, ...	*Paris.*
Count Leon de la Borde, ...	"
Alex. Vattemare, ...	"
A. Calderon de la Barca, ...	*Spain.*
Pedro de Angelis, ...	*Montevideo, South America.*

CORRESPONDING MEMBERS.

Col. Jose Arénales, ...	*Buenos Ayres, South America.*
J. Mora Moss, ...	" "
Jno. R. Baltzell, ...	*Frederick, Maryland.*
Jas. McSherry, ...	" "
W. F. Lynch, ...	*U. S. N.*
Thos. G. Pratt, ...	*Annapolis, Md.*

THE ORIGIN AND GROWTH OF CIVIL LIBERTY IN MARYLAND.

A DISCOURSE

DELIVERED BY

GEO. WM. BROWN,

BEFORE THE

Maryland Historical Society,

Baltimore, April 12, 1850,

BEING THE

FIFTH ANNUAL ADDRESS TO THAT ASSOCIATION.

BALTIMORE:
PRINTED BY JOHN D. TOY,
Corner of Market and St. Paul-sts.

1850.

DISCOURSE.

Mr. President and
Gentlemen of the Historical Society:

In this age and country we do not much love to contemplate the past. The legends and time-honored traditions which form so large a part of the intellectual store of many nations have no place in our literature. Society is so constituted that most of us seek and therefore find little leisure for rest or recreation, and still less for looking backward. Every hour brings with it so much engrossing labor, or such a variety of pursuits and cares, and the age is so crowded with startling events, that the transactions of the present time only, seem to be worthy of our serious attention, and, contrasted with them, those of the past fade into insignificance as if they were mere shadows and unrealities.

Twice a day the never resting press spreads before our eyes the current history of the whole civilized world. Not a battle is fought, nor a dynasty subverted, nor does any other event of real or supposed importance happen any where within the outermost boundaries of civilization, but the account speeds back to us faster than the winds can waft it, borne aloft over land and ocean by the mighty arm of steam, or shot through the wires of the telegraph with a rapidity so great that it defies calculation. As the sun in the short cycle of twenty-four hours looks down upon the inhabitants of the whole earth, making one and the same solar day for all, so we, by the wonderful agency of steam and magnetism, may be almost said to live on the same actual day in the midst of events which occur among other people and in distant lands. A happy effect of this wonderful circulation of thought and intelligence is, doubtless, to expand our views beyond the narrow confines of our own homes and country, and to enlarge our sympathies so as to enable us to embrace within them the interests of the whole human family, but its effect also is, to concentrate our thoughts still more intensely upon the occurrences of the present time to the exclusion of the past.

The existence of this Society and of associations of a similar kind, which have recently been established in many of the States, and the encouragement which they have received, amounting to something more than a permission to live, may be regarded as a favorable omen. They not only embody in themselves a protest against the practical and utilitarian spirit of the times, but are an evidence of a reverent desire on the part of their members to do justice to the memory of our forefathers who have left us so largely their debtors.

No people are connected with the past by stronger and more endearing ties than ourselves, although, at first sight, it might seem to be otherwise. We justly attribute to the free institutions of our country the extraordinary prosperity which as a nation we have always enjoyed;—but whence came those institutions? The distinctive character which they possess was impressed upon them at a recent period, but their origin lies hid in the distant past, and they were developed slowly and gradually by the events of many centuries. It may be said of them as has been said with reference to the intellectual treasures which we possess, that we who now live,

> "Are the heirs of all the ages,
> In the foremost ranks of time."

All history shows that few things are of slower growth than civil liberty, and that it is easier either for individuals or nations to submit to be ruled by others, than to learn to control themselves. In some measure we, as a people, have learned the duties of self-government, and to practice them, under the favorable circumstances in which we are placed, seems to be so easy, that we can hardly comprehend that the habit was acquired by slow degrees and a transmitted experience. If we had attempted the experiment for ourselves, without the benefit of the instruction which we have derived from those who preceded us, we should have failed signally as others have done.

In order to establish a republic, much more is required than to set men free from the bonds of despotism, and to put the reins of authority in their own hands. Nor is it enough that the true interest of all requires that law and order should be the unvarying rule, nor even that a liberal and wise written constitution should be solemnly adopted. Our sister republics on this continent, if indeed such travesties of free governments can be called republics, furnish an instructive lesson on this subject. Spain, while they remained her colonies, endeavored to trample out every spark of freedom, and, now that they have thrown off her yoke, they are not fitted for the new duties which they have assumed.

Nor is the case much better in enlightened Europe. Within a short space of time the old dynasties there have been shaken to their foundations. A veil has fallen from the eyes of men. The divine right of kings to govern, and the heaven-appointed duty of the people to submit to be governed without reference to the general welfare, have come to be regarded as impostures too gross to be seriously maintained out of Russia and Turkey. Even fortifications and standing armies, with which monarchs have been accustomed to hedge themselves round, have, in times of trial, proved, like the rest, a delusion. Late events have shown that in most of the countries of Europe there are destructive agencies at work, quite sufficient to subvert the old governments which have so long elevated the few at the expense of the many. They are permitted to stand, not through their own strength, but because there is not sufficient constructive power in the people to rebuild after a revolution. Men must learn self-control, self-government, before they are prepared to be republicans. True liberty is the farthest thing possible from anarchy and licentiousness. Those who have grown up in bondage can hardly be made to assume the port, and practice the moderation of men educated in the habits of regulated freedom.

Only two of all the men of Israel, who, in Egypt, had been hewers of wood and drawers of water for their tyrannical task-masters, were permitted to assist in laying the foundations of the Jewish commonwealth. Slaves they had been, and had been taught to submit and obey, but self-control, self-denial they could not learn, even from the teaching of their inspired lawgiver. The privations which their new freedom imposed, soon made them pine for their former slavery, and it was not until the old generation had died completely out, and a new and brave race, composed of those who had left Egypt in their youth and those who were born and nurtured in the free air of the desert, had taken its place, that the chosen people were permitted to enter and take possession of the promised land.

The men who laid the foundations of civil liberty, broad and deep, in this their land of promise, were the early colonists and their immediate successors, and they are worthy of all honor from us who have entered into their labors. They were not fully aware of the consequences destined to result from the work in which they were engaged, but our gratitude is not the less due to them on that account. The real benefits which mankind were to derive from the discovery of a new continent, were not, as was at first supposed, in a large increase of wealth, nor even in finding an outlet for the crowded population of Europe. They were to spring from the new order of things, socially and politically, which has here been developed, aud which is fast modifying the civilization of the world. More precious seeds were never sown in the fallow field of time than the English colonies which, in the seventeenth century, were planted along the eastern coast of North America. As the child is the father of the man, as the acorn enfolds within its shell the future oak, as the bubbling fountain gives birth and direction to the mighty river, so those insignificant colonies, the work mainly of individual enterprise, feeble in numbers, neglected in their infancy, struggling for existence against Indian foes, diseases, hardships and privations, contained within themselves principles of liberty, which in their development, naturally produced the free institutions under which we live and which we justly prize as the most valuable of our possessions.

But I pass from these general considerations to the subject to which I desire more especially to call your attention, the origin and growth of civil liberty in Maryland. It is a theme which I cannot hope to make generally interesting, for it will necessarily carry me into somewhat minute details, and, unfortunately, the early records of our State are not only few and scanty in themselves, but are barren of striking and romantic incidents, which are essential to render the pages of history animated and attractive.

The charter of Maryland bears date on the 20th of June, 1632. It was drawn in the lifetime of George Calvert, the first Lord Baltimore, for whose benefit it was designed, but he having died about two months before its execution, it was granted by Charles the First to Cecilius, the eldest son of George Calvert, to whom the title and fortune of his father had descended. Very different views have been taken and earnestly maintained of the true meaning of this instrument. It has been described by some as embodying a scheme of the strongest government known throughout the American Colonies, and has been praised by others as being not only liberal but even democratic in its character, and as making ample provision for the rights of the settlers. This difference of opinion has arisen from the ambiguity of some of its provisions, but I think that it is not difficult to shew that the charter was designed to establish a government resembling that of England in the days of James the First, in which still more extensive powers were vested in the rulers than were claimed by the English executive, and fewer rights were secured to the people, than were then enjoyed in the parent country; and, indeed, it would be strange if it were otherwise, if we consider the source from which it originated. It is generally admitted either to have been the work of the first Lord Baltimore himself, or to have been prepared under his immediate direction, and it bears, in all its parts, the strongest intrinsic evidence that such was its origin. He was first knighted, and afterwards created Baron of Baltimore, by James the First, for about six years was one of his secretaries of state, and, through the life of that arbitrary and capricious monarch, continued to be a favorite. He was twice returned to parliament, in which body he was known as a supporter of the royal prerogative, and as a member of the court party as opposed to the country party. He is universally conceded to have been an able and conscientious man, but it is no reproach to him to say, that his sympathies and opinions, so far as they are known to us, all inclined him to favor a strong rather than a popular government.

The charter conveys, according to specified boundaries, which afterwards and for a long time were the source of much trouble and litigation, "a certain region," "in a country hitherto uncultivated in the parts of America." It was a compact between the sovereign and the proprietary, in which the latter undoubtedly had the best of the bargain, but as the former voluntarily parted with that which to him was of little value, and to which, at best, he had but small right, he certainly had no cause to complain. The grantee and his heirs were made true and absolute lords and proprietaries of the soil, and all that the sovereign reserved to himself was two Indian arrows of the country, to be delivered at the castle of Windsor every year, on Tuesday of Easter week, in token of allegiance, and the fifth part of the gold and silver—the latter, as it proved, a barren right.

The laws and institutions of the province were not required to be submitted to the crown for its approbation, and the right of taxation by it was expressly and forever abandoned. This last was a remarkable provision, and greatly strengthened the popular cause in the subsequent controversy with England, growing out of the right which it asserted of taxing the colonies.

Thus a government almost independent of the parent country, was created by the charter itself.

Maryland was, in the quaint language of the instrument, to be "eminently distinguished above all regions of that territory, and decorated with more ample titles." And to carry out this purpose, the proprietary was clothed with powers almost royal in their character and extent. He was to be the fountain of honor, and was permitted to adorn well deserving subjects inhabiting within the province, with whatsoever titles and dignities he should appoint, provided only that they were not to be such as were then used in England. There doubtless glittered before the imagination of the proprietary a long line of transatlantic nobility, of which he was to be the acknowledged head and founder. Their functions are not designated in the charter, but we must suppose that they were designed to be appropriate to elevated rank. The proprietary, if he so willed, had the power of establishing the feudal system perfect in all its parts. Express provision was made for manors, lords of manors and manorial-courts. Various manors were in fact granted, and in one or two cases, manor-courts appear to have been held, but this is the extent to which this feature of the charter was in practice preserved. It is, however, doing no injustice to the proprietary to suppose that he designed to create a new and vigorous aristocracy, who would sit as an upper house in the future parliaments which he intended to assemble, would fill the most important offices of the State, and by their wealth, power and dignity would form the surest support and brightest ornament of the vice-royal court, which he and his descendants were authorized to hold in the fair province of Maryland.

The proprietary had the power of creating ports of entry, of erecting towns into boroughs, and boroughs into cities, with such privileges and immunities as he might deem expedient, of pardoning offences, of taking command in chief of the forces, with as full and unrestrained power as any captain general of any army ever had, of declaring martial law, and of granting lands on such terms and tenure, as he thought proper.

He was the source of justice. He had the power of establishing courts, of abolishing them at will, and of determining their jurisdiction and manner of proceeding; and all process from them ran in his name and not in that of the king.

He was not only the head of the executive branch of the government, but he had the power of appointing officers of every description, and of creating and abolishing the offices themselves at his own pleasure.

He was the head of the church. That is, he had the power of erecting and founding churches, and was entitled to the patronage and advowsons appertaining to them.

He had also in certain cases and to a limited extent, the dangerous power of promulgating ordinances which were to have the force of laws; and he also claimed as a part of his prerogative, and occasionally practised, the equally dangerous power of dispensing with laws actually existing.

He was invested with all the royal rights which the Bishop of Durham enjoyed within the County Palatine of Durham, and this among other things gave him the right to all the game within the province.

In the end of the instrument, there is a sweeping clause, that in case any doubt shall arise as to the true meaning of any word of the charter, an interpretation was to be put upon it most *beneficial*, *profitable* and *favorable* to Lord Baltimore, his heirs and assigns.

Amid this imposing array of powers conferred on the proprietary, those granted to the people were neither numerous nor explicit. The most important right secured to them, was that the laws were to be enacted by the proprietary, with the advice and approbation of the freemen, or more properly freeholders of the province, or of their deputies.* The proprietary understood this clause to mean that *he* had the right of originating all laws, and that the people had nothing to do but *accept* or *reject* those which *he* might choose to propose.

But whatever may be the true meaning of the charter in this respect, it is clear that the legislative assemblies were to be called together at such times only as the proprietary might prescribe and in such form as he might think best, and he had the power of adjourning and dissolving them at pleasure. Thus their organization was left as indefinite as their functions.

It is a fact worthy of notice, as illustrative of the character of those

* The charter is in Latin, and it has been a matter of doubt whether the expressions "Liberi Homines" and "Liberi tenentes," which are therein used to indicate the same class persons, should be translated Free-men or Freeholders. As, however, the proprietary, by his ordinance of 1681, restricted the elective franchise to persons who were either freeholders or had a given amount of visible personal estate, and as this ordinance was always acquiesced in and became the settled policy of Maryland, it would seem to have been the established construction that all freemen were not as such entitled, by virtue of the charter, to vote for delegates to the General Assembly. If they had been so entitled, none could have been excluded for want of property.—*Charter of Maryland*, §§ 7 *and* 8; 2 *Bozman's Hist. of Md.* 47 *note*; *McMahon's Hist. of Md.* 443, *note* 1.

times in which political rights were comparatively little discussed, that amid all the various and tempting allurements, held out by Lord Baltimore to induce the adventurous to enlist in the enterprise of planting the colony of Maryland, not a word is said of the form of government intended to be established. The conversion of the Indians was presented as a primary object. The land was described as being white unto the harvest, prepared to receive into its fruitful bosom the seed of the Gospel. The air was represented as mild and serene, of a medium temperature between the cold of New England and the burning heat of Florida. The bays and rivers were extolled as abounding in delicious fish, innumerable, the forests as swarming with game, the swine and deer as so abundant that they were troublesome rather than advantageous, and the soil so fertile that it afforded three harvests of Indian corn, or King's corn, as it was then called, in one year. But whether those who were invited to occupy this Western Paradise were to participate in the affairs of government, or to be ruled wholly by others, it was not considered material to communicate.*

If the view of the charter which I have given be correct, the people of Maryland are not mainly indebted to it for the freedom which they have always enjoyed.

We must look elsewhere for an explanation of the fact, and we find it in the character of the men who planted the colony, and the circumstances by which they were surrounded. The colonists consisted of some two hundred, for the most part Roman Catholics. They brought with them stout English hearts, in which were cherished fundamental principles of liberty, learned in a land where four hundred years before, *magna charta* had been extorted by the sturdy barons from the fears of King John, where parliaments met, and where trial by jury was established. They spoke the language in which Shakspeare had written. They belonged to the same period which produced a John Milton, whose "Speech for the liberty of unlicensed printing," rings even now in our ears like the voice of a trumpet. They were part of the same generation which a few years afterwards, appalled all Europe by a spectacle never before seen, the trial, condemnation and execution of an anointed king, for a violation of the rights of his subjects. It mattered little to such men whether their rights were more or less definitely settled by the parchment title under which the land was acquired. The

* See the Report of Maryland prefixed to Father White's narrative.

very ambiguity of the instrument operated in their favor, for it opened wide the door to a construction which became more and more liberal, as their strength and numbers increased. All the circumstances by which they were surrounded, favored the growth of free principles. They had settled themselves in a wilderness, where the artificial distinctions of life, must, to a great extent, be laid aside. The best man was he who was the bravest, the most useful, the most enterprising. All had to labor for subsistence, and nearly all with their own hands. The charter provided for nobles, but none were to be found, for nobles cannot live in a wilderness. There, stars and garters are out of place, and a coat of frieze is worth more than a coat of arms. The inhabitants consisted chiefly of planters, small farmers, mechanics, redemptioners, (or persons who were bound to render personal service for a term of years, to those who had paid the expenses of their emigration,) and a few official personages sent out by the proprietary. Some of them were persons of education and gentle birth, but the majority were doubtless such as usually compose the materials of which colonies are formed, men of little or no means, who go abroad in the hope of bettering their condition. They could not be called poor, for they had the means of comfortable subsistence in abundance around them, but their wealth consisted mainly in their capacity for labor.* The tendency of such men so situated was necessarily and inevitably towards the establishment of freer institutions than were contemplated by the charter. All that they needed was to be left free to work out their own destiny without foreign molestation, and this was secured to them for a considerable time, by the fact that the political and religious contest waged between the contending parties at home,

* The act of 1638, ch. 16, furnishes an illustration of the scanty means of the colonists. A water-mill having become necessary for the use of the people instead of the hand-mills which had previously sufficed to grind their corn, the Governor and Council were authorized to contract for its erection, provided the cost should not exceed 20,000 pounds of tobacco, or $333 33⅓ cents, which was to be raised by general taxation in two years. *McSherry's Hist. of Md.* 56. 2 *Bozman*, 156. Education was not very extensively diffused among the settlers. The return of the election of a burgess for Mattapanient hundred, dated 14th of February, 1638, was signed by seven persons, of whom only one could write his name, the rest affixed their marks; and out of fifteen persons whose names were subscribed to the return for St. Mary's hundred, seven made their marks. On this Mr. Bozman remarks: "This gross deficiency in literature among our colonists is not however to be imputed to their colonial state. These persons, for the most part, were born and bred in England, and had left their country after the common period of acquiring literary attainments. It was the defect of the age in which they lived." 2 *Bozman*, 99.

left the British government little leisure to look after its remote and insignificant colonies.

For about a year after the colony was planted, the settlers were too busily occupied with building, planting, reaping, and the various other labors incident to their new situation, to find leisure for any thing else, but on the 26th of February, 1635, they were called together by the Governor for the purpose of making laws. Various bills were passed, but unfortunately no memorial of them remains, as most of the early records of the colony were seized and carried off to Virginia, in the outbreak known as Clayborne and Ingle's rebellion, where they were either lost or destroyed. But the bills passed never became laws, as the Proprietary refused his assent to them, for the reason, as is supposed, that they did not originate with himself.

The important business of legislation was thus put off for two years longer. In the year 1637 the second legislative assembly was summoned by the Governor, to meet at the little town of St. Mary's. It was a strangely constituted body. It met in one chamber. Governor Leonard Calvert, the brother of the Proprietary, presided, and his three councillors took their seats as members. All the freemen of the province, who chose to do so, were invited to attend in person, or to send delegates in their place, or to give their proxies to any individual of their own selection, authorizing him to vote for them. Thus was as near an approach made to a purely democratic body, as could well exist, and indeed from the condition of the colony it would not have been easy to form one of a different character. Some of the entries on the journal of the house sound strangely to us at this day. On the first day of their meeting, proclamation was made "that all freemen omitted in the writs of summons, that would claim a voice in the general assembly, should come and make their claim." Whereupon we read that "claim was made by John Robinson, carpenter, and was admitted." On the next day, "came Edward Bateman, of St. Mary's hundred, ship carpenter, and claimed a voice as a freeman, and made Mr. John Lewger, secretary, his proxy." "Also came John Langford, of the Isle of Kent, gentleman, high constable of the said island, who had given a voice in the choice of Robert Philpot, gentleman, to be one of the burgesses for the freemen of that island, and desired to revoke his voice, and to be personally put in the assembly, and was admitted." And so, by this simple process, Edward Bateman, the ship carpenter, by his proxy, John Robinson, the carpenter, and John Langford, the high constable, were admitted to their seats as legislators, although the last had already voted for a regularly appointed delegate.

It is fortunate, perhaps, that political aspirants, even at this enlightened day, find it not quite so easy to obtain seats in the legislature of the State, either for themselves or their favorite candidates.

The house being at length organized, proceeded to business, and most pressing business it had on hand. For three years the colony had been struggling on in the midst of difficulties. Clayborne, who has been called the evil genius of Maryland, had not only set up a claim to the Isle of Kent, but is charged with having instigated the Indians to hostilities. The colonists were increasing in number, and were gradually extending themselves beyond the settlement at St. Mary's. There was urgent need of laws. They were surrounded by new circumstances, a new social relation, that of slavery unfortunately had, probably even then, sprung up among them, their dangerous Indian neighbors seemed to threaten them, their infant agriculture, commerce and institutions were all sadly in want of laws adapted to their situation. And a greater want in a community cannot well exist. Those who live under a system of just laws duly enforced do not, until deprived of them, appreciate the benefits which they confer. Like the common blessings of water and sunshine, they come to be regarded as things of course, for which no gratitude is due. But if they were suspended for a single day, we should then learn to estimate, more correctly, their importance. The laws, in truth, surround us like the atmosphere, they attend our steps when we walk abroad, and shield our homes from harm when we are absent; by a thousand unseen and unfelt influences, they minister to our comfort, protection and happiness. They are the embodied wisdom of the age which enacts them, its sense of justice speaking in enduring words.

But a serious difficulty stood in the way of the colonists. They had already, two years before, passed a series of laws which in mass had been rejected by the proprietary, and now, in his turn, he had prepared in England, a Code for their government, which they were assembled to ratify and adopt. The question was, would they do it, and important consequences for many years hung upon their decision. It does not appear that the laws proposed were, in themselves, objectionable. The proprietary had at heart the good of the colony, on which he had lavished large sums of money, and it was, doubtless, his desire to promote the welfare of the inhabitants while he protected what he deemed his own rights.* The colonists, on their part, manifested for him, on various occasions, a high degree of respect and affection. But an important principle was involved. If they yielded to him the privilege of originating all laws, and reserved to themselves a mere negative on such as he might choose to propose, they surrendered, so long as the charter should endure, the dearest and most important right of freemen.

If, on the other hand, they rejected the Code, they must be prepared not only to engage in a serious controversy with their beneficent patron, but to forego the advantages of all legislation for an indefinite period. The matter is very briefly stated, but it is clear from the record, that the sturdy Marylanders did not hesitate for a moment. They could endure, if need were, to go without laws, but not to have laws made for them by another. When the question was taken, the Code of the proprietary was promptly *rejected*, but two of the members present voting for it, and those two were Governor Calvert himself, and Mr. Lewger, his Secretary. It is true that the two increased their vote by the proxies which they held; but I speak of the votes of the members present. Thus early was fought and won, the first battle for civil liberty in Maryland. The head of the popular movement appears to have been Captain Thomas Cornwaleys, one of the Governor's Council, and for a long time a man of note in the colony, and its military leader. It is to be lamented that a more full memorial of this brave soldier and patriot has not come down to us.

The house soon afterwards proceeded to pass laws for itself, but as the bills had not been matured in committee, the Governor proposed an adjournment, in order that the members might attend to their other business, while the bills were preparing. This was opposed by Cornwaleys, who replied significantly, that, "they could not spend their time in any business, better than in this for the country's good."

The bills were at length got ready and passed, forty-two in all, but, as the colonists probably anticipated, they shared the fate of their predecessors, and were in a body rejected by the proprietary. Their titles, however, have come down to us, and show that the fathers of Maryland set themselves in earnest to the great work of legislation. There is a bill providing for the probate of wills, another regulating the descent of land, another in restraint of liquors, and another for the liberties of the

* During the first two or three years of the colony, Cecilius Calvert, the proprietary, expended upon it upwards of £40,000 sterling.—*McMahon*, 197.

people. The colonists being thus deprived of the power of making laws for themselves, neither gave up in despair, nor had recourse to lynch-law, but resorted to a better expedient than either. They claimed that they brought with them, and were to be governed by, all the laws of England which were applicable to their situation, and this claim they never relinquished although the proprietary opposed it, on the ground that a wholesale adoption of the laws of England would interfere with his legislative rights. From this difference of opinion, a controversy arose long afterwards, in the year 1722, which lasted for ten years. As the courts only could decide what laws of England were applicable and what were not, the people of Maryland were advocating a principle, the establishment of which would give a large and somewhat dangerous discretion to the judges, especially, as their appointment and tenure of office rested entirely with the proprietary, but the people greatly preferred to encounter this danger and inconvenience rather than risk the liberties which were enjoyed in the mother country, by surrendering the protection of the laws under which those liberties had grown up. It is a note-worthy circumstance that the most serious controversy which ever arose between the proprietary and the people of Maryland, originated in the assertion by them of their right as English subjects, to be governed by the laws of England. The fact is a high practical testimonial to the substantial character of English liberty, which is the parent stock of our own.

At last both of these questions were determined in favor of the people. It was soon settled* that all legislation should originate in the legislature of the province, and not with the proprietary, but it was not settled until the year 1732, that in cases not otherwise provided for, "the rule of judicature was to be according to the laws, statutes, and reasonable customs of England *as used and practised within the province*."†

Some time necessarily elapsed before the various departments of government became fully organized, as is singularly illustrated by an anecdote which is related of an early period of the colony. In 1648, a Miss Margaret Brent, on the death of Governor Leonard Calvert, was

* In 1639.

† *McMahon*, 127. From this period until the revolution, the courts continued to exercise the power of adopting and giving effect to such of the English Statutes as were accommodated to the condition of the province, without regard to the inquiry whether they had been practised upon, or enacted previously to 1732. *Ib.* 128.

appointed his administrator, and as the Governor had been the agent of his brother, the proprietary, under a power of attorney from him, it was judicially decided that Miss Brent was duly authorized to act as attorney in fact for the absent proprietary. She is described as having been possessed of a "masculine understanding," and at least appears to have been addicted to masculine pursuits; as she is said "to have been very actively employed in taking up lands, and in affairs of all kinds relating to property." To her great credit it is related, that by her personal influence and by a timely appropriation of a small sum from the estates of the proprietary, of which she had the management, she, on several occasions, pacified the soldiers in garrison at St. Inigoe's fort, who were ready to mutiny on account of the non-payment of their wages. Armed thus with a double right, Miss Brent presented herself before the legislature of the province, which was then in session, and made her application to have two votes in the house, one for herself and another as his lordship's attorney. But although the merit of this remarkable lady and her public services, were on a subsequent occasion handsomely acknowledged by the legislature, yet they probably thought that by granting the request they would establish a precedent, dangerous even at that early day, in favor of female rights, for we are told that the application "was refused peremptorily by the Governor Greene, and that the lady protested in form against all the proceedings of that assembly, unless she might be present and vote as aforesaid." Mr. Bozman, the learned historian of Maryland, endeavors to justify this proceeding on the part of the legislature, but whether successfully or not, I shall not stop to consider. Our Maryland lady, he thinks, may in character be aptly compared to Queen Elizabeth; if this be so, that fact may probably have weighed as strongly with the assembly and governor in the peremptory refusal with which they met her request, as the reasons on which the historian relies in vindication of the ungallant decision.*

I shall not weary you by a detail of the various difficulties which beset the founders of our State, or of the intestine commotions by which they were harassed. The controversies in England between Charles I. and his people, and Cromwell and the parliament, were not without effect on the affairs of the colony, and although strife and commotion were the immediate result, the progress of free principles in England undoubtedly gave an additional impulse to them here.

* 2 Bozman, 323.

It is every where in this country recognized as a fundamental principle of government, that the legislative, executive and judicial functions should be kept separate and distinct, but this wholesome rule was wholly disregarded in the proprietary government of Maryland.

The governor was at first in the habit of summoning by special writs such persons as he thought proper, to sit in the legislative assembly. This was an arbitrary power, liable to great abuse, and it happened that in the session of 1642, the number thus summoned gave the governor a majority over the regularly elected burgesses, thus taking the whole legislation out of the hands of the people. To remedy this inconvenience, the burgesses demanded that the assembly should be divided into two bodies, of which they should constitute the lower house. This reasonable request was at first refused, but about the year 1659, the division was permanently effected. Subsequently to this, the lower house was composed of delegates regularly elected by the people, and the upper house of the governor and his council, and the right of each individual to appear in person or by proxy, wholly ceased. In 1681, the proprietary, by a positive ordinance, restricted the elective franchise to freemen having a small property qualification, and this restriction was continued down to the adoption of the State Constitution, and was incorporated in it.*

The judiciary was strangely blended with the executive, and never became properly independent of it. The governor and his council sat as the High Court of Appeals of the province, and the inferior judges who were appointed by the proprietary, were removable at his pleasure. Still they could on occasions act with firmness and independence, for, in 1765, we find Frederick County Court deciding the British stamp act to be unconstitutional and void, and proceeding in the transaction of business without paying the least regard to its provisions.

The governor was the chancellor of the province, although his previous occupation might have been such, as, according to our notions, to have furnished a very unsuitable preparation for the performance of the responsible duties appertaining to the office. The last colonial governor, Robert Eden, a brother-in-law of the then Lord Baltimore, had previously been a lieutenant in the Coldstream Guards.†

* 2 Bozman, 216, 297 note ; McMahon, 449, note 8.

† 1 Bland's Rep., 625, note.

The main security for the liberties of the people was in the house of delegates, who alone of the public servants were elected by the people, and who took care so to exercise their powers, as constantly to strengthen the popular cause. They claimed the right of originating all money bills, and an equal rank in point of privilege with the English house of commons. One of the expedients to which they resorted to increase their power, was to pass important laws with a proviso that they were to continue only for short and limited periods, which made frequent sessions of the general assembly, and a constant resort to it for the enactment of indispensable laws, absolutely necessary.

The intention of the charter to establish in Maryland a mixed form of government, of which a hereditary nobility was to be a prominent feature, was overruled by circumstances. Such a class can be sustained only in a country where the ownership of the soil is mainly vested in them, and where the masses are reduced to the condition of tenants, dependent on the landholders for support.* But in Maryland there were vast uncultivated tracts of land, lying in their primitive state, which the proprietary was more anxious to sell than the people were to purchase. Every man who chose, became a landholder, a proprietor in his own right. He had no occasion to look up to any other man for patronage, and still less for support or protection. Labor was the passport to independence and wealth. There was no place then for an aristocracy, for there was nothing to support it. Aristocracy is a plant which flourishes only in the sunshine of courts, here it was an exotic, and it died at once in the shade of our vast forests. So we find that the manors which were actually granted, subsisted only in name, and the lords of manors had, only for a short time, even that unsubstantial existence. The aristocratic provisions of the charter being thus incapable of being carried out in practice, were soon lost sight of by the proprietary, and excited no opposition on the part of the people; but in them the proprietary lost what would have been of material assistance in sustaining him in the exercise of the royal prerogatives with which he was clothed.

The proprietary government established by the charter, lasted, with slight interruptions, down to the American revolution; but long before that event the proprietaries, one after another, had silently relinquished the exercise of those powers which, as set forth in the charter, seemed

* This subject is more fully discussed in Burnap's Life of Leonard Calvert, Chapter X.

to threaten the liberties of the inhabitants. They usually resided in England, and in Maryland had no other means of enforcing their authority than through the agency of civil officers, who, although appointed by them, were generally selected from among the people, and shared their feelings and opinions. The charter itself soon became an object of jealousy to the British government, in consequence of the extensive privileges which it lavished on a subject; so that the proprietaries frequently encountered opposition, and seldom received support from that quarter, while, in Maryland, the people opposed a steady resistance to the exercise of every thing approaching arbitrary power. They were uniformly quick in perceiving, and prompt and tenacious in resisting, the slightest infringement of what they considered their rights—which they claimed to be not only those which were conferred by the charter and laws of the province, but all those, in addition, which were enjoyed by English subjects at home. No right or privilege once acquired by them was ever relinquished, but, on the contrary, became a means of increasing their power in all future controversies. The consequence was, that although Maryland continued to have a hereditary executive, it became, in essential matters, republican, and instead of being subjected to an arbitrary government, enjoyed one of mild and equal laws. The people were protected in their persons and property, and the latter was so distributed, that few were found who were either very rich or very poor—a condition of things most favorable to the growth and maintenance of civil liberty.

The discipline which they had undergone during the colonial period, was of incalculable service in the revolutionary struggle in which they were about to engage. They approached that great crisis not with the timid and hesitating steps of novices in public affairs, but with the resolute tread of men who from long experience in matters of government, and by the habit which they had acquired of resisting oppression from whatever quarter it came, and of weighing and judging of their rights, were fully prepared to engage in the fearful strife which awaited them, and, in the event of success, to lay wisely and well the foundations of a free commonwealth. No better proof can be adduced of the progress which the principles of true freedom had made among them, than the wisdom and moderation which they then exhibited.

In illustration of this, I shall for a short time ask your attention to a few of the events which occurred in the town of Baltimore previously to, and in the early part of, the revolutionary war. Although they are not in themselves of much magnitude or importance, they possess some degree of interest for us, both on account of the local associations connected with them, and because they carry us into the heart, as it were, of a great movement, and show, by the manner in which it was conducted, the reason of the wide difference which exists between the American revolution and every similar occurrence of modern times. The time to which I refer embraces the critical and important period extending over rather more than two years, during which the committee of observation for the town and county of Baltimore sat here, and performed many important functions which, in a regularly constituted government, devolve upon the tribunals and officers of the law.* The province was then in a transition state; for the colonial government had virtually ceased to exist, and another had not yet been established in its place. Society was therefore, in a great measure, resolved into its original elements, and temporary expedients had to be resorted to, until a permanent constitution could be adopted. At the commencement of this period, when, in the face of domestic disorganization, every energy of the people had to be called forth to meet the impending war with Great Britain, the committees of observation came into existence. They were regularly elected by the qualified voters of the province who assembled for the purpose at the different county towns, and were sustained throughout in all their proceedings by the force of public opinion.†

They were, in fact, revolutionary tribunals, acting with vast force and efficiency, and for a time were the main spring of the popular movement.

In common with most of the public servants at that day, they were clothed with large discretionary powers, but they acted under the pressure of a responsibility, which was relied on as a sufficient guarantee against the abuse of the confidence reposed in them. The exigency of the crisis demanded that confidence should be freely bestowed, although in some cases it was withheld, or very reluctantly given. When, for instance, the assembly of South Carolina resolved to appoint deputies to attend the Continental Congress, a proposition was made to instruct heir delegates as to the point to which they might pledge the colony.

* I have had the advantage of consulting the original records kept by the committee, which have been kindly lent to me for the present occasion by their owner, Peter Force, Esq., of Washington.

† See Appendix, note 1.

John Rutledge, the eminent patriot and orator of South Carolina, warmly opposed the proposition. But what shall we do, asked its advocates, if these delegates make a bad use of their power? Hang them! was his decided and impetuous reply.* John Rutledge was right, and it was somewhat in the spirit in which he spoke, that the people of Maryland acted, in the authority with which they invested the committees of observation.

These committees originated in a resolve of the Continental Congress, which met at Philadelphia, in September, 1774, in pursuance of which the delegates acting for themselves and the inhabitants of the several colonies which they represented, entered into an association, the object of which, among other things, was to put a stop to all trade with Great Britain and its possessions, to discontinue the purchase and use of East India tea, to encourage frugality, agriculture, arts and manufactures, and to discourage every species of extravagance and dissipation, and especially all kinds of gaming and expensive diversions and entertainments. As part of the plan to carry out this agreement, committees were to be chosen by the qualified voters in every county, city and town, whose business it was attentively to observe the conduct of all persons touching the association, and the names of all persons who violated its articles were to be published in the newspapers, to the end that all such foes to the rights of British America might be publicly and universally contemned as the enemies of American liberty, and that all dealings with such persons might be broken off.

Previously to this,† however, on the 27th of May, 1774, a public meeting had been called in Baltimore, at which the inhabitants had agreed to unite in an association of non-intercourse with Great Britain, had elected a committee to attend a general meeting of delegates from all parts of the province, to be held at Annapolis, and had appointed a committee of correspondence for the city and county of Baltimore.

But the resolve of Congress was intended to create a concert of action throughout the colonies, and the committees of observation thus established were, in Maryland, from time to time, clothed with such additional powers by the Provincial Convention at Annapolis, as were necessary to meet the emergency of the times.‡

* 4 Graham's History of the United States, p. 370.

† See Purviance's Narrative, pp. 12 and 13.

‡ See the Proceedings of the Convention, published in 1836.

They not only exercised all the authority requisite to carry out the measures agreed on by the articles of association established by Congress, but their permission was necessary in many cases before suits could be brought or executions issued. They were empowered to purchase arms and ammunition, and to raise money for that purpose, and others which were specified, by subscription, or in any other voluntary manner. They were authorized to enroll and equip troops, to impose fines not exceeding ten pounds on all disaffected persons who refused to enlist, to disarm such persons, as well as all those who refused to subscribe certain articles of association of the Freemen of Maryland, promulgated by the Provincial Convention, and to exact from non-associators, as they were called, security for their good behavior.

They were required to see that traders did not monopolize goods, or exact unreasonable prices for them; to hold up to public censure and odium those who, by acts or words, manifested hostility to the country, and to arrest, imprison and hand over to the council of safety, those who were guilty of offences calculated to disunite the inhabitants, or dangerous to their liberties.

A part of their duty, was to appoint sub-committees of correspondence, by means of which, at a period when neither the press nor the mails circulated information as rapidly as they now do, intelligence was communicated to every part of the country. When, for example, the harbor of Boston was closed by the arbitrary edict of the British Parliament, the committee of Philadelphia sent the news by express to Baltimore. It excited a determined spirit of resistance here, and the Baltimore committee of correspondence sped the alarming tidings onward to Annapolis, Alexandria, Norfolk, Portsmouth and Charleston.* It passed through the length and breadth of the land, like the fiery cross by which, on a sudden outbreak of war, the Scottish clans were in former times rallied around the banner of their chief; and with similar results. A thrill of indignation and resentment pervaded the whole people, and thus gradually were their hearts prepared for the impending war.

Immediately on the arrival of a vessel at the port of Baltimore, the

* This committee, however, was not appointed by the committee of observation, but at the public meeting, before mentioned, held in Baltimore previously to the election of the latter.—See Purviance's Narrative, p. 13. The incident is referred to here only as an instance of the efficient action of the revolutionary committees of correspondence.

master was required to appear before the committee, and state, on oath, whether or not he had imported goods contrary to the resolve of Congress, which prohibited all trade with Great Britain. If such goods were discovered, as they sometimes were, they were taken possession of by the committee and sold. The cost of the goods and charges, were, out of the proceeds of sale, paid to the importer, and the profits, if any there were, were, in conformity with the recommendation of Congress, remitted to Boston, for the benefit of the poor of that town, who were suffering under the oppression of the Boston port bill. Baltimore, although then a small town containing only about five thousand inhabitants, was engaged in a large and profitable commerce, the interruption of which inflicted a heavy blow on her growing prosperity; but such was the patriotism of her citizens that they cheerfully submitted to it, and fairly carried it out. It is to the credit especially of the mercantile part of the community, who were the greatest sufferers, that they were among the most prominent supporters of the measure: but their sacrifices have not received from posterity the gratitude to which they are justly entitled. The merchant princes of Tyre and of Florence, are inseparably associated in the memories of all, with the former glories of those cities, but the merchant patriots of Baltimore are already almost forgotten in the city where their ashes repose, and by whose fortunes they stood so steadfastly in the hour of her greatest need.

If it was reported that a trader had taken advantage of the necessities of the times to demand exorbitant prices for his goods, he was summoned to appear before the committee, and the matter was investigated. If the charge was proved, and a satisfactory atonement was not at once made, the offender was liable to be published to the world as an enemy of his country; and this was no trivial punishment, for it was equivalent to civil and social excommunication. No good citizen would associate or deal with one who in the time of trial had deserted the cause of American liberty.

The colonies were engaging with fearful odds against them, in a war with the leading power of the world, and it seemed to many here, as well as in Great Britain, that they would be annihilated at a single blow. They had more than a foreign enemy to contend with. In every part of the country there were intelligent and conscientious men, occupying the highest places in society and public office, who could not sympathize with the popular movement, and who held it to be their duty to oppose it as far as they dared. Many were bound to the parent country by the closest ties of relationship and affection, and there was then, moreover, as there always is in every community, a strong conservative force which upholds the established order of things whatever it may be, because it is established. To this class belong the timid, the prudent, the selfish and unenterprising, and not a few of those who have much to lose and little to gain by change. There is always beside a baser crew, which on the first outbreak joins the popular side, but in the hour of danger can only be kept in the ranks by the fear of the fate which awaits deserters. Some, but not many of all these classes there were in Baltimore, and with them the committee had to deal. In a war like that of the revolution, whoever is not for it is against it, and the most dangerous enemies are those, who while they take no active part in the strife, occupy themselves in sowing seeds of disaffection and discontent, and by their influence and example, operate on the fears and scruples of the timid and vacillating. An unpublished letter of General Washington, which has been placed in my hands by a gentleman of this city,* contains some pointed remarks on this subject. It is dated on the 6th of June, 1777, from his head quarters at Middlebrook, and is addressed to Major Apollos Morris, of Philadelphia, who appears to have been what was called in the language of that day, a neutral character, but which was generally understood to mean an enemy in disguise. "I must," says General Washington, "tell you in plain terms, that at this time a neutral character is looked upon as a suspicious one; and I would therefore advise you to leave a country, with the majority of whom you cannot agree in sentiment, and who are determined to assert their liberties by the ways and means which necessity, and not the love of war, has obliged them to adopt."

As in times of public commotion, martial law may rightfully supercede the office of the civil magistrate, so, on occasions of extreme peril, even liberty of speech may have to yield to the exigency of public safety. The Baltimore committee did not hesitate to act on this principle, and for the first application of it they selected a man who occupied a prominent position in the community. Information was given to them that the Rev. Mr. Edmiston† had publicly approved of the Quebec bill, and had also publicly asserted that all persons who mustered were guilty of treason, and that such of them as had taken the oath of alle-

* Brantz Mayer, Esq.

† Mr. Edmiston was the pastor of St. Thomas' Parish, in Garrison Forest, Baltimore county.

giance to the king of Great Britain, and afterwards took up arms, were guilty of perjury. The committee decided that such declarations had a tendency to defeat the measures recommended for the preservation of America, and that it was their duty to take notice of persons guilty of such offences. Whereupon, a copy of the charge was sent to Mr. Edmiston, and he was summoned to appear before them, which he accordingly did. After taking two hours to consider the matter, he admitted that he had spoken the words, but excused himself by alleging that they were uttered in the heat of political excitement. He explained away, as well as he could, the offensive charge contained in them, and solemnly promised in writing, to avoid, for the future, all similar cause of offence. The committee were satisfied with the apology and promise, and Mr. Edmiston was effectually silenced.

Soon afterwards the case of a man named James Dalgleish was brought before the committee. He had, on different occasions, manifested, in offensive language, his hostility to the country, and expressed an intention of joining the British forces. The committee "resolved that he had discovered an incurable enmity to his country, and that it was dangerous to the common cause to encourage a person of such principles;" and they accordingly "published him to the world, as an enemy of the liberties of Americans." After this we hear no more of James Dalgleish. A man thus stigmatized, was stripped of the power to harm. Further punishment was unnecessary. A stain was imprinted on his name which he carried with him wherever he might go.

But the committee did not rely wholly on moral suasion, or the force of public opinion, though it was seldom that any thing more efficient was required. If other means became necessary, it was not difficult to obtain a file of soldiers to enforce their decisions. And the name of a young officer, on whom special reliance seems to have been placed, appears more than once on the records of the committee. When its bold and able chairman, Mr. Samuel Purviance, undertook, on his own responsibility, and rather irregularly it must be confessed, to seize the person and papers of Governor Eden, the last proprietary governor of Maryland who was still living at Annapolis, though no longer in the exercise of his office, this young officer was selected to take charge of the enterprise. It failed through no fault of his, but because the zeal of the chairman of the Baltimore committee, overran the limits of prudence marked out by the authorities at Annapolis. They suffered the governor to depart in peace. The officer to whom I allude, was then

Captain Samuel Smith. Subsequently, he earned for himself an honorable place in his country's history, and his name is inseparably connected with the annals of this city, which he defended in 1814, as commander-in-chief against the British forces, and of which he was subsequently elected chief-magistrate. Those among us who marked the courage and fire which, at the advanced age of eighty-three, the veteran General Smith, then a private citizen, displayed, when in 1835 he was summoned in haste from Montebello, his country residence, to quell a frightful mob which had well nigh obtained possession of the city of Baltimore,* will know that in the youthful Captain Smith, the Baltimore committee had one to rely on who could not be turned aside from his purpose by fear or favor, while he was engaged in the service of his country.

The committee felt it especially incumbent on them to denounce the use of tea, but to banish this article was a work on which they required the co-operation of those against whom neither their best soldiers, nor public denunciation could avail. As wise and experienced men they knew that conciliation will often prevail where a command would only offend, and, therefore, they mildly and persuasively address the ladies of Baltimore, as follows: "However difficult," say the committee, "may be the disuse of any article which custom has rendered familiar and almost necessary, yet they are induced to hope that the ladies will cheerfully acquiesce in this self-denial, and thereby evince to the world a love to their friends, their posterity and their country." It is to be feared, however, that this advice was not always followed, for there is a tradition, which I have often heard, current in the family of a sturdy patriot, an ancestor of my own, who was a member of the committee, that the forbidden beverage frequently made its appearance even at his table, but, as it was always served in the coffee pot and poured out under the name of coffee, which he did not drink, and as he took instead of tea a cup of milk and water which was provided for him, neither the committee man, nor the community was the wiser, and his daughters thought that no great harm was done. It must not be supposed, however, that these ladies were deficient in patriotism. On the contrary, they cheerfully bore their share of the hardships and privations of the war, and, in common with the rest of the ladies of Baltimore, helped

* See Appendix, Note 2.

with their own hands to clothe the destitute soldiers whom, in 1781, La Fayette was leading to take part in the Virginia campaign.*

The committee sat, as I have said, for more than two years, during which period they exercised a large and somewhat indefinite power over the persons and property of the people, encountered and overcame domestic opposition, gave a powerful impulse to the war, and, when the town was threatened by the enemy, were mainly instrumental in putting it in a state of defence. Their records are not stained by a single act of violence or oppression. The highest fine which they inflicted, did not exceed £10 and seldom reached that amount, and only in a few instances did they exercise their power of making arrests, or of publishing in the newspapers the names of those who had manifested hostility to the cause of the country. Their proceedings, when contrasted with the bloody atrocities which characterized the revolutionary tribunals of France in the last century, demonstrate, as forcibly as any thing can, the wide difference between the people of the two countries, in their fitness for the enjoyment of civil liberty.†

The citizens of Baltimore, on their part, submitted with alacrity and cheerfulness to the control exercised by the committee, and, throughout the war, were honorably distinguished for their devotion to the cause of their country. They performed their full share in achieving its independence and in the establishment of the free institutions, state and national, under which we live.

* La Fayette, on his way to Virginia, passed through Baltimore, where he was hospitably entertained. The incident alluded to is thus related in McSherry's History of Maryland, p. 299. "Being invited to a ball, he was there remarked to be grave and sad. On being questioned by the ladies, as to the cause of his gloom, he replied, that he could not enjoy the gaiety of the scene, whilst his poor soldiers were without shirts and destitute of the necessaries of a campaign. 'We will supply them,' exclaimed these patriotic women. The pleasures of the ball-room were exchanged for the needle, and, on the next day, they assembled in great numbers to make up clothing for the soldiers out of materials advanced by their fathers and husbands."

General La Fayette preserved through life a grateful sense of the assistance thus generously rendered. On his visit to Baltimore in 1824, when the surviving officers and soldiers of the revolution were introduced to him, he remarked to a gentleman near him, "I have not seen among these, my friendly and patriotic commissary, Mr. David Poe, who resided in Baltimore when I was here, and out of his own very limited means supplied me with five hundred dollars to aid in clothing my troops, and whose wife, with her own hands, cut out five hundred pairs of pantaloons and superintended the making of them for the use of my men." On being informed that Mr. Poe was dead, but that his widow was still living, the General expressed an anxious desire to see her. The venerable lady heard this with tears of joy, and, on the next day, an interesting and touching interview took place between them.—*Niles' Register of 24th October*, 1824.

† See Appendix, Note 3.

We, of this generation, have received those institutions by direct inheritance, but like ungrateful heirs we too often forget the source from which they were derived. Towards such institutions the human race, through centuries of toil, has been gradually struggling upward and onward against oppressions, discouragements and disappointments innumerable. Every inch of ground has been won by hard contest against steady opposition, and whole generations have passed away without perceptible progress having been made. In vain efforts to hasten their advent, thousands of brave hearts have shed their blood in battle, or, less fortunate, have broken in dungeons in despair. To us they have descended by the accident of birth, not as our own property which we may waste or destroy, but as a sacred trust which posterity will demand at our hands, in all their integrity as we have received them.

They are not perfect, because they are the work of imperfect men and by such are administered; but it is one of their chief excellences that they are not cast in an unalterable mould, and that they embody no evils which time may not remedy. Time, according to Lord Bacon, is the greatest of all innovators, and he who would innovate wisely, must imitate time. The Creator himself deals thus with evil, an enemy and intruder though it be in his universe, patiently he bears with it, and is content to banish it at last by slow degrees and by the beneficent agency of good. But fanaticism will not wait a single day nor hour. Driven onward by the suggestions of its own ungoverned passions, which it mistakes for the whisperings of a divine voice, it engages in a fierce crusade against some one evil which it is determined to exterminate, although to do so it may first be necessary to perpetrate a crime. Thus a faction at the North would rend asunder the sacred ties which bind this people together for a senseless Wilmot Proviso, and a faction at the South would do the same thing for an equally senseless Slavery Proviso.

We have studied the lessons of the past in vain, if they do not teach us that civil liberty and all that is most valuable in the institutions under which we live, rest for their surest support and protection on the preservation of the Union. But for it, this country would have continued to this day a remote and feeble dependency of the British empire. The thirteen disunited colonies have grown to be thirty united States. If union was necessary once as a defence against the oppression of the mother country, it is incalculably more necessary now as a protection against domestic commotion and fraternal strife. There are, happily, some things which are felt to be degraded by an attempt to subject their worth to the cold process of calculation, and among these should be numbered all that pertains to the honor and welfare of our common country. Unless we have some standard by which we can estimate the loveliness of peace and the wretchedness of war, the glory of national honor and the shame of national disgrace, the gain of progress and the loss of decline, it is in vain for us to attempt to calculate the value of the Union.

With us, here, the effort has never yet been made, and we may hope that it never will be. Even although the love of others should grow cold, it is natural and fitting that Maryland, which has been called the Heart State, because her place is in the very bosom of the Union, should cherish in her heart of hearts a loyal devotion and an unchanging affection for that Union which has been to her the source of countless blessings, by which the great achievements of the past have been accomplished, and through which alone the auspicious promises of the present can be fulfilled.

APPENDIX.

NOTE 1 TO PAGE 20.

A MEETING of the qualified voters of Baltimore county and town was assembled, after public notice, at the Court House, on Saturday the 12th of November, 1774.

Andrew Buchanan was chosen Chairman, and Robert Alexander, Clerk. The following persons were chosen the Committee of Observation:

FOR BALTIMORE TOWN.

Andrew Buchanan, Robert Alexander, William Lux, John Moale, John Merryman, Richard Moale, Jeremiah Townley Chase, Thomas Harrison, Archibald Buchanan, William Smith, James Calhoun, Benjamin Griffith, Gerard Hopkins, William Spear, John Smith, Barnet Eichelberger, George Woolsey, Hercules Courtenay, Isaac Griest, Mark Alexander, Samuel Purviance, Jun'r, Francis Sanderson, John Boyd, George Lindenberger, Isaac Vanbibber, Philip Rogers, David McMechen, Mordecai Gist, and John Deaver.

FOR BALTIMORE COUNTY.

Hundreds.

Patapsco, Lower—Charles Ridgely and Thomas Sollers.

Patapsco, Upper—Zachariah McCubbin, Charles Ridgely, son of William, and Thomas Lloyd.

Back River, Upper—Samuel Worthington, Benjamin Nicholson, T. C. Deye, John Cradock, Darby Lux and William Randall.

Back River, Lower—John Mercer and Job Garretson.

Middle River, Upper—Nicholas Merryman and William Worthington.

Middle River, Lower—H. D. Gough and Walter Tolley, Sen'r.

Soldier's Delight—George Risteau, John Howard, Thomas Gist, Sen'r, Thomas Worthington, Nathan Cromwell and Nicholas Jones.

Middlesex—Thomas Johnson and Maybury Helm.

Delaware—John Welsh, Rezin Hammond and John Elder.

North—Jeremiah Johnson and Elisha Dorsey.

Pipe Creek—Richard Richards, Frederick Decker and Mordecai Hammond.

Gunpowder, Upper—Walter Tolley, Jun'r, Jas. Gittings and Thos. Franklin.

Mine Run—Dixon Stansbury, Jun'r, and Josiah Slade.

And the following resolutions were passed:

Resolved, That the same, or any seven of them, have power to act in matters within the town of Baltimore, and that any five may act in matters, without the said town, in the said county.

Resolved, That T. C. Deye, Capt. Charles Ridgely, Walter Tolley, Jun'r, Benjamin Nicholson, Samuel Worthington, John Moale, Doctor John Boyd, and William Buchanan, or any three of them, be a committee to attend the General Meeting at Annapolis, on Monday, the 24th of this month.

Resolved, That Robert Alexander, Samuel Purviance, Jun'r, Andrew Buchanan, Doctor John Boyd, John Moale, Jeremiah Townley Chase, William Buchanan and William Lux, be a Committee of Correspondence for Baltimore county and Baltimore town, and that any four of them have power to act.

At a subsequent meeting of the voters of Baltimore county and town, held at the Court House on the 16th of January, 1775, the following persons were added to the Committee of Observation:

FOR BALTIMORE TOWN.

James Sterett, Charles Ridgely, Jun'r, William Goodwin, Dr. Charles Weisenthal and Thomas Ewing.

FOR BALTIMORE COUNTY.

Hundreds.

Patapsco, Lower—Charles Rogers, John Gorsuch, William McCubbin, William Wilkinson, Thomas Todd.

Patapsco, Upper—James Croxall, John Ellicot, Edward Norwood.

Back River, Upper—John Cockey, Edward Talbot, Joshua Stevenson, Edward Cockey and Ezekiel Towson.

Middle River, Upper—Benjamin Rogers, Robert Cummings, Benjamin Buck, Joshua Hall, Gist Vaughan, Benjamin Merryman.

Back River, Lower—George Mathews, John Buck.

Middle River, Lower—Moses Galloway, George Goldsmith Presbury, Abraham Britton and Nicholas Britton.

Soldier's Delight—Thomas Cradock, Charles Walker, Samuel Owings, Jr. Christopher Randall, Jr. Benjamin Wells.

Middlesex—Jacob Myers, Richard Cromwell, Thomas Rutter.

Delaware—Christopher Owings, Benjamin Lawrence, Nicholas Dorsey, Jr.

North—John Hall, Stephen Gill, Jr.

Pipe Creek—John Showers, George Everhart.

Gunpowder, Upper—Samuel Young, Jesse Bussey, Thomas Gassaway Howard, James Bosley, William Cromwell, Zaccheus Barret Onion.

Mine Run—Edmund Stansbury, John Stevenson, Daniel Shaw, William Slade, Jr. Joseph Sutton, John Stewart.

At a subsequent meeting, held on the 18th of May, 1775, the following persons were added to the Committee:

FOR BALTIMORE TOWN.

Daniel Bowley.

FOR BALTIMORE COUNTY.

Hundreds.

Middle River, Lower—John German, William Andrews, Edward Day, William Allender.

Patapsco, Upper—Zachariah McCubbin.

Soldier's Delight—Doctor William Lyon.

This Committee served until the month of September in the following year, at which time a new election for Committees of Observation was held in the several counties throughout the Province, in pursuance of a resolution of the Provincial Convention, at Annapolis, which limited the number of the Baltimore Committee to thirty-seven.

The following is an extract from the records of the Committee:

"SATURDAY, 23 *September*, 1775.

"The poll for electing a Committee of Observation for this county, (Messrs. Robert Alexander, Jere. T. Chase, Thomas Harrison, John Moale and Wm. Buchanan, five of the delegates for this county in the late Provincial Convention, being judges of the election,) was this day closed, and the following gentlemen declared duly elected, viz:

1. John Moale,
2. Jeremiah Townley Chase,
3. James Calhoun,
4. Benjamin Nicholson,
5. Andrew Buchanan,
6. Thomas Sollers,
7. John Cradock,
8. James Gittings,
9. Robert Alexander,
10. Samuel Purviance, Jun'r,
11. William Wilkinson,
12. Charles Ridgely, son of Wm.
13. Walter Tolley, Jun'r,
14. Darby Lux,
15. John Cockey,
16. William Smith,
17. William Buchanan,
18. William Lux,
19. John Boyd,
20. John Smith,
21. Zachariah McCubbin, Jun'r.
22. Capt. Charles Ridgely,
23. Thomas Harrison,
24. Benjamin Griffith,
25. William Randall,
26. Thomas Gist, Sen'r.
27. Stephen Cromwell,
28. Isaac Griest,
29. Thomas Cockey Deye,
30. Mordecai Gist,
31. John Stevenson,
32. Ezekiel Towson,
33. Jeremiah Johnson,
34. William Asquith,
35. John Eager Howard,
36. George Risteau,
37. Abraham Britton.

"And the following gentlemen were chosen Provincial Delegates, to continue for one year, viz:

Robert Alexander,
Benjamin Nicholson,
John Moale,
Walter Tolley, Jun'r,
Jeremiah Townley Chase.

"N. B.—The poll was kept open eleven days to give every freeholder and freeman full and sufficient time to vote."]

The following persons of those elected as above, declined to serve:

Thomas Cockey Deye, William Smith, Ezekiel Towson, William Randall, Stephen Cromwell and Jeremiah Johnson. Mordecai Gist became disqualified by the acceptance of a commission as Major in the regular forces, raised by order of the Convention.

The Committee, therefore, on the 4th of March, 1776, filled up the vacancies by electing the following persons:

John Gillis, Frederick Decker, John Merryman, Jr. John Sterrett, Gist Vaughan, Thomas Rutter, Samuel Worthington.

Capt. Charles Ridgely also resigned, but it does not appear that the vacancy thus created was filled by the appointment of another person in his place.

The last meeting of the Committee, elected on the 23d of September, 1775, so far as appears from the minutes, was held on the 12th of Oct., 1776.

The Bill of Rights and Constitution of the State of Maryland were completed and adopted by the Provincial Convention on the 3d of November, 1776, but as some time must necessarily elapse before the Government thus organized could go into full operation, the Convention, on the 11th of November, 1776, directed that new Committees of Observation should be elected for the different counties, with the same powers which they previously possessed, and that they should continue to act until the 10th of March next ensuing.

The records to which I have had access, contain no reference to the election of a Committee under this resolution, or of their proceedings.

NOTE 2 TO PAGE 26.

A more striking instance than the one referred to, could hardly be found, of the influence which, in a time of danger, may be exerted by an individual of strong will and of known conduct and courage. The Bank of Maryland had failed disgracefully, inflicting heavy and widely diffused losses on the people of Baltimore. A deep and just indignation was felt throughout the community, which was artfully directed against certain individuals who had been connected with the bank as directors or otherwise, and who were wrongfully suspected of a participation in the fraudulent conduct by which it had been ruined. Encouraged and sustained by this feeling, a mob threatened to destroy the houses of the obnoxious individuals. The city authorities had ample notice, but they made the fatal mistake of attempting to quell the outbreak by a show of force, without the reality. Citizens who were called on to defend the threatened houses, had wooden batons placed in their hands, and the use of arms was strictly forbidden. But the rioters were not to be thus overawed, and the defenders, of course, had the worst of the conflict which ensued. Bricks and stones were showered upon them and many were seriously injured, until, at last, recourse was had to fire-arms, by which a number was killed and wounded, and the mob was subdued for a single night. But, on the next day, the use which had been made of weapons was denounced by those who should have sustained it, and the rioters became bolder and intent on greater mischief. Various houses were destroyed, the lives of many individuals were threatened, and for twenty-four hours civil authority was completely at an end in Baltimore. No one could tell what acts of violence would next be perpetrated, but the city was filled with rumors of meditated outrage. At this crisis, a few individuals called a meeting of the citizens at the Exchange, but when they came together they had no leader, and were uncertain how to act. A proposition was made and adopted to send for Gen. Smith, who was then at his country seat, two miles from the city, and the meeting waited with anxiety for his arrival. He came with alacrity, and his presence wrought an instantaneous change in the state of affairs. There was no longer any doubt, fear or uncertainty. He would allow no time to be lost in framing resolutions, and making speeches, and would hear of no temporizing with those who were setting all law at defiance. A leader had been found, who, aged as he was, at once took the direction into his own hands. In a few energetic words he insisted that an armed force should at once be organized, and that the rioters should be put down by force if necessary; but, he maintained, that they would not dare to attempt resistance. His plan was adopted by acclamation, and the meeting marched at once in a column with him at its head, to the neighborhood of the Washington monument, where it was organized into companies, who chose their own leaders. Arms were brought out from every receptacle where they could be found, and were in many instances placed in hands which had never used them before. Hundreds flocked to the rescue, and in a few hours, and for many nights afterwards, the whole city was patrolled by armed defenders ready to put down the mob, and anxious to find one. But none appeared. It vanished out of existence the moment that a competent force with a courageous leader was prepared to oppose it.

NOTE 3 TO PAGE 27.

The following extracts from the Minutes are given to illustrate more fully the manner in which the committee performed some of the various duties assigned to them.

The committee were watchful to protect the morals of the people, so far as lay in their power.

At a meeting on the 10th of April, 1775, the following resolution was passed:

"*Resolved,* As the fairs usually held at Baltimore town are hurtful to the morals of the people and are a species of extravagance and dissipation which are forbid by the Continental Congress, that the committee of correspondence be directed to give public notice to the inhabitants of the town and county, that the committee advise them not to erect any booths, or be in any manner concerned in countenancing the holding said fair during the continuance of our public distractions."

Complaint having been made to the committee, that a certain John Burns kept a billiard table, and that shuffle-boards are kept at John Smith's and at Abraham Gorman's, at all of which houses encouragement was given to gaming, and great disorders committed to the injury of the militia and the sailors and mariners employed in the public service as well as others, and the same being contrary to the regulations and resolves of the honorable, the Continental Congress, it was on the 17th of June, 1776,

"*Resolved,* That the chairman issue his summons for the said persons to attend the committee on the following day to answer the complaints alleged against them."

This summons probably had the desired effect of abating the nuisances in question, as no further action appears to have been taken by the committee in the matter.

A night watch for the town of Baltimore being found necessary, it was supplied by the public spirit of the inhabitants and the organization thereof was made by the committee, as appears by the following extract from their minutes.

"At a meeting of the committee on the 26th June, 1775, present Mr. SAMUEL PURVIANCE, Chairman, and forty-two members. WILLIAM LUX, Sec'y.

"The inhabitants of Baltimore town having found it absolutely necessary to establish a nightly watch in the said town, for the preservation of their property from robbery or fire, as well as to prevent any hostile attempts in this time of public confusion, and having had several meetings to digest a proper plan for the purpose, they unanimously agreed to recommend the same to the committee for their approbation and superintendence, which being done the committee highly approved of the measure. And a subscription being signed by every inhabitant, wherein he obliges himself to conform to the regulations adopted, and to attend personally, or provide a sufficient man in his room, which said man, so provided, to be a subscriber, or to pay seven shillings and six pence. The committee received the said subscription, and divided the subscribers into six companies for the Town, and one company for the Point, and then directed a general meeting of the subscribers to elect a captain for each company, which being done, the following gentlemen were returned, viz.

JAMES CALHOUN,	1st,	BARNET EICHELBERGER,	4th,
GEORGE WOOLSEY,	2nd,	GEORGE LINDENBERGER,	5th,
BENJ'N GRIFFITH,	3rd,	WILLIAM GOODWIN,	6th,

for Baltimore Town, and ISAAC VANBIBBER for the Point. But his district being thought rather too extensive, the committee thought it necessary to appoint JESSE HOLLINGSWORTH and GEORGE PATTEN to assist him in the arrangement of the watch.

"The committee then determined that the said watch shall consist of sixteen persons under the direction of a captain, to be appointed for the night, and that they shall patrol the streets from 10 o'clock at night until day-light next morning, and that the companies take it in rotation."

The following is a specimen of the manner of proceeding of the committee when complaint was made that goods were sold at exorbitant prices.

"Cornelius Garritson lodged an information before the committee against Messrs. Usher & Roe, charging them with having sold to him, the said Garritson, certain goods at a higher price than he had usually paid for them, and that they had sold the same kind of goods to himself and others some time ago at a much lower rate than he had now paid. Mr. Roe appeared to answer this charge, and said that Mr. Garritson had asked him for certain buttons which he confesses he had formerly sold to Mr. Garritson and others, at 2*s.* 6*d.* per dozen, but for which he now asked 3*s.* 6*d.* not being willing to sell the buttons, without, at the same time, selling some cloth to which they matched, but that he did at length agree to let Mr. Garritson have them at the price he formerly sold them. Mr. Garritson departed, and soon after returned and took the buttons from a young man who attended in Messrs. Usher & Roe's store, who insisted on having 3*s.* 6*d.* for them per dozen, which said Garritson paid. But as soon as Mr. Roe understood what his clerk had done, he called after Mr. Garritson with an intention to return him his money, but Mr. Garritson refused to return. Mr. Roe afterwards sent the money to said Garritson but he declined accepting it, choosing rather to lodge a complaint to the committee for the imposition. From the above representation it appeared to the committee that the same kind of goods have been incautiously sold at Messrs. Usher & Roe's store at different prices, and, in this instance, above the limitations ascertained by the Provincial Congress—but as it appears to have happened by mistake of their clerk, and as Mr. Roe offered immediately to rectify the mistake, the committee thought proper to dismiss the complaint, with a caution to Messrs. Usher & Roe that they be more careful in future in giving cause for the like complaints."

The committee endeavored to sustain the paper currency issued by the Province. Information having been lodged against Mr. James Moore, of Gunpowder, for refusing to take money issued by the Provincial Convention, tendered to him by Mr. Nathaniel Britain, the committee on the 29th of January, 1776, "*resolved,* that Messrs. Moore and Britain be summoned to attend on Monday next."

"On the 12th of February, 1776, Mr. James Moore appeared according to summons, and Messrs. Nathaniel Britain, Tunis Titus, and Jesse Bussy, appeared as evidences against him, all and each of whom being sworn, deposed, That Mr. Jas. Moore had refused to take bills of credit emitted by the Provincial Convention, when tendered to him, alleging that he was afraid they would not pass, else he should have no objection, and that the said James Moore had asserted, that he would not pay any tax towards the support of American measures, and that he thought all those who had taken the oaths of allegiance and mustered, when holding a place under government, guilty of perjury and rebellion. It being represented by Mr. Gittings, that Jesse Williams was a material witness on the occasion, it was *resolved,* that the further examination of this affair be postponed until Monday next, Mr. William Lux being security for Mr. Moore's attendance."

"Mr. James Moore, agreeable to promise, appeared again before the committee on the 19th of February, and, (after admitting the veracity of the charges exhibited against him in the depositions of Messrs. Nathaniel Britain, Jesse Bussy and Tunis Titus, taken before the committee,) voluntarily signed the following recantation:

"Whereas, I the subscriber, have unfortunately and inadvertently been guilty of actions tending to depreciate the currency emitted by the Convention of this Province, for the express purpose of defending those inestimable privileges transmitted to us by our ancestors, and expressed an aversion to pay any taxes for sinking said currency, and other ways discouraged people from mustering, enrolling and associating, but am now satisfied and convinced that such conduct is highly unbecoming the duty of an American, and tends immediately to obstruct the measures calculated to preserve the liberties of this country from the cruel and unrelenting oppressions of the British ministry, do most sincerely acknowledge the heinousness of such offence, beg pardon of my countrymen, and do hereby solemnly engage and promise not to be guilty of a like offence in future, but to conform to such measures as shall be adjudged necessary by the Continental Congress, or Conventions of this Province, for the preservation of the rights of America. As a further atonement for my misconduct, I request this acknowledgment to be published, in hopes it may deter others from committing the like offence. Witness my hand this 19th of February, 1776. James Moore."

Whereupon it was "resolved that the above is satisfactory."

The following energetic proceedings were taken against Mr. Francis Sanderson, who had been elected a member of the first committee of observation, but who afterwards gave great offence by the manifestation of tory principles, and by accepting an appointment from the Proprietary government to the office of a justice of the peace, after those who had been previously in the commission had been summarily dismissed from office on account, it would seem, of their taking sides with the popular movement.

"May 8th, 1775. Mr. Francis Sanderson, once a member of this committee, but who, for some time past, had neglected his duty, by refusing or declining giving attendance at their meetings and other exceptionable conduct, did this day again unexpectedly appear among them. The committee reflecting on his late conduct, and uncertain as to the design of his coming among them at so critical a juncture, plainly informed Mr. Sanderson of their sentiments, that they could not but suspect a man of so variable principles and questionable conduct—that as matters of great moment frequently were agitated among them, they did not think it prudent or safe for them to sit in council with a person in whom they could have no confidence, and that therefore they would wish him to withdraw himself from the committee, till the sense of the county should be known concerning him at a future election.

"Mr. Sanderson declared that he was sensible of the impropriety and mistakes of his late conduct, but was now heartily disposed to concur in every measure that his countrymen should adopt for the preservation of their rights—that in the meantime he acquiesced in the intimation of the committee, and would, for the future, so conduct himself as, if possible, to recover the good opinion of his countrymen, and convince them of the sincerity of his present declarations."

The voters of the town and county were assembled on the 18th of May, 1775, "when the proceedings of the committee on the 8th of May, respecting Mr. Francis Sanderson, were read to the freemen of the county now convened, and their sentiments taken on the propriety of the committee's request to Mr.

Sanderson to decline acting as a committee man, till the sense of their constituents should be known on the matter; the freemen having heard what Mr. Sanderson had to offer, unanimously approved of the committee's prudent conduct, and do further resolve that until Mr. Sanderson shall give unequivocal evidence of his sincere attachment to the cause of his injured country, by a steady and uniform acquiescence in every measure which has or may be generally adopted for her preservation, they cannot approve of him as a man to act for them in committee, leaving it to the committee to determine how far he is otherwise entitled to public favor. The committee accordingly, (the business of the county having been finished,) fifty-two members being present, proceeded to consider and judge of Mr. Sanderson's case; and were of opinion, that as he had already acknowledged to the committee his error and late misconduct, and was sincerely sorry for the same, and was now willing to satisfy his countrymen by a public declaration of his present political opinion, as contained in a paper which he handed in, Mr. Sanderson be restored to the good opinion of his countrymen."

The paper handed in by Mr. Sanderson, was as follows:

"I hereby declare that I have resigned the office of a Justice of the Peace for Baltimore county, being now sensible that my appointment to that office, with others, in the manner, and at the time the same was done, was disagreeable to my friends, and tended to injure the cause of my distressed country. I further declare my readiness to engage heartily in the measures now carrying on for the preservation of American liberty, and for that purpose I have contributed to the purchase of arms and ammunition, and also to the poor of Boston and enrolled myself a soldier in a company of militia; and I trust my future conduct will evince the sincerity of my present declarations, and restore me to the favor and esteem of my countrymen, an event most ardently wished for by FRANCIS SANDERSON."

But Mr. Sanderson, encouraged probably by the success of the British forces in New York, sometime afterwards again brought himself into trouble, as appears by the following extract from the minutes of the committee:

"At a special meeting of the committee on Saturday, 12th October, 1776—Present: Samuel Purviance, Chairman, William Lux, Vice-Chairman—W. Buchanan, B. Nicholson, T. Rutter, W. Asquith, J. Calhoun.

"Information being given to the committee, on oath, by Mr. David Evans, that Francis Sanderson had, in a conversation with him, spoken words 'tending to disunite the good people of this State, in the present opposition to Great Britain,' by order of the committee, 12th October, 1776, Francis Sanderson is required to attend this committee at Mr. Purviance's immediately, to answer a complaint exhibited against him for several words spoken by him, and tending to disunite the people of this State in their present opposition to Great Britain, and, in case he don't attend, Captain Cox is directed to bring him by force.

Per order W. L., V. Chr'n.

"The said Francis Sanderson appeared in consequence of the warrant, and having nothing to offer in vindication of the charge, he was committed to the custody of the guard for this night, in order to be sent to the Council of Safety, agreeably to the resolves of the Convention, in July, 1775.

Attested, GEO. LUX, Sec'y."

The Council of Safety appear to have referred the case to the Provincial Convention, then in session at Annapolis, by which body the following proceedings were had:

"October 16, 1776. The Convention met.

"On reading a letter from Samuel Purviance, Jr., chairman of the committee of observation, from Baltimore county, respecting the conduct of Francis Sanderson, the same was taken into consideration, and the said Francis Sanderson called before the Convention, and on the examination of several witnesses, and hearing him in his defence,

"On motion of Mr. Paca, the question was put, That the said Francis Sanderson is guilty of delivering sentiments tending to discourage the American opposition to the hostile attempts of Great Britain; that therefore he be reprimanded at the bar of this house by the president; that he give bond in the penalty of one thousand pounds, with good security, to be approved of by the committee of Baltimore county, to the president, conditioned, that he will not hereafter speak or do any matter or thing in prejudice or discouragement of the present opposition; that he pay all the expenses incurred on account of his being apprehended, guarded, and brought to this Convention, and that thereupon he be discharged. Resolved in the affirmative."

"Francis Sanderson was then called to the bar of the house, and reprimanded accordingly."

The Committee manifested great energy and judgment in all their proceedings, and especially in enrolling and arming troops, accumulating munitions of war, and in placing the town of Baltimore in a condition of defence when in March, 1776, it was threatened with an attack from the enemy; but a further selection from the minutes would swell this Appendix to an unreasonable size. The object of the insertion of the extracts which have been given, has been to gratify a reasonable curiosity, which has been expressed, to see in print the names of those in Baltimore who were prominent in the early revolutionary movement, and to exhibit the calm, determined and business-like manner in which a committee—chosen indiscriminately from the various walks of life, and responsible for all their proceedings to the people whose sentiments and feelings they represented—deliberated and acted in the very dangerous and difficult emergency in which they were placed, and the moderation and ability with which they exercised the large and somewhat indefinite powers with which they were clothed.

A SKETCH

OF THE

LIFE AND SERVICES

OF

Gen. Otho Holland Williams,

READ BEFORE THE

Maryland Historical Society,

ON THURSDAY EVENING, MARCH 6, 1851.

By OSMOND TIFFANY.

BALTIMORE:
PRINTED BY JOHN MURPHY & CO.
No. 178 MARKET STREET.
1851.

MR. PRESIDENT:

THE events of the American Revolution are so nearly connected with our own times, that the actors in that great struggle seem yet to be to us as living men. We open the portal of the past century, and are with those who once like ourselves, breathed and thought, and who now, lie not silent or forgotten in the tomb.

Their deeds live in our memory; their examples are glorious as of old: their words of hope in dark hours, and of their joy in success, still burn before us:—they have become the great historians of their age. Among this band of gallant men, who gave themselves with all their soul to liberty, I could name none of our native State, who displayed a more patient, disinterested, and zealous spirit, than the pure and chivalrous Otho Holland Williams.

He was born in the county of Prince George's, in March, 1749. His parentage was highly respectable, his ancestors emigrating from Wales, and he being of the second generation after their settlement in Maryland.

Had his days been wholly passed in the enjoyment of peace, his influence would not have been lost. He would still have left to his friends the same invaluable legacy of a good name, but it was his fortune to deserve and gain a wider celebrity. He was his father's oldest son, and in the year succeeding his birth, his home was changed to the mouth of the Conococheague Creek, in Frederick, near Washington county. In that beautiful region of country, watered by the stream that lends its name to the valley, were spent the few short years of his boyhood. There he learned to love the aspect of fields and groves, the memory of which was his solace long after, in many dark and trying hours, for we find in the midst of the toils of the camp, that his spirit yearns for rural peace and solitude. The love of nature is ever ennobling; it perhaps contributed to form the character of the future hero.

It is a favorite theme with biographers to dwell on parental precepts, especially on those of the mother. We have no anecdotes of this period, but we may yield to a happy idea, and imagine young Williams listening to the accents of a mother's lip, with the true deference which he always paid to goodness. We may see him, among his little playmates on his father's farm, already showing those traits of character, which guided him in the path to honor: that love of truth, that physical and moral courage, which won in time the confidence of his great commander-in-chief, who had himself early shone in the same qualities. We may picture him crossing the fields, at early morning hours, to the rustic school, there to recite the simple lesson, and to be instructed in his mother tongue, which he afterwards used with the grace of a scholar. But the sunshine of his boyhood was soon clouded—his father, Joseph Williams, died, leaving but a small property to seven children; and Otho at the age of thirteen, was thrown upon his own exertions. He was placed with his brother-in-law, Mr. Ross, in the Clerk's Office of Frederick county. Here he remained several years, diligently occupied in studying the duties of the bureau, and when he was duly qualified, took charge of it himself, for a while, until removed to a similar situation in Baltimore. It was in this vocation that he acquired those habits of regularity and method, which were so signally manifested when called to situations of the highest trust.

His appearance at this time, when about eighteen years of age, is thus described by his friend and fellow-soldier, Gen. Samuel Smith: "He was," says the writer, "about six feet high, elegantly formed; his whole appearance and conduct much beyond his years; his manner, such as made friends of all who knew him."

Thus does he appear before us, while to use Burke's apt expression, he was yet in the gristle, and had not hardened into the bone of manhood. But he was already a man in his high sense of honor, his unsullied integrity, and the polish of his address: if he had not won laurels, he had acquired the esteem of the worthy.

Thus endowed, we learn that he entered into commercial life, in Fredericktown, shortly before the commencement of the American Revolution. There is little doubt, that had this course been pursued, it would have been crowned with eminent success, for he afterwards united, to an extraordinary degree, military genius with scientific business habits. But when the clouds, which had so long been gathering over the sun of peaçe, burst at last, all thought of pursuing quiet trade was abandoned. The spirit that prompted Putnam to reverse the Scriptural promise, and beat the plough-share into the sword, kindled kindred feelings in the breast of Williams. A company was formed in Fredericktown, and under the command of Capt. Price, marched for Boston. Williams might easily have obtained the captaincy, but with the modesty which always kept pace with his success, he declined to press a claim to command, saying to the committee, that though ambitious to lead, he was willing to serve. This spirit uniformly attended him—he deferred cheerfully to authority himself, and exacted obedience from those whom he commanded. He was a strict disciplinarian, as all good officers are, but governed his own conduct by his rigid adherence to the rules of superiors. In reporting an officer to Gen. Greene, for disobedience, he says: "When orders are received with contempt, and rejected with insolence, examples are requisite to re-establish subordination, the basis of discipline."

But, before attempting to trace the career of the soldier, it will be by no means uninteresting, or uninstructive, to depict the man. His letters to his family and friends, are true mirrors in which he was reflected, and we cannot more fully present him, than by a few sentences from his correspondence. Indeed, I have found his letters so graphic and elegant in style, so illustrative of any subject on which they touch, that I have made large extracts, believing that they would be of much greater historic value, concerning the scenes and actions of which they treat, than any description of mine. His views of life were most cheerful and happy—he writes to his brother thus:

"I have seen a great variety of life, and profess most seriously, that there is more true felicity to be found in a bare competence and domestic industry, than in any other circumstances. My observations on others confirm this opinion, and I wish to have an opportunity of experiencing the satisfaction which I am sure is to be found in rural employments. We should not hope to be wealthy, or fear to be poor; we never shall want; and whoever considers the true source of his happiness, will find it in a very great degree, arising from a delicate concern for those dependent upon him, useful employments, and the approbation of his friends."

He was ambitious, but his ambition never led him astray: and through all circumstances of life, he was governed by a deeply religious faith. His own words precisely express his feelings: "It would give me pain, if the world should believe any person, with the same advantages, may do more than I may. Fortune does a great deal in all military adventures, and, therefore, I am not to say whether this reproach will come upon me or not. But you may rely upon it, my good friend, discretion and fortitude shall govern my conduct; and in the interim, I commit myself to that Power whose eye is over all his works, and by whose goodness I have been preserved in numerous perils."

We do not learn that Williams was engaged in any very noted service until the following year, but he acquired the confidence and esteem of his superiors—among others Gen. Gates, whose friendship often professed, was afterwards proven. In 1776 he was promoted to the rank of Major, in a rifle regiment formed from Maryland and Virginia troops, and we learn that his first trial in actual battle, occurred at the fall of Fort Washington, on the Hudson River. He was stationed in a wood with his troops, in advance of the Fort, and was attacked by the Hessian allies. They were several times repulsed with heavy loss, but being reinforced, they succeeded in beating back Williams and his company into the Fort, where all were eventually taken prisoners. The enemy accomplished this by reinforcements, as has been already mentioned, and from the unfortunate condition of the rifles of the attacked party. By long continued and incessant fire, these had become so foul as to be nearly useless, and Williams reluctantly retreated at the last moment, only to delay capture for a short period. The feelings of an officer, when obliged to yield his sword, and suffer an imprisonment, he knows not how long or cruel it may be, must be sufficiently agonizing to feel that utter inactivity is forced upon him, at the very instant that his country is most in need of the services he would cheerfully render. In the last attack of the Hessians, Williams received a severe and dangerous shot wound in the groin, though he entirely recovered from its effects in due time. His career was suddenly checked, and he was doomed to languish fifteen months, before he again saw the sun shine on his freedom. The first half of his captivity, though painful enough to an ardent patriot, was not total eclipse.

He was placed on Long Island on parole, and among many annoyances, there occurred some incidents which cheered him in captivity. He formed the acquaintance of Major Ackland, a British officer, and they became firm friends. The elegant person, and finished manners of Williams, procured him access to circles as a gentleman, which would have closed to him solely as a prisoner; and under the guidance of Ackland, visiting the opposite city of New York, he sometimes appeared in the fashionable houses, which reversing the present order,were then measured on the scale of style, by proximity to the battery.

It is related that on one occasion, after Williams had been dining with Lady Ackland, his good friend the Major, and he, sallied forth for a ball, and that although the company were much struck with the elegant figures and demeanor of the two friends, and although the Briton made all effort to introduce the captive, the gentlemen of the party could not forget the enemy to welcome the stranger, and the ladies treated him with extreme coldness. Ackland finding that all his efforts were vain, took Williams by the arm and led him from the room, saying, "Come, this company is too exclusive for us." This was not the only occasion on which Major Ackland proved his friendship and sympathy for Americans.

His fate was a melancholy one, and such as he little deserved. After the war of the Revolution, and when he had returned to his own country, on the occasion of a dinner, the valor of American soldiers became the subject of conversation. On their merit being denied, Ackland defended them, and in the warmth of argument with a brother officer, to some assertion, replied that he lied. The insult was of course unpardonable, and could only be settled by a duel, in which he was shot dead.

During the period of Williams' confinement on Long Island, it was the pleasure of some of the British officers to stroll among the American prisoners, and tauntingly ask them in what trade they had been employed. When Williams was asked this impertinent question by a titled officer, he replied, that he had been bred in that situation which had taught him to rebuke and punish insolence, and that the questioner would have ample proof of his apprenticeship on a repetition of his offence. The noble did not attempt it, or demand satisfaction for the contempt with which he had been treated, but it is probable, that through his instrumentality, Williams was accused of carrying on a secret correspondence with Washington. There was, indeed, some apparent foundation for suspicion in Williams' superior ability, and from the respect paid to him by his fellow-prisoners. He was seized, and without one word of defence on his part being listened to, without being suffered to confront his accusers, he was suddenly removed to the provost jail in New York.

Here he was delivered to the tender mercies of harsh turnkeys, and confined in a room about sixteen feet square that was seldom visited by the breath of heaven, and always remaining in a state of loathsome filth. Among other prisoners, was the celebrated Ethan Allen, and he shared the miserable den, in which Williams was confined. Their only visitors were wretches who came to glut their brutal curiosity, and to torture their victims with loud sentiments of delight in the anticipation of seeing them hanged. Letters complaining of such cruel treatment were repeatedly but vainly addressed to the commandant of New York, and they thus suffered for seven or eight months.

Their health was much impaired, for their food was of the vilest sort, and scarce enough to keep soul and body together, and to add to these discomforts, the anxiety that preyed upon their minds, was terrible in the extreme. The naturally fine constitution of Williams was much impaired, and he never recovered entirely from the effects of his imprisonment. But he is still full of hope, to which, though not written at the time of his incarceration, his own words to one of his family thus bear witness: "I flatter myself I shall still see a day, a prosperous day, when we shall all be assembled in some agreeable spot in the neighborhood of Hagerstown, where we shall mutually embrace each other, with joy and tenderness, and cheerfully recount the tedious hours which the distresses of our country oblige us to pass in absence, and when the dangers that are passed will serve as a subject for an evening tale." But finally, the doors of his prison-house were thrown asunder and he was free.

After the surrender of Burgoyne, Gen. Gates proved his friendship by stipulating positively for Williams' release, and he was exchanged for his old friend Major Ackland, who had been taken prisoner with the British army. Gen. Phillips, the commandant of New York, anxious to offer some excuse for the rigor with which Williams had been treated, asked him to dine with him, but the invitation was properly rejected. During his captivity his native State had not been unmindful of him, he had been appointed to the command of the 6th regiment of the Maryland line, and he joined the army in New Jersey, shortly before the battle of Monmouth, fought in June, 1778. The result of this engagement is well known: it gave great encouragement to the American troops, and Col. Williams has left a little description of the joy with which the following anniversary of Independence was celebrated, a joy enhanced by the favorable issue of the late conflict, and moreover, is one of the few instances on record in which the day has been celebrated without a patriotic oration.

His letter is dated Camp New Brunswick, July 6th, 1778:—"On the 4th inst. the anniversary of American Independence was celebrated in the following manner. At 3 o'clock in the afternoon, a cannon was discharged as a signal for the troops to get under arms, half an hour afterwards, the second fire was a signal for the troops to begin their march, and at four the third signal was given, for the troops to drawn up in two lines, on the west side of the Raritan, which they did in beautiful order. A flag was then hoisted for the *feu de joie* to begin. Thirteen pieces of artillery were then discharged, and a running fire of small arms went through the lines, beginning at the right of the front line, catching the left, and ending at the right of the second line. The field pieces in the intervals of brigades, were discharged in the running fire, thus affording a harmonious and uniform display of music and fire, which was thrice well executed. After the *feu de joie* the general officers and officers commanding brigades, dined with his Excellency. Yesterday a number of field officers shared the same fate, and I had the satisfaction of seeing the old warrior in very fine spirits."

During the remainder of Col. Williams' sojourn in the Northern States, we do not learn that he was in any position to prove his skill as a soldier, excepting in those qualities which are too often under-estimated by the public. His regiment when he took command of it, was rather noted for looseness of discipline, and did not stand upon a mark with others of the line, but in a very short time, under Williams' prompt and active organization, it became equal if not superior, in thorough discipline, to any in the whole army.

A soldier should certainly not be deemed unable, who has few opportunities of any brilliant success, and who is only known by the admirable order of his troops.

From several of Williams' letters written about this time, we learn that if there was little chance of fame, he found time to fall in love, proving that though ambitious of the glory of Mars, he was not insensible to the blandishments of Venus.

But it is time, that we approach the sphere of action in which Williams was particularly distinguished, and where he acquired such honor, as to raise him to eminence among the greatest Generals of this country. We allude to the war in the Southern States, particularly the Carolinas, in which some of the bloodiest and most obstinate battles were fought, during the whole revolution. The entire country in that portion of the States, was completely reduced and subdued by the superior generalship of

Sir Henry Clinton, who had left New York, for the express purpose of subjugating the Carolinas. He had been eminently successful, and it will not be unimportant to pass briefly in review, the condition to which those States had been reduced, when Congress determined to succor them, by reinforcements of Northern troops, among which were the Maryland and Virginia lines. On receipt of the news of Clinton's expedition, Charleston, then in possession of the Americans, had been placed in a state of defence, in the manner deemed best calculated to resist the enemy, though the garrison was enfeebled by disease, want of money, and want of enthusiasm among the soldiery. Many refused to serve again, after the late campaign in Georgia, unwilling to leave their homes, and having no faith in their own strength, against a powerful and amply munitioned foe. They also had strong grounds, through the proclamations of the English, to believe that non-resistance to the Crown would purchase security from fire and pillage, for it was the policy of the English utterly to destroy, as far as possible, all kinds of property belonging to the Republicans. The garrison of Charleston consisted of scarcely five thousand men, under command of General Lincoln, while Clinton's force alone, amounted to upwards of eight thousand. The garrison, after an obstinate defence of forty days, was obliged to surrender to the enemy, before which time, all hope of succor or escape was reluctantly abandoned. Various expeditions were planned by the American troops, but almost every one was prevented, or destroyed, by the ceaseless vigilance and activity of the British, among whom none was ever more conspicuous than the well remembered Tarlton. No sooner did the British standard wave over the ramparts of Charleston, than Clinton determined to use the most energetic means, to ensure the reduction of the entire province. To this end, he planned several expeditions, all of which succeeded even beyond his own hopes. The royalists joined his army in great numbers, and the Americans were defeated at all points. The complete rout and terrible slaughter of the Republicans, under Col. Buford, at Wacsaw, the enemy being led on by Tarlton, for a time utterly prostrated the vigor of the Carolinians, who thereupon submitted in despair. Clinton, then by promise of amnesty, endeavored to maintain the authority which British bayonets had again acquired, but he excepted those who had been instrumental in the defence of Charleston. This measure was productive, as we shall see, of the most fatal consequences, and in time overturned all hopes of those which he so strenuously endeavored to introduce. His object was to put down the slightest attempt at rebellion, and those who had lately fought for Congress, were forced to take up arms for the Crown, instead of being suffered to remain as prisoners of war, on parole.

This unexpected act of tyranny produced a state of society of which, at this period, we can have but little idea.

Those who had fought bravely in defence, were treated with the most cruel persecutions, their property plundered and destroyed, while those who submitted supinely to their fate, were sometimes rewarded, or at least suffered to remain undisturbed. This naturally engendered a bitter feeling, even between families, and the complete separation of members of the same flock, were but the happiest results: their hate was frequently kindled into a flame, only quenched in blood. Williams has left a graphic picture of the state of society at that time, and it may be remarked, that his opinion of the inhabitants was by no means high.

He says, writing to his brother:—"There are a few virtuous good men in this State, and in Georgia; but a great majority of the people is composed of the most unprincipled, abandoned, vicious vagrants that ever inhabited the earth. The daily deliberate murders committed by pretended Whigs, and reputed tories, (men who are actually neither one thing nor the other in principle,) are too numerous and too shocking to relate. The licentiousness of various classes and denominations of villains, desolate this country, impoverish all who attempt to live by other means and destroy the strength and resources of the country, which ought to be collected and united, against a common enemy.

"You may rely on it, my dear brother, that the enemy have had such footing and influence in this country that their success in putting the inhabitants together by the ears, has exceeded even their own expectations: the distraction that prevails surpasses any thing I ever before witnessed, and equals any idea, which your imagination can conceive, of a desperate and inveterate civil war."

But horrible as this state of society was, it had some redeeming features; fire might consume, a savage soldiery might plunder, the sun might scorch and not gladden, and the rivers might run with blood, instead of water, but the women of the Carolinas stood superior to their husbands, their sons, and their brothers, and were unconquered, unconquerable. They indeed, bore the fiery trial, and preferred exile to submission, death to slavery. They incited their kindred never to lay down their arms, until the last foe had vanished from their soil. They would with the courage of Joan of Arc, have grasped the sword, and perished at the stake. They would not give their hand in the light dance to a Briton; they gave their heart with their hand to the meanest of their countrymen. They threw the gold bracelet into the scale to lighten the iron fetter. They feared not the contagion of the prison ships, nor the damp of the dungeon. They instilled into their drooping relatives new hopes, and urged them once more to draw the sword, and throw away the scabbard. It is related that Col. Tarlton once asked a lady in Charleston, the name of the Camomile blossom. "It is called," answered the noble woman, "the Rebel flower, because it flourishes best when most trampled on." The influence of woman prevailed, the sword seemed sharpened, instead of blunted by the blows it had taken, and the spirit of '76 again animated the soldiery. The arrival of Lafayette about this period, was most welcome: he brought encouraging news, and instilled into the colonists hopes which were soon verified by the arrival of the French fleet, commanded by Admiral de Tiernay, in Newport harbor. Then the people once more flew to arms, and

> The war that for a space did fail
> Now trebly thundering swelled the gale.

General Gates took command in July, 1780, superseding Baron de Kalb; and Col. Williams with his regiment appears at the seat of war, in the Southern States, about that time. He assumed by appointment the important post of deputy Adjutant

General, which added greatly to his duties, but which he discharged through his whole period of service, with exemplary fidelity. He has left a detailed narrative of the campaign of 1780, (published in Johnston's Life of Greene,) and his letters give most graphic accounts of the battles in which he was engaged, and the trials in other forms, through which he passed. The sharp action where blows were given and taken, proved less arduous and scarce more dangerous, than the sufferings of the army without an enemy in sight. He writes soon after his arrival—"The affairs of our little southern army are much deranged, and we find ourselves under very considerable embarrassments in our present position; the want of provisions is an inconvenience we have often experienced, but we have never been in a country so unwilling to supply us as at present. By military authority, we collect a kind of casual subsistence that can scarcely be called our daily bread. The fatigue of campaigning in this country is almost inconceivable. I have slept, when I have had time to sleep, in my clothes. I seldom divest myself of my sword, boots or coat; my horse is constantly saddled, and we eat when provisions are to be got, and we have nothing else to do. The dangers of the field are neither more frequent, nor more fatal, than those attending the fatigues and accidents that reduce an army—from long experience, I find myself so capable of sustaining the fatigue, and by my good fortune (the favor of Providence) I have so often escaped the danger, that I am contented to do my duty, and submit myself to that fate which Heaven ordains."

The campaign of 1780 was a most unfortunate one for the Southern States, as that of 1776 was for the Northern. Soon after General Gates took command, the battle of Camden was fought, which resulted in the total defeat of the Americans. Col. Williams gives an account of it in his sketch of the campaign, but I have not been able to find any of his private letters on the subject. The battle was fought on the 16th of August, and from returns which Williams collected, the actual number of fighting men or rather of able bodied troops, for some did not fight at all, amounted only to three thousand and fifty-two, about one-half of the nominal strength of the army. The numbers of the enemy were much superior, and at the very time that Gen. Gates had determined to march upon Camden, Lord Cornwallis, commander-in-chief, (Clinton having returned to New York,) apprised of all that was passing in the interior of the States, determined to march himself to reinforce Lord Rawdon, thinking it highly probable from the position of the American army, that Camden would be a point of speedy attack. He arrived there two days before the battle, and unwilling to hazard an assault, determined to surprise the rebels in their place of encampment at Clermont. Thus both armies, ignorant of each other's intentions, moved about the same hour of the night, and approaching each other, met half way between their respective encampments at midnight. An exchange of fire between the advanced guards was the first notice that either army had of the other. Hostilities were for the time suspended, and from one of the prisoners taken in the skirmish, Williams learned that Lord Cornwallis led the army with three thousand troops under his especial command, besides those of Lord Rawdon's.

This intelligence threw consternation into the American army, and Gen. Gates called a council of war. It was decided that the time had passed for any course but fighting. Frequent skirmishes occurred throughout the night, which served to display the relative force and situation of the two armies. Col. Williams narrates another circumstance which contributed to distress the Americans, and he says:

"Nothing ought to be considered as trivial in an army which in any degree affects the health or spirit of the troops, upon which often, more than upon number, the fate of battles depends. The troops of Gen. Gates' army had frequently felt the consequence of eating bad provisions, but at this time a hasty meal of quick baked bread and fresh meat, with a dessert of molasses mixed with mush or dumplings, operated so cathartically as to disorder very many of the men, who were breaking the ranks all night, and were certainly much debilitated before the action commenced in the morning."

On the morning of the 16th, the two armies came together, and Williams at the very onset distinguished himself by his valor, and by his suggestion to Gen. Gates that the enemy should be attacked while displaying by Gen. Stevens' brigade, already in line of battle, as first impressions were very important. Gen. Gates at once replied, "that's right, let it be done." This, however, could not be accomplished until the right wing of the British was discovered in line, too late to attack them while displaying. Williams at the head of forty or fifty men then commenced the attack, and kept up a brisk fire. But the militia no sooner beheld the enemy advance impetuously, than they threw down their arms without firing and fled instantly. This was followed by others, acting in the same pusillanimous style, and at least two-thirds of the army never fired a shot. Williams writes:

"He who has never seen the effect of a panic upon a multitude can have but an imperfect idea of such a thing. The best disciplined troops have been enervated and made cowards by it. Armies have been routed by it, even where no enemy appeared to furnish an excuse. Like electricity, it operates instantly; like sympathy, it is irresistible where it touches."

The regular troops, including those of Maryland, stood their ground, and by tremendous fires of musketry kept the enemy for a while in check. Several times did the British give way and as often rallied. But two brigades of American troops remained firm upon the field. Williams called upon his regiment not to fly; he saw that to avoid retreat was impossible but wished it to be accomplished with credit. The troops stood well and returned the hot fire of the enemy with zeal, until Cornwallis, charging with his whole force of dragoons and infantry, put them to total rout. Not a company retired in good order, but Williams attributed this not to want of courage; they had fought against desperate odds, besides having to fight for those who so ingloriously fled, but it appears that there was no command to retreat from any general officer until it became too late to retire in order. Williams gained in this action, unfortunate as it proved, a character for cool courage, for discretion, and that thorough knowledge of tactics so essential in the officer, and without which impetuosity would be but an explosive gas, but which, guarded by the master-hand of the philosopher, burns steadily through the thickest gloom. Never off his guard, he knew when and where to strike, and when to reserve the blow that opportunity only served to encourage; for it is hard for the brave in battle to retain the gauntlet of defiance, and so armed, "out of the nettle danger pluck the flower safety."

General Gates never entirely recovered from the odium showered upon him by the event of the battle of Camden, and the consequences finally led to his displacement, and the appointment of Gen. Greene to the command of the Southern army, but Williams always continued his firm friend, and speaks of him in several instances as the "good old man."

(It is impossible, in a sketch so brief as this, to give any detailed account of the war in the Carolinas; it will be sufficient to introduce successively Col. Williams' graphic pictures of the battles and scenes in which he was engaged.)

The tide of fortune could not flow forever with the English, and at the battle of King's Mountain, in which Williams took part, they were utterly defeated; this victory proved a severe blow to the interests of Lord Cornwallis. Sometimes by good luck, advantages were gained, as in the following circumstance during the same year, and of which Williams gives this account, dated 7th Dec. 1780:

"A few days ago Gen. Morgan, with the Light Infantry of our army and a party of Light Dragoons under Lieut. Col. Washington, moved towards Camden. Col. Rugely's farm was defended by a strong block house, which was garrisoned by Col. Rugely and a party of new levies. A good block house is proof against musketry and sometimes against light artillery. Therefore Gen. Morgan would not risk his troops in an assault, but had recourse to stratagem, and Lieut. Col. Washington executed the plan. He paraded the cavalry in view of the block house and mounted the trunk of a pine tree upon three prongs, instead of a field piece, and which he manned with dismounted dragoons, then summoned Rugely to surrender, which the poltroon did, without hearing a report of this new invented piece of ordnance, and submitted himself with about 100 officers and men to be taken as prisoners of war."

The battle of Cowpens was another blow—perhaps the most decisive victory gained by the Americans during the whole war, and in which the hitherto terrible and fortunate Tarlton was put to total rout.

The retreat of the army through North Carolina, which, so admirably executed, had the effect of leading Cornwallis into Virginia, followed the battle of Cowpens, and gave Williams an opportunity of displaying those qualities of tact, vigilance and prudence, which gain for an officer a fame as deserved as the laurels won in battle. He commanded the rear guard, and succeeded in eluding every effort of the enemy in pursuit. Greene, with a keen eye, early distinguished his abilities, and he became, as long as he remained with the army, one of his general's few and constant advisers. He appointed him Adjutant General, as he had been Deputy under Gates.

The next engagement of consequence is that of Guilford Court House, and Williams has left a short account of it in a hasty letter to his brother. His letter is dated from Camp at Speedwell's furnace, ten miles from Guilford Court House, 1st March, 1781:

"The Southern army has once more come off second best in a general action. Gen. Greene being reinforced with a few small detachments of new levies, which gave the regular battalion a respectable appearance, and a sufficient number of militia to make his force apparently superior to the British army, made the best possible arrangement of his troops, and for many reasons which rendered it almost absolutely necessary, came to a resolution of attacking Lord Cornwallis the first opportunity. When both parties are disposed for action all obstacles are soon overcome. The two armies met at Guilford Court House yesterday at 12 o'clock. Our army was well posted; the action was commenced by the advanced parties of infantry and cavalry, in which our troops were successful, but the situation of the ground not being favorable in our front, our army kept its position and waited the attack of the British. They were opposed wherever they appeared. The militia of North Carolina behaved as usual, but those of Virginia distinguished themselves by uncommon bravery. The regular troops were the last that had come to action and generally behaved well, but as these were the most inconsiderable in number, the general chose rather to retire than risk a defeat. The retreat was made in tolerable good order, and so stern was the appearance of our regular force, that the enemy did not think proper to press our rear, nor continue the pursuit more than three miles. Our greatest loss is four pieces of artillery and the field."

During the next month another ineffectual attempt was made upon Camden, and pursuing the plan formed of allowing the actors in these scenes to speak for themselves, we have Col. Williams' account of the efforts of the army as follows:

"Camp before Camden, 27 *April*, 1781.

"*Dear Elie*—We have been here ever since the 19th instant, and have made several manœuvres, upon different quarters of the town, but have neither been able to discover advantages, that promised success by a storm, nor to completely invest the place. The town is flanked on the West by the Wateree, and on the East by two deep creeks; the other quarters are strongly fortified. A villain of a drummer went in to the enemy on the the 24th, when we were encamped within a mile of the town, and gave them such information of our circumstances, position and numbers, as induced Lord Rawdon to sally with all his best troops the next morning, about eleven o'clock.

"This was what we wished, and the only hope we had of a speedy reduction of the post. Lieut. Col. Washington was ordered to pass the right flank of the enemy with his cavalry, which he did, and threw himself in their rear. Capt. Kirkwood, with two small companies of light infantry, was behaving bravely in front, and the picquets were doing their duty upon the flanks, when the line was ordered to advance, and the artillery to play upon the enemy. The first Maryland regiment particularly, was ordered to charge bayonets, without firing, but for some cause not yet clearly ascertained, the regiment received orders to retire and then broke. The second regiment retired in consequence. The second Virginia regiment was ordered off, and the first broke. The unfavorable consequences were, that the army lost a glorious opportunity of gaining a complete victory, taking the town, and biasing the beam of fortune greatly in favor of our cause.

"The action was at no time very warm, but it was durable, and our troops by the gallant exertions of our officers, were rallied frequently, but always fought at long shot. A convincing testimony that this was generally the case, is that none or very few of our men were wounded with buck shot or bayonet. The baggage of our army was sent off to Rugely's, and the troops halted at Saunder's Creek, about two miles South of where we fought last year, and about five miles from Camden. The loss was nearly equal on both sides, if we do not consider the loss of opportunity. We lost about 130 killed and wounded, and from every account the enemy were not more lucky.

"The cavalry, the light infantry, and the guards, acquired all the honor, and the infantry of the battalions all the disgrace that fell upon our shoulders. The cavalry, led on by Washington, behaved in a manner truly heroic. He charged the British army in the rear, took a great number of prisoners, sent many of them off with small detachments, and when he saw we were turning our backs upon victory in front, by a circuitous manœuvre, he threw his dragoons into our rear, passed the line and charged the York volunteers, (a fine corps of cavalry,) killed a number and drove the rest out of the field. Washington is an elegant officer; his reputation is deservedly great. Many of our officers are mortally mortified at our late inglorious retreat. I say mortally, because I cannot doubt that some of us must fall, in endeavoring the next opportunity, to re-establish our reputation. Dear Reputation, what trouble do you not occasion, what danger do you not expose us to! Who but for it, would patiently persevere in prosecuting a war, with the mere remnant of a fugitive army, in a country made desolate by repeated ravages, and rendered sterile by streams of blood. Who but for reputation would sustain the varied evils that daily attend the life of a soldier, and expose him to jeopardy every hour. Liberty, thou basis of reputation, suffer me not to forget the cause of my country, nor to murmur at my fate."

The events of this campaign being active, and following in quick succession, we have an account of the siege of Ninety-six, a very important post. The fortunes of the war had turned generally in favor of the Americans, although their troops were several times defeated in this campaign. Lord Rawdon was forced to abandon Camden shortly after the events narrated by Williams, and the posts of Fort Watson, Fort Mott, Fort Granby, Nelson's Ferry, Georgetown, Fort Dreadnought and Augusta were all reduced or deserted, and there remained only Charleston and Ninety-six in South Carolina, and Savannah, in Georgia, in the hands of the enemy. The post of Ninety-six was closely besieged for three weeks, and without reinforcements, which the Americans hardly expected, would certainly have been taken. But it so happened, unfortunately, that the garrison was strongly reinforced by Lord Rawdon, and the Americans were obliged to abandon the siege. Col. Williams writes thus:

"Bush River, *June* 23*d*, 1781.

"*Dear Bro.*—The circumstances of the war, in this part of the world, have had a material alteration since I had the pleasure to write you. After Lord Rawdon's retreat from Camden, Gen. Greene pushed his operations southwardly, and has obliged the enemy to abandon or surrender all their posts in South Carolina, except Charleston and Ninety-six. On the 22d ult. our little army invested the last mentioned place, and continued the siege with infinite labor and alacrity till the 20th inst., when we were obliged to relinquish an object, which, if attained, would not only have given peace to this distracted country, but would have added a lustre to our former services, sufficiently brilliant to have thrown a proper light upon the character of our excellent General, and reflected a ray of glory upon the reputation of each inferior officer. Though we have been greatly disappointed, no troops ever deserved more credit for their exertions. The operations were prosecuted with indefatigable zeal and bravery, and the place was defended with spirit and address. Our loss is Capt. Armstrong, of the Maryland Line, killed; Capt. Benson, dangerously wounded, and Lieut. Duvall, also wounded. Besides officers, we lost fifty-eight men killed, sixty-nine wounded, and twenty missing. From this account you will conclude that a day seldom passed without execution, and

I can assure you that each night rather promoted than diminished the mischief. We succeeded so far as to take one of the enemy's redoubts, and in all probability a few days more would have happily concluded the business. But Lord Rawdon had received a strong reinforcement, and by making forced marches, arrived in time to avert the impending fate of the garrison. I cannot ascertain the loss the enemy may have sustained, but judging by our own, it cannot be inconsiderable. Our approaches were carried by two trenches and a mine to within a few feet of the ditch of their strongest fort, and our troops once took possession of it, but their works were too strong to be escaladed. Instances of consummate bravery were exhibited, but their fire was too fatal for our people to remain in their fosse, and we were obliged to leave it with loss."

But the most important battle, and the last of consequence, was that of Eutaw. It was by no means as decisive as that of Cowpens, but it was instrumental in putting an end to the war. Col. Williams displays his knowledge of the enemy, and his skill as a soldier, in this prognostic of the battle, which happened four days after that he writes as follows from

"Fort Mott, on the Congaree River, *Sept. 4th*, 1781.

"I wrote last from the high hills of Santee, from which the army moved the 23d of August, with the view of attacking the enemy at Thompson's Farm, which is within half a mile of this place, but having a large circuit to make before we could pass the Wateree and Congaree rivers, which lay between us, the enemy took the opportunity of retiring to Nelson Ferry, which is on the Santee River, about forty miles below the confluence of the first mentioned rivers, which form the last, within sight of our present position.

"Having got the enemy so low down the country, a great point is gained, and puts the laboring oar into their hands.

"We shall not be under the necessity of fighting, neither shall we avoid it if a favorable opportunity offers. These large rivers, which have all extensive marshy shores and but few ferries, embarrass us on account of transporting our baggage, and will subject the army to some inconvenience, but our circumstances, taken altogether, are very different from what they were three months ago, and are indeed a perfect contrast to the adverse fortune that followed the heels of our retreating troops last winter. If Col. Stewart, who has commanded the army since Lord Rawdon's departure for Europe, thinks proper to risk an action, he will be beaten."

Here we have his account of the battle itself:

"The British army, being reinforced by the 3d regiment, contrary to my expectations, advanced from Orangeburgh to Congaree, and encamped at Col. Thompson's, about one mile from Fort Mott, which we had reduced some time before. It is said they exultingly gave three cheers upon regaining that position. The two armies remained neighbors, and were separated by the Santee, from early in August till the 23d of that month, when Gen. Greene took the resolution to remove Col. Stewart, (who succeeded Gen. Rawdon in command,) or give him battle.

"It was impossible to pass the rivers Wateree and Congaree immediately in front, and as their confluence is but a little to our left, it was not considered eligible to cross the Santee below the enemy for obvious reasons: we had a junction to form with the State troops and militia, whose numbers were not ascertained, and without them we were greatly inferior in force to the enemy. Therefore the General ordered us to march by the right, and we passed the rivers above, which induced the British army to retire to Eutaw Springs, about thirty-five miles from Thompson's and about two from Nelson's Ferry over the Santee. Gen. Greene did not approve of their holding that post, and as his forces were now collected, he determined to prosecute his plan of giving battle or removing them to a more peaceful distance. By easy marches we arrived at Burdell's, seven miles from Eutaw, in the afternoon of the 7th inst., and orders were given for marching again next morning, at four o'clock, to attack the enemy.

"At four o'clock next morning we were under arms, and moved in order of battle about three miles, when we halted, and took a little of that liquid which is not unnecessary to exhilarate the animal spirits upon such occasions. Again we advanced, and soon afterwards our light troops met the van of the enemy, who were marching out to meet us.

"Very serious, very important reflections began to obtrude. But liberty or death; peace and independence; or glory and a grave. The enemy's van was soon driven to their line, and our troops displayed. Our militia, which composed the front line, seconded the attack, and behaved better than usual. The North Carolina brigade of Continentals were next engaged, and acquired honor by their firmness. The Virginians advanced with impetuosity, and beat their foes wherever they found them. And the little remnant of Maryland troops, with an intrepidity which was particularly noticed by our gallant commander, advanced in good order, with trailed arms, and without regarding or returning the enemy's fire, charged and broke their best troops. Then, indeed, we fired and followed them into their camp, near which is a thick wood, very unfavorable to cavalry. But Col. Washington, impatient perhaps for a more favorable opportunity, charged upon the enemy's right, where unluckily their flank companies were posted. He received a very galling fire, by which his horse fell in front of his dragoons. In an instant his breast was pierced by a bayonet, which however wounded him but slightly. His cavalry was repulsed, and that excellent officer became a captive.

"Our loss in officers killed and wounded was very considerable, and the eagerness of the pursuit had thrown most of the troops into disorder, which could not now be remedied. Some were taking prisoners, and others plundering the enemy's camp, while they in despair sought refuge in and about a strong brick house which stood in the midst of it, and from whence their fire began to gall us exceedingly. About this time General Greene had brought our two six pounders within one hundred yards of the house, and I believe by accident or mistake, two others which we had taken were brought to the same place. At this critical juncture the enemy made a conclusive effort, which not only did them great honor, but, in my opinion, was the salvation of their whole army. Major Majoribanks sallied briskly from behind a picket garden, charged our artillery, and carried the pieces, which they immediately secured under the walls of their citadel.

"As our two three pounders and one which we had taken in the field, were all dismounted, it was useless to attempt any thing further with the small arms. The General, therefore, ordered the troops to retire, which was done gradually, the enemy not presuming to follow. The cavalry of the legion kept that of the enemy in awe, but found no good opportunity to cut them.

"The Delaware battalion and legion infantry acted with their usual vivacity, and were among those who did the most execution. As the Eutaw Spring was within fifty yards of the house, and there was no other water nearer than Burdell's, we retired in the afternoon to that place, which gave the enemy an opportunity of burying as many of their dead as their stay would admit. They abandoned the post early on the night of the 9th, leaving upwards of sixty of their dead unburied, and sixty or seventy wounded that could not be carried off. We pursued them about thirty-five miles, and though their army was reinforced by Major McArthur's detachment of 300 or 400 men from Monks' Corner, they thought proper to retire to a strong position on the south side of Ferguson's swamp, in the night of the 10th, when we lay at the Trout Spring, within five miles of them.

"They retired to Fair Lawn, below Monks', and on the morning of the 13th the General ordered the army to return to its former position at the high hills of Santee. This expedition was made in the season of the year which is most sickly in this country; and you cannot conceive how much more lamentable it is to lose an officer in sick quarters, than to see him fall in the field. There, there is no duration of that toilsome anxiety which we suffer for a languishing friend, besides his exit is glorious and, we believe, happy.

"Upon re-perusal of this circumstantial sheet, I do not think I have said enough of the bravery of the American troops. To have an idea of their vivacity and intrepidity, you must have shared their danger and seen their charge, which exceeded any thing of the sort I ever saw before.

"The battle of Eutaw, was an example of what I conceive to be obstinate fair field fighting, and it is worthy of remark, that it happened on the same spot of ground where, according to the tradition of this country, a very bloody, desperate battle was fought about a century ago, between the savage natives and the barbarous Europeans who came to dispossess them of their property, which, in soil, is as rich as any upon the continent, or can be any where else. On the spot where the conflict of bayonets decided the victory, is a monument or mound of earth, said to have been erected over the bodies of the brave Indians who fell in defence of their country. Will any such honorable testimony be erected to the memory of our departed heroes?"

Both parties claimed the victory, and according to Gen. Tarlton's narrative, it was a most brilliant triumph for the British. It had, however, great weight in favor of the Americans. Williams' conduct in this engagement was most distinguished, and won for him the entire approbation and praise of General Greene and the army. Indeed, Greene says: "I cannot help acknowledging my obligations to Col. Williams for his great activity on this and many other occasions, in forming the army, and for his uncommon intrepidity in leading on the Maryland troops to the charge." Williams might, indeed, well be proud of such commendation, but he now knew that he had done all in his power for the country, and he yearned to return to the bosom of his family. A sense of duty alone made him a soldier; there was in him no desire of mere military distinction, but of

"that good fame,
Without which glory's but a tavern song."

He would have chosen to live on the old homestead, had not the cry of his country rung in his ears, and when he was at last free to set his face homewards, how gladly did he depart. He writes to his brother:

"My disposition is wholly domestic; my feelings flow with excess of tenderness whenever I indulge the thoughts of home. There I will be as soon as I can quit the field with honor, and sooner you don't expect me. The hope of terminating this tour of service with a little good fortune, and of returning once more to my friends, supports me under all my anxiety and danger. I am happy in my office, in my command, and in my connections. My health is seldom impaired, though my feelings are wounded every day by such circumstances as I have frequently related—so that I have a mixture of pleasure and pain in the exercise of my profession, which I ardently wish I may soon have an honorable opportunity of changing for some silent, sweet domestic occupation. Then will I take you and my fond sisters in my arms, and live with you in peace."

The military career of Williams now drew rapidly to a close, and the remainder of his days were passed in the repose he so ardently loved. But toward the close of the war he was sent by Greene with despatches to Congress, and became Brigadier General by brevet. Much as he merited the honor, it caused some dissatisfaction among his brother officers, and Greene writes to him on this subject, in connection with others, as follows:

"I wrote you, my dear General, some time past, in answer to your letter. In mine I congratulated you on your promotion, from which I felt a singular happiness, but observed at the same time, that the manner was more honorable to you, than satisfactory to the other Colonels of the army. Your right of promotion, which took place from the United States being formed into districts, was repealed before your promotion took place, and being promoted upon a principle of merit, the Colonels feel an injury in the comparison that their merit is less conspicuous than yours. Col. Pinkney wrote me on the subject, and I believe has written to Congress. I gave him copies of my letters to Congress, which were satisfactory. I expect other Colonels will feel the same injury, and very likely make the same application.

"The love of rank is so strong a principle in the breast of a soldier, that he who has a right to promotion will never admit another over his head upon a principle of merit. You are not to expect that every body will subscribe to the justice of your promotion. You must content yourself with having obtained it, and that no man is without his enemies but a fool. I am glad to hear the sentiments of the public are so flattering to the Southern army. The Southern States have acted generously by me, and if I can close the business honorably here, I shall feel doubly happy, happy for the people and happy for myself. I think the public are not a little indebted for our exertions. The Southern States were lost, they are now restored; the American arms were in disgrace, they are now in high reputation. The American soldiery were thought to want both patience and fortitude to contend with difficulties: they are now remarkable for both. That sentiment had taken deep root in Europe, but it is now totally changed. Indeed, the change of British administration is in a great degree owing to our efforts, and the consequences resulting from them.

"I hope I don't arrogate too much in saying this, and in saying we have contributed not a little to the glory of the nation and the American arms. I find by a Parliamentary Register, that there were 18,000 troops and upwards, in the Southern department last year, besides the militia which acted with the enemy, and those amounted to not less than 2,000, exclusive of the negroes, and they had more than 1,000 of them on the different military departments of the army. This includes Lord Cornwallis' army in Virginia. At the time the battle of Eutaw was fought by the enemy, from returns laid before Parliament, it appears they had in Charleston and in their advanced army, 6,700 men fit for duty, besides all the militia and negroes. What an amazing difference between their force and ours! From these authorities, I find our operations were much more glorious than ever we considered them."

Gen. Greene and Gen. Williams were equally zealous in defending each other's reputation, and at a later period when Greene himself was made the subject of animadversion, Williams defends him in a strain of indignation and sarcasm, in the following letter to Maj. Edwards:

"The late revolution in South Carolina is owing not only to a change of circumstances, but to a change of men in the government of that country. How daringly impudent it is for those who have been rescued from misery and dejection, to arraign the virtue that saved them. Gen. Greene exercised a superior judgment, changed the system of military operations in that country, and used the only possible means of recovering it—

and dare the ingrates now accuse him of any interested design, or any view of ambition, other than that which receives its highest gratification from the thanks and approbation of a free people? And do the devils dare to treat with neglect and contempt that little corps of gallant men who saved them from despair and slavery? Their ingratitude proves manifestly, how well they deserved the chains which have been taken off their necks. There are many sensible, amiable characters in Carolina, but I always feared the majority were envious, jealous, malicious, designing, unprincipled people. Come one, come all of you away and leave them. I am glad to hear the Northern troops are returning. Though I cannot flatter myself with the pleasure of seeing them rewarded as they deserve, there will be something done for them, they will not starve on the same fields in which they have bled."

It will not be of purpose to dwell much longer upon the subject before us, for Gen. Williams did not live many years more to enjoy the fruits of his hard toil. He settled in Baltimore and was appointed to the collectorship of the port, by the Governor of the State, the duties of which he discharged with the same exemplary fidelity which had attended his military career. When the Federal Constitution was adopted, he was re-appointed to the same office, which he continued to hold as long as he lived. In 1786, he was happily married to the second daughter of Mr. William Smith, a very wealthy and influential merchant, and his union was productive of the complete felicity he so well deserved. His habits of industry, economy and method, joined to the lucrative office he held, enabled him among much other property, to buy the old home of his father, on the banks of the Potomac, which in the midst of the battle field's "dreadful array," he had so often fondly returned to in imagination. Here he was pleasantly employed in improving the condition of the farm, and in laying out the present town of "Williamsport," called after his own name. It was at one time thought that the seat of government would be at Williamsport, and there are several letters from the General's brother on the subject, and written in a very hopeful strain: one of great length detailing an account of Gen. Washington's visit to Springfield's farm, (for such is its name,) with speculations on the site of the Federal seat. On this letter Gen. Williams has endorsed the words "All a Hum," and Williamsport has remained to this day, rather a village than a city of magnificent distances.

The health of Gen. Williams became much impaired, and disease attacked his lungs, but he still continued his duties. He had many friends in and out of the army, and he delighted to keep up a correspondence with them. None thought more highly of him as a soldier and a man, than Washington, and such names as Greene, Knox, Lincoln, Lee, Steuben, Kosciusko, and many more, form those of intimate and tried associates. Nor was he less solicitous to preserve unbroken friendship with many unknown to fame, and with a large family circle. The wealth that he acquired was liberally dispensed, and his bounty was always readily extended to the deserving. To his brother he says in one of his letters—"Whatever is mine in Maryland is yours, and I really don't know what you mean by my money in your hands." So highly was he esteemed by Gen. Washington; that in 1792, on the refusal of Gen. Morgan to accept the actual rank of Brigadier General, Gen. Knox being then Secretary of War, wrote to Williams that the President would be highly pleased to appoint him to the post, which would make him the eldest Brigadier General, and second in command, and he was accordingly actually so nominated. But this honor he positively declined in several letters to the President and Secretary Knox, on account of ill health and family duties; and he also adds that it would be no stimulus to his ambition to be second in command. His illness still increasing upon him, he was induced in 1793 to try the effect of sea air, and a voyage to Barbadoes had some benefit, but of very short duration.

And now the light which he created and shed around him, was to be withdrawn from those who looked as upon the rainbow's glories after a stormy day; for just as they were encircled by its arch of splendor, in radiant promise of sunny skies, they beheld its brilliant hues melting into air, as the luminary whence they emanated sunk solemnly from their sight. In the next year, 1794, while on his way to the Sweet Springs, in Virginia, on reaching the little town of Woodstock, he became too ill to proceed farther, and on the 16th of July, at the early age of 45, he died. He was prepared; he had lived the full measure of his fame; his life had been glorious and happy; he had shrunk from no responsibility; he had feared nothing but to do wrong; he had gained "honor, love, obedience, troops of friends," and when at last he met the unconquerable foe, it was with the same calm courage and reliance on a higher power, that had been his trust when he had rushed into mortal battle.

He left an ample fortune to his four sons, and committed them to their mother's father, saying in his will, that he could do so with entire trust, "as soon as it should please Heaven to remove him from that endearing office." In the eloquent language of the Spaniard, himself a soldier as well as a poet,

"As thus the dying warrior prayed,
Without one gathering mist or shade
Upon his mind;
Encircled by his family,
Watched by affection's gentle eye
So soft and kind—

"His soul to him who gave it, rose:
God lead it to its long repose,
Its glorious rest!
And though the warrior's sun is set,
Its light shall linger round us yet,
Bright, radiant, blest."

On the banks of the lordly Potomac his remains repose, beneath a simple monument crowning the summit of a hill, overlooking a wild expanse of waving woods and pleasant fields, and distant mountains, which he once delighted to look upon. The setting sun sheds its glories over that peaceful landscape; the river flows calmly by many a pleasant village, by the marble palaces of the busy Metropolis, and by the tomb of him who has given it his name. Heroes, patriots and friends, both sleep by the same river; both firm in love of peace but hatred of tyranny, and both spared to be cheered by the smiles of their country, whose battles they had fought while she pined in fetters and in tears.

MEMORIALS OF COLUMBUS,

READ TO THE

Maryland Historical Society,

BY

ROBERT DODGE,

3 April, 1851.

BALTIMORE:
PRINTED FOR THE SOCIETY.
MDCCCLI.

JOHN D. TOY, PRINTER.

COLUMBUS.

AUTOGRAPH LETTERS AT GENOA.

At the meeting of the New York Historical Society, held at its rooms, on the evening of the fifteenth day of January, 1850, I had the honor of presenting to the Society a copy of one of the very few remaining autograph letters of Christopher Columbus, in the original and beautiful Italian.

Upon the nineteenth day of January, 1848, during my stay at Genoa, I had the opportunity of examining that city's proudest treasury,—its Custodia of the Memorials of Columbus, which with Parmegiano's Portrait in the Royal Gallery at Naples, compose some valuable relics of him, the results of whose sublime achievement may well fill coming centuries for their development.

During the brief space that the Custodien allowed me to hold the letter in my hand, I succeeded in making a correct copy of the original, which, as one of but three landmarks of his history supplied by himself, and left for us, is justly regarded by his countrymen with no ordinary veneration. Perhaps their famous Emerald Vase or the ashes of St. John, do not meet with equal regard.

I presented the copy that I thus had myself made, to the Society, without any accompanying data, which might be useful to demonstrate the originality and authenticity of the donation, as well as its historical importance.

Favorable opportunity has since, through the courtesy of Mr. Brantz Mayer, of Baltimore, and from other sources, placed in my hands some evidence thereof, which I now ask permission succinctly to detail.

It may perhaps, be as well here to premise a short history of the collection and preservation of the few autograph Memorials of the Great Discoverer of the New World.

Of the Autograph Letters of Christopher Columbus, there are but *three* as yet known to the world; the residue, though long desired, have never yet been brought to light.

The priceless value of an autograph letter from the accomplished mind of Him, who was confessedly at the head of physical science, at that period of the awakening of the human intellect; which speaks to us, at the vast distance of near three centuries and a half, of his daily griefs, hopes, and plans of beneficence; in that most mellifluent of human tongues, the daily speech of his cotemporaries, Michael Angelo, Titian, Corregio and Raphael, and whose harmonies were even as Columbus wrote, flowing in immortal grace from the pens of Ariosto and Machiavelli, must be manifest to all, and more especially in this land—the scene of his glory, now so rapidly hasting foward in that grand career, predicted in the sublime visions of his own prophecies.

We are told by the Decurions of Genoa, that the library of the Count Michael Angelo Cambiasi, a former Senator of that city, was, after his death, in July, 1816, advertised for sale. Its catalogue contained as one of its Nos. the "Codice dei Privilegii del Colombo." The Decurions of Genoa, anxious to procure this treasure, had the public sale adjourned until the King's answer had been received to their memorial on the subject. The King of Sardinia, Victor Emanuel, earnestly seconded their wishes, ordering the originals to be deposited in the archives of the Court at Turin; where an accurate copy having been taken, at the solicitations of the Decurions of Genoa, the originals were given up to them and the copy left at Turin. The originals were received by Genoa, on the 29th day of January, 1821, and shortly after a beautiful monument or *custodia*, being a marble pillar surmounted by a bust of Columbus, was erected as their honored depository, and placed in an apartment in the beautiful marble palace of the Doges of Genoa.

A small door of gilded bronze in the centre, opens to still another door of similar material, behind which, in their golden receptacle are preserved these sacred relics. The closet is secured by two keys, which are kept respectively as appurtenances of office, by the Senator and by the Cardinal Legate of Genoa, during their terms of office. To see the relics, both keys must be obtained on written application to these dignitaries.

The reflecting stranger who has the happiness of visiting "Genova la Superba," as she is so well designated, and looks with admiration on that beautiful palace, the seat of the pomps of its long line of illustrious Doges, still so fresh and well preserved, despite French Vandalism; may now, as he walks through its classic corridors, colonnades and porticos, well hesitate to attribute the inspiration of the scene, to the thronging memories of the great Doria, the deliverer of his country, the Crusades, the capture of Constantinople, the rescue of the Holy Sepulchre, or to these memorials of Genoa's greater Son, who made her the mother of a New World.

The documents contained in this monument to Columbus, consist of forty-four separate charters, warrants, orders and grants of privileges, beautifully engrossed on vellum, by the art of the copyist and illuminator of that age, and also the autograph letters of Columbus, of which we purpose to speak.

These documents are enclosed in a bag of richly gilt and embossed scarlet Spanish leather, with a silver lock; being the "book of copies of his letters and of his privileges" which in 1502, when he set off upon his fourth and last voyage, he entrusted to the care and guardianship of Signor Francesco di Rivarolo, to forward to his intimate friend at Genoa, "the most learned doctor," as he styles him, and "the ambassador" Signor Nicolo Odérigo, for his safe keeping and preservation.

In the TWO autograph letters, which are *all* that were published accompanying the copy of these documents of Columbus, printed by order of the Decurions of Genoa, in 1823; (entitled "Codice Diplomatico Colombo-Americano,") Columbus addresses both letters to Signor Nicolo Odérigo, the *first* dated March 21st, 1502, just before he sailed upon his fourth and last voyage of discovery; and the *second*, dated the 27th of December, 1504, two months after his return; as will appear by the copies of these letters annexed.

In *the first* of these letters, bearing date Seville, March 21, 1502, he says: "I gave the book of my Privileges to Signor Francesco di Rivarolo, in order that he might forward it to you, along with a copy of the missive letters. I beg of you as a particular favor to write to Don Diego, to acknowledge their receipt and to mention where they are deposited."

In the *second* of these letters, bearing date Seville, December 27, 1504, he says: "At that time, when I set off upon the voyage from which I have just returned, I gave to Francesco di Rivarolo, a book of copies of my Letters, and another of my Privileges, in a bag of colored Spanish leather, with a silver lock; and *two letters for the Bank of St. George*, to which I assigned the tenth of my revenues, in diminution of the duties upon corn and other provisions: no acknowledgment of all this has reached me. Signor Francesco tells me, that all arrived there in safety. If so, it was uncourteous in these gentlemen of St. George not to have favored me with an answer, nor have they thereby improved their affairs, which gives me cause to say, that whoever serves the public, serves nobody."

The magistrate of St. George, at Genoa, on the 8th day of December, 1502, writes him at great length, acknowledging the receipt of a letter from him, in which he gives orders to his son, Don Diego, that the tenth part of his annual revenues should be paid to the city of Genoa, in diminution of the duties on corn, wine and other provisions, for which they render suitable acknowledgments to the Admiral, replying in detail to his said letter.

This letter of the magistrate of St. George, of Genoa, of which we append a translation, therefore could not have been received by the Admiral.

These three letters form all the letters that are printed by the Decurions of Genoa, in their publication of 1823, of autographs *by*, or addressed *to* the Admiral.

The manifest hiatus of meaning in this correspondence, can only be explained by the production of that letter *from Columbus to* the magistrates or *Bank of St. George*, mentioned by himself in the second letter, and acknowledged on receipt, and answered at length by the letter of the magistrate of St. George.

It may be as well here to observe, that on examination of the printed volume of the Decurions of Genoa, it appears from the detailed history of the documents furnished on page 138, et seq. that they print *only* the contents of the book of Privileges, and book of copies of Letters, and such autograph letters as are found therein, and attached to the leather case of the book, and no others.

The letter of Columbus, of which I had the honor of presenting a copy to the New York Historical Society, in Italian, copied from the autograph, was by the Custodien, taken out of the same depository, but was not attached to the book of Privileges.

This letter bears date the 2d day of April, 1502, at Seville; addressed to the Governors of the Bank of St. George, at Genoa; gives directions to Don Diego to pay the one tithe of his revenue to the Bank, in diminution of the taxes; informs them of his having sent to Signor Nicolo Odérigo a copy of his Privileges and Charters; and is thus, as will be seen by the copy appended, *the missing letter*, referred to by Columbus himself in his second letter, and fully acknowledged and answered in detail by the magistrate of St. George, on the 8th day of December following.

Condensing a few leading events of the life of the great navigator, may throw more light upon this intrinsically interesting letter.

Biographers have not as yet determined whether it was in 1446 or 1447, or earlier, that Columbus was born. Their theories are indeed numerous. Dr. Robertson, in note 11 to page 62 of Vol. I. of his History of America, says: "The time of Columbus' birth may be nearly ascertained by the following circumstances. It appears from the fragment of a letter addressed by him to Ferdinand and Isabella, A. D. 1501, that he had at that time been engaged forty years in a seafaring life. In another letter he informs them that he went to sea at the age of fourteen: whence it follows that he was born April, A. D. 1447,"—and cites Ferdinand's Life C. Col. Mr. Prescott, although not venturing in his text positively to state it, in his History of Ferdinand and Isabella, Vol. II. page 115, note 6, and Vol. III. page 242, note 16, sums up all the authorities, and comes to the same result. It seems that Mr. Irving's date of 1435, based on the hypotheses of Navarrete and Bernaldez is conjectural, and opposed to the great weight of authorities. The last writer appears unwilling to allow that the infirmities of the declining years of the Admiral were not the natural result of his numerous mental and bodily hardships, and therefore adds ten years to his life. Spotorno and others say 1446: the rest 1447. However, after much controversy, it seems agreed that he was the son of the wool-carder, Domenico Colombo, and his wife, Susanna, and that the place of his nativity was in the present street of St. Andrew's Gate, or Lane of Mulcento, in the Parish of St. Stephen, being the suburbs of Genoa.

From the age of fourteen until the age of sixty, or 1506, when he died at Valladolid, his habitual pursuit was navigation. The facts and speculations of all the existing science of the age were applied by him, in the study and practice of his favorite occupation.

These memorials of him, and the still lingering historic reminiscence of his age, establish his character, to have been immeasurably superior to his fellow men: that his mind, enriched by a long experience in navigating the seas of Europe, and by the contemplation of the phenomena of nature, and the laws of the physical world, had risen to an unalterable conviction of the truth of that ever memorable and grand conclusion, from those laws and phenomena, which shone upon his own mind with the clearness and directness of a sunbeam.

How he, of whom his own age was not worthy, toiled and wandered: how much privation and suffering, how many griefs and sorrows he endured; how many long years he begged his way from door to door, and from court to court; how his clear reasoning was derided; and how often baffled in the effort to gain a hearing among the ignorant and selfish sovereigns of Europe; how his great heart and hope outlived this all; and how at last, the gracious queen of Castile, lifted him up from the dust of his abasement, and staking the jewels of her crown, set him forth upon that voyage, which at once opened the area of a world, and covered him and her with a more resplendent glory than all human diadems;—is familiar to us all.

The great navigator, made in all, four voyages to this Continent, or, as it was then called, the Indies.

His *first* voyage began on the 3d* day of August, 1492, from Palos; and he returned to Lisbon, on the 4th day of March, 1493.

His *second* voyage started from Cadiz, the 25th day of September, 1493; and he returned to Burgos, in Spain, on the 14th of June, 1497.

On his *third* voyage, he sailed from San Lucar, on the 30th day of May, 1498; the reins of power in Hispaniola, were then in the hands of his vindictive enemies; and the student of the life of this really sublime hero and prophet of his age, reads with weeping heart, how he was reviled, persecuted, disgraced, and sent home a prisoner to Cadiz, in Spain, where he arrived a captive in chains, on the 20th day of November, 1500.

Two long and weary years, were then spent by him in repeling the malicious falsehoods of his jealous foes, before the tribunals and court of Spain, which had but two years before showered upon the discoverer dominion and honors equal to royalty. The truth, finally, as ever, when facing falsehood, triumphed. The royal favor was restored, and on the 9th day of May, 1502,

* All these dates being prior to A. D. 1582, the epoch of the Gregorian Calendar, or change to the New Style, eleven days are therefore to be added to bring them to the modern reckoning, the present or New Style.

with a still greater equipment, and still greater glory, though his conscious satisfaction of victory over his enemies was saddened by his experience of their malice, he set forth on his *fourth voyage* to the Indies from the same port of Cadiz.

He returned home to San Lucar, in the month of September, 1504; the precise day of his arrival is not ascertained.

This fourth voyage was an addition to his glory; as he therein first saw the main land of this Continent in voyaging along the South American coasts. This was his last voyage. The great Mariner returned no more. In less than two years afterwards, and on the 20th day of May, 1506, at Valladolid, his mighty heart surrendered to "the last enemy, which is death."

In a codicil to his will, which codicil was written by the testator himself at Segovia, August 15, 1505, and executed at Valladolid, the 19th day of May, 1506, (the day before his death,) Columbus declares that his will had been made and executed on the 1st day of April, 1502, and deposited in the keeping of father Gaspar Certosa, at Seville. Another codicil, called the military codicil, written on the blank leaf of the Breviary, presented to him by Pope Alexander VI., dated at Valladolid, the 14th day of May, 1506, has also been published. This will itself has never yet seen the light; but a previous will, dated in 1498, has been, of late years, discovered and published.

Perhaps this may be charged to the wilfulness of that crowd of selfish claimants, who started so many wild and dubious stories, and unfounded litigations for the succession to his wealth and honors, and prosecuted their finally unsuccessful suits for generations after his decease. In this will, he declares Genoa to be his birth-place, and directs his son Don Diego, therefore to honor and be serviceable to that city. The controversy was created by a race of claimants from Cuccharo or Cogoletto, who attempted to deprive Genoa of the honor of his birth-place, to fix it at Cuccharo, and thereby to make out their own lineal descent and title to the succession, to the honor and wealth of the great Admiral of Genoa. The explicit declarations of his will, that he was a native of Genoa, stood in their way; and it is easy to believe that to protract their pertinacious litigation, they found it convenient to suppress the will.

This epitome of the leading events of his life points clearly to the character of this letter of the 2d day of April, 1502. It appears that the month of April, 1502, was selected by the Admiral for making the final disposition of his earthly affairs. On the 1st day of the month, at Seville, in Spain, where he was occupied in the business of his last expedition, he executes his will, the most solemn record of humanity, and therein speaks with affection of his own distant and native Genoa. During the month of March, he had given diligence to have all the charters, warrants and grants, from the crown and others to him, accurately copied, authenticated by a public notary, and sent by the trusty hand of intimate friendship, to his son, Don Diego, at Genoa, there to be carefully deposited and preserved. After thus honoring his native city, by its selection as the depository of his most valuable muniments of title, he seeks to confer a more substantial favor upon his fellow-citizens. To diminish the burthen of the taxes upon food, which bore heavily on the poor, he, by this letter, voluntarily yields up to the city one *tenth* of all the revenues he derived from this source; and entrusts his son, Don Diego, with the honorable office of executing his plan of beneficence. The letter is therefore *testamentary* in its character; and was more efficient than if he had included it in his will, which became the prey of the avarice of litigants.

It is addressed, like the others, to Signor Nicolo Odérigo, his intimate friend; an accomplished fellow-citizen of Genoa, who was one of its Senators, and had been honored by its embassy to the Court of Spain, then the first power of the world.

Mr. Irving, in the second volume of his History of Columbus, alludes generally to this subject; states the fact that Columbus sent two letters to the Bank of St. George, assigning to it the one-tenth of his revenues, to be employed in diminishing the duties on corn and other provisions, but does not furnish any copies of the autograph letters of the Admiral or the Bank, nor any additional information.* A very material confirmation has however, been furnished me.

*I am informed by Mr. Irving, that he has not visited Genoa, since the discovery of these relics of Columbus, and therefore has had no opportunity of personal inspection.

In Niles's National Register for June 15th, 1839, it is stated, on the authority of the New York Gazette, that Captain Baker, of the Baltimore Brig Helen McLeod, recently arrived from Genoa, had furnished to the Editor of the Gazette a translation of an autograph letter from the great discoverer of our Continent, which translation had been given to Captain Baker by Mr. Robert Campbell, who at that period was United States Consul at Genoa. This letter is dated 2d April, 1502, addressed to the Bank of St. George, at Genoa. The Editor remarks that it will be perused with interest as an original from Christopher Columbus, *never before published*, and appends (without, however, giving the Italian) a very fair rendering into English of the identical letter, which I have translated and inserted as No. 4 in the Appendix to this paper. As evidence from an independent source and high character, this additional testimony of the authenticity of the autograph is entitled to great weight and respect.*

The letters speak for themselves, their contents require no commentary; and least of all, can the gap of meaning between the letters printed by the Decurions of Genoa, be supplied by the cool assertion of D. Giovanni Batista Spotorno, in his Memoir of Columbus, that the letter of the magistrate of St. George refers, and is an answer to the first letter of Columbus, bearing date at Seville, March 21st, 1502, which is addressed to Nicolo Odérigo, upon a subject entirely distinct.

It may be pertinent to add that the Bank of St. George at Genoa, whose banking house, girt with the Pisan chains, the trophy of Genoa's ancient fame, is still a conspicuous monument at the side of the Porto franco, arose about A. D. 1400, as a means of providing the Republic with funds to repel the aggressions of the exiled nobles, who then in great force threatened its destruction.

The Republic pledged the whole revenues of the state, to a company of merchants, called the Compera or Banco di San

* Mr. Robert Campbell was in office as United States Consul at Genoa, in September, 1839. See U. S. Official Register for 1839, p. 11.

Georgio, for the payment of the advances of money required by the exigencies of the State. The bank was for loans and deposits. Its transactions were on a grand scale; many of the European States, and Spain in particular, were its debtors, and its income exceeded ten millions of French livres. The administration of its concerns was committed to eight directors, and it had jurisdiction over its own officers. The product of the imposts, pledged by the State to the Bank, for the payment of its loan and interest, when inadequate, was constantly increased.

At the time of its failure, its rents amounting to 3,400,000 Genoese Lire, or about seven hundred thousand dollars, the property of its creditors was transferred to the account books of France.

The Bank had all the nature and powers of the English East India Company, being both a financial and trading corporation. Its colonial administration and power extended to the Crimea, Asia Minor, and over the Island of Corsica.

This great engine of the State, was managed with power and integrity; its bills continued current throughout Europe, until French Vandalism overran the territory of the Republic and seized on Corsica; until the year 1750, when the Bank failed; the artery of life to Genoa ceased to furnish aliment when the other powers of the venerable Republic were destroyed.

The interest of the subject is my excuse for the length of this paper, whose conclusion I now form by copies of the three letters of Columbus, and of the letter of the Magistrate of St. George to the Admiral.

APPENDIX.

No. 1

"To the Ambassador Signor Nicolo Oderigo."

"*Sir:*

"It is impossible to describe the solicitude which your departure has caused among us. I gave the book of my Privileges to Signor Frco. di Rivarolo, in order that he might forward it to you, along with a copy of the missive letters. I beg of you as a particular favor, to write to Don Diego, to acknowledge their receipt, and to mention where they are deposited. Another copy shall be furnished and sent to you, in the same manner, and by the said Sig. Franco. You will find another letter in it, in which their highnesses have promised to give me all that belongs to me, and to put Don Diego in possession of it, as you will see. I am writing to Signor Gian Luigi, and to the Signora Caterina, and the letter will accompany this. I shall depart, in the name of the Holy Trinity, with the first favorable weather, with a considerable equipment. If Girolamo di Santo Stephano comes, he must wait for me, and not entangle himself with any one, for they will get from him whatever they can, and then leave him in the lurch. Let him come here, and he will be received by the king and queen until I arrive.

"May our Lord have you in his holy keeping.

"March 21, 1502, in Seville.

"At your commands,

S.
S. A. S
X. M. Y.
X*po* FERENS."*

* It may explain this peculiar signature, which is so indicative of the fashion of his age, to add, what I believe comes originally from his son Ferdinand's Life of the Admiral; that Columbus, always, when trying his pen, before writing, wrote these words:

"Jesu cum Mariâ,
Sit nobis in viâ."

No. 2.

"To the most learned Doctor Nicolo Oderigo.

"*Learned Sir:*

"When I set off upon the voyage from which I have just returned, I spoke to you fully: I have no doubt you retained a complete recollection of every thing. I expected upon my arrival to have found here letters, and possibly a confidential person from you. At that time I likewise gave to Francesco di Rivarolo, a book of copies of my letters, and another of my Privileges, in a bag of colored Spanish leather, with a silver lock, *and two letters for the Bank of St. George, to which I assigned the tenth of my revenues, in diminution of the duties upon corn and other provisions.* No acknowledgment of all this has reached me. Sig. Francesco tells me that all arrived there in safety. If so, it was uncourteous in those gentlemen of St. George not to have favored me with an answer, nor have they thereby improved their affairs; which gives me cause to say, that whoever serves the public, serves nobody. I gave another book of my Privileges, like the above, in Cadiz, to Franco Cattaneo, the bearer of this, in order that he might likewise forward it to you; and that both of them might be placed in security wherever you thought proper. Just before my departure, I received a letter from the king and queen, my lords; a copy of which you will find there. You will see that it came very opportunely; nevertheless, Don Diego was not put in possession, as had been there promised.

"While I was in the Indies, I wrote to their highnesses an account of my voyage, by three or four opportunities; one of my letters having come back to my hands, I send it to you inclosed in this, with the supplement of my voyage in another letter, in order that you may give it to Signor Gian Luigi, with the other of advice; to whom I write that you will be the reader and interpreter of it. I would wish to have ostensible letters, speaking cautiously of the matter in which we are engaged. I arrived here very unwell, just before the queen, my mistress, died, (who is now with God,) without my seeing her. Till now

I cannot say how my affairs will finish. I believe her highness has provided well for them in her last will; and the king, my master, is very well disposed. Franco Cattaneo will explain the rest more minutely to you.

"May our Lord preserve you in his care.

Seville, 27th December, 1504.

S.
S. A. S.
X. M. Y.
Xpo FERENS.

"The Admiral of the Ocean, Viceroy, and Governor General of the Indies, &c."

No. 3.

Copy of a Letter written by the magistrate of St. George's to Columbus.

"Ill. Vir, et clarissime, amantissimeque
Concivis, et Domine memorandisseme.

"The distinguished Juris Consult, Messer Nicolo di Odérigo, on his return from the embassy to which he was appointed from our illustrious Republic, to the most excellent and glorious monarch, (of Spain,) delivered me a letter from your Excellency, which gave me singular pleasure, from the affectionate regard, so conformable to your disposition, which your Excellency therein exhibited towards your native country, to which you have shown most singular love and charity, in wishing it to be partakers of the favors which it has pleased Divine Providence to bestow upon your Excellency. Your aforesaid country and people must feel what singular profit and advantages they will derive from the orders you have given to Don Diego, your son, that the tenth of your annual revenues should be paid to this city, in diminution of the duties on corn, wine and other provisions. Nothing could be more charitable, nor more memorable than this, or will tend more to the remembrance of your glory, which, in other respects, is as great and extraordinary, as according to history, any man in the world has ever acquired, having by your own perseverance, energy and prudence discovered so large a portion of this earth and globe of the lower world, which for so many centuries past had remained unknown to the people of that which we inhabit. But this great exercise of your extraordinary glory, is in truth much more memorable and complete, as proceeding from the humanity and benignity which it proves you possess towards the country of your birth, on which account we praise, as it deserves, your disposition, and pray to God to preserve you many years. We shall always bear that affection towards your most illustrious son, Don Diego, which he is entitled to, as being your son, and from the splendor and glory of your actions of which this our common country is proud of having its part. To Don Diego we have expressed by letter, as we now do to your Excellency, our readiness to do everything in our power for the honor and advantage of your illustrious family. The above mentioned Messer Nicolo has related to us many things respecting your Favors and Privileges, of which he has brought copies here, with which we were much gratified, and return you everlasting thanks for those of which you had made us partakers.

"From Genoa, the 8th of December, MDII."

Here ends the publication by the Decurions of Genoa, in 1823. The following is a copy of the letter in the original Italian, and translation obtained by myself from the same depository, in Genoa, January 19, 1848.

No. 4.

ALLI MOLTO NOBILI SIGNORI
DEL MOLTO MAGNIFICO UFFICIO
DI S. GIORGIO
A GENOVA.

Al di dentro
Molto nobili Signori:

Benche il corpo cammini qua, il cuore sta li da continuo. Nostro Signore mi 'ha fatto la maggior, che dòpo David abbia fatto a nessuno. Le cose della mia impresa, giá risplendóno, e piu risplendérebbero, se la oscuritá del Governo non le coprisse.

Io torno alle Indie, in nome della Santissima Trinitá, per tornare subito; e perché, Io son mortale, lascio, a D. Diego, mio figlio, che di tutta la rendita, vi corresponda corti, per il decimo del totale, di essa, ogni anno, per sempre, in sconto, del prodotto, del grano, e vino, edaltre vettovaglie commestibile. Se questo decimo sará molto, ricevetelo, e se no, ricevete la volontá che io tengo. Vi prego, per grazia, che tengniàte riccomandato questo mio figlio. Messer Nicolo Odérigo sa dei fatti miei piu che io stesso, e lui ho mandato la copia dei miei privilegii, e carte; perche li pongo in buona guardià, avrei piacere, che li vedreste.

Il Re e la Regina, miei Signori, mi vogliono onora piú che mai. La San. Trin. guardi le vostre nobili persone, e accresca in molto magnifico uffizio.

Fatto in Seviglia le 2 di Aprile 1502.

L'Ammiraglio Maggure del Mare Oceano, e Vice Re, e Governatore Generale delle Isole, e della Terra Ferma, del Asia, e delle Indie, del Re, e della Regina, miei Signori, e suo Capitano Generale del Mare, e del suo Consiglio.

S.
S. A. S.
X. M. Y.
$X_{\rho o}$ FERENS.

Supplex.
Servus. Altissimi Salvatoris.
Xristi. Mariæ. Josephi.
Christo Ferens.

TRANSLATION.

TO THE MOST NOBLE GENTLEMEN OF THE ILLUSTRIOUS BANK OF ST. GEORGE AT GENOA.

To the within

Most noble Gentlemen:

Although the body travels hither, the heart remains with you for ever. Our Lord hath shown me greater grace than after David hath he shown to any one. The affairs of my enterprise are now resplendent, and will be more so, if the darkness of the government shall not overwhelm them.

I go again to the Indies, in the name of the Most Holy Trinity, to return speedily: and forasmuch as I am mortal, I leave in charge to Don Diego my son, that annually, for ever, he shall account to you for the one-tenth of all my Income, in order to reduce the taxes on corn, wine and other provisions. If this Tenth shall be considerable, accept it; and if not, accept the regard I entertain for you. I solicit your gracious consideration for my son. Signor Nicolo Odérigo, knowing of my affairs more than I do myself, I have sent him the copy of my Privileges and Charters; and as I thus place them in good guardianship, have the kindness to examine, when you see them.

The King and Queen, my Lords, treat me with more favor daily than ever. May the Most Holy Trinity safely keep your noble persons, and magnify you in your illustrious office.

Done at Seville, the 2d of April, 1502.

The High admiral of the Oceanic Sea, and Vice Roy and Governor General of the Islands, and of the Terra Ferma, of Asia, and of the Indies, of the King and Queen, my Lords, and their Captain General of the Sea, and of their Council.

S.
S. A. S.
X. M. Y.
X$_{po}$ FERENS.

EXPLANATION OF THIS SIGNATURE.

Supplex.
Servus. Altissimi Salvatoris.
Xristi. Mariæ. Josephi.
Christo Ferens.

The Suppliant
Servant of the Most High Saviour
Christ, of Mary, of Joseph
Christo Ferens or
Christopher.

MARTIN BEHAIM AND HIS GLOBE,

AT NUREMBERGH.

I TRUST that I may be allowed in connection with the Memorials of Columbus, to add a brief detail and description of a memento of his age, at Nürembergh in Bavaria; which during my stay at that interesting city, by the courtesy of resident friends, on the thirteenth day of September, 1847, it was my good fortune to visit and inspect. I allude to the celebrated Terrestrial Globe there, made by Martin Behaim, a native of that ancient imperial city; a most eminent navigator and discoverer, constructed by him in August, 1492, and left with his family there, with whose descendants in their ancient mansion, it still remains.

Apart from its originality and antiquity, it has attained a greater interest; having through misrepresentation, been made the prominent material for controversial detraction of the fame of Columbus. In this brief and unassuming paper, I purpose succinctly to detail the information afforded by others, of the personal history of the maker of this globe, Martin Behaim; and a few extracts from the controversial authors, so far as may be useful, in showing the importance of concluding with a simple and truthful description of this globe by an eye witness.

This spirit of detraction survived in 1786, when in April, M. Otto, a French gentleman, then residing in the city of New York, addressed to Dr. Franklin his able and ingenious "Memoir on the Discovery of America," in which the claims of Behaim to priority of discovery are presented with as much force as they are susceptible of. In my extracts from the memoir, it will be perceived that the statements of M. Otto, in his loose description of the globe, are contrary to the fact, and show that he, like other writers on this subject, has failed to examine the globe itself, although it is one of his chief arguments. But all mementos of a man of science and practical navigator, eminent for his own discoveries, and for the intimate friendship of Columbus, kindred in spirit and pursuit, cannot fail, however presented, to secure an abiding interest.

His name is variously given, Behain, Behem, Boehm, Behen and Behenira, but the name now of the family at Nürembergh is written "Behaim."

Martin Behaim was born at Nürembergh, in Bavaria, about A. D. 1430, and died at Lisbon, A. D. 1506, the same year as his great cotemporary Columbus. His ancestors were of an ancient and honorable family of Nürembergh. His genius and education were early inclined to diligent study of the master subject of that age, geography, which, after the Crusades, had opened the treasures of the east to the enterprise of awakening Europe, for which oriental commerce, his own native Nurembergh, was, until the passage of the Cape of Good Hope, in 1497, one of the chief marts, became a subject of increased attraction, by the marvellous histories of Marco Polo, Sir John Mandeville and other travellers of the preceding age. About the year 1481, he is supposed to have entered the service of King Alphonso V. of Portugal; no doubt attracted thither by the fame of the then late Prince Henry's munificent patronage, and the discoveries of the Portuguese, who had in 1471, crossed the Equator in their voyages of discovery on the Coast of Africa. Appointed by John II. the successor of Alphonso, to the Council or Department for the Improvement of the Art of Navigation, he is, by some authors, alleged then to have invented or at least to have introduced the Astrolabe, the forerunner of the Sextant, into nautical use. Without discussing his title to the discovery of the Island of Fayal in 1460, in the service of Isabella, Regent of Burgundy and Flanders, from whom he is said to have obtained a grant of the Island, a matter of some question; it is more material to state that as Cosmographer for the King, in 1484, he accompanied Diego Cano, on his voyage, which discovered the Western Coast of Africa, as far as the Coast of Congo, and for his eminent service was, on his return in 1485, knighted by the King John II.; the ruling policy of whose reign was to extend the area of discovery, and by her newly acquired colonies, to elevate Portugal to a great commercial power, and fitting rival to Genoa and Venice. During this voyage, Behaim is alleged by several authorities to have extended his course to the great South Western Sea, discovered and followed the Coast of Brazil, Patagonia and the Straits through which Magellan, whose name it bears, in 1519, passed to the Pacific, in his memorable voyage, the first circumnavigation of the Globe.

As a curious subject, it may be worth while to state such evidence as is urged; prefacing that his own Globe is the best refutation of a claim, which reaches us mainly from German Authors, and was unheard of in Portugal, where Behaim long lived, and was so widely known and honored; and is therefore only capable of affording entertainment to the student of his age.

The chroniclers of Nürembergh, anxious to add new laurels to their already distinguished fellow burgher, speak from the archives of that ancient city, that "Martin Behem, traversing the Atlantic Ocean for several years, examined the American Islands, and discovered the Strait, which bears the name of Magellan, before either Christopher Columbus, or Magellan sailed those seas, and mathematically delineated on a geographical chart for the King of Lusitania, the situation of the Coast around every part of that famous and renowned Strait." Apparently this record must have been written after the year 1519; the epoch of Magellan's voyage. It is asserted, that the archives of Nürembergh contain letters from Behaim, dated in 1486, confirming this record; but it is at least singular that they have never yet seen the light. To show that this story loses nothing in its German progress but

"Vires acquirit eundo,"

allow me to add a few more of the alleged authorities. Hartman Schedel, a chronicler of Nürembergh, writing about the time of Behaim, after describing the outfit of the celebrated expedition in 1484, by John II., under Behaim and Diego Cano, for discovery on the West Coast of Africa, already mentioned, says of Behaim, that he "was a man very well acquainted with the situation of the globe; blessed with a constitution able to bear the fatigues of the sea, and who by actual experiments and long sailing, had made himself perfect master of the longitudes and latitudes of Ptolemy in the West. These two," (Behaim and Cano,) "by the bounty of heaven, coasting along the Southern Ocean, and having crossed the Equator, got into the other hemisphere; where, facing to the Eastward, their shadows projected towards the South, and right hand. Thus by their industry, they may be said to have opened to us another world, hitherto unknown, and for many years attempted by none but the Genoese, and by them in vain."

This assertion of the chronicler, who might with his learned tomes well sleep in his native dust; has, we are told, been quoted and enlarged beyond his limits, which must be confessed are somewhat vague, by two famous men of their time: Eneas Sylvius, afterwards Pope Pius II., and Cellarius, but neither show any wish to verify their oracles. With them, the case on *authorities*, set up to mantain Behaim's priority of discovery of America, closes. Is it not a little singular, that such a claim should have survived till the close of the last century?

Another theory, the natural sequent of the former, and gathered about the memory of Behaim, cobweb-like, will, by your permission, detain us a moment, before passing to the conclusion of the whole matter,—the description of Behaim's Terrestrial Globe in Nürembergh. A once celebrated astronomer, Riccioli, an Italian, who surely might be presumed to have possessed better means of knowledge, is brought into the field to say that "Christopher Columbus never thought of an expedition to the West Indies until some time before, while in the Island of Madeira, where amusing himself in forming and delineating geographical charts, he obtained information from Martin Boehm, or as the Spaniards say, from Alphonsus Sanchez de Huelva," (the father-in-law of Behaim,) "a pilot, who by mere chance had fallen in with the island afterward called Dominica," and "let Boehm and Columbus have each their praise, they were both excellent navigators; but Columbus would never have thought of his expedition to America had not Boehm gone there before him. His name is not so much celebrated as that of Columbus, Americus or Magellan, although he is superior to them all."

It is also frequently asserted, with indeed some show of probability, that Magellan made great use of the practical and scientific knowledge and charts of Behaim: some say, that when Magellan, in 1519, in the audience chamber of Emanuel, king of Portugal, proposed his grand idea of voyaging westerly to the Indies of the east, by which in his memorable voyage he so signally accomplished the hopes of Columbus and his age, he there saw a chart of the coasts of America, drawn by Behaim, which at once made plain his path before him; and others say that Magellan carried either these charts, or this very terrestrial globe with him as his companion. It is enough to say that our sequel will show that this globe would not have been of much service to Magellan.

In 1486, Martin Behaim married, at the island of Fayal, the daughter of Alphonsus Sanchez de Huelva, (the name is sometimes given as Job de Huerta) of that island, likewise eminent as an experienced navigator. Christopher Columbus had previously married the daughter of Bartholomew Palestrello, of the island of Madeira, where Columbus spent much time in study and preparation of charts; and all authorities agree that from the year 1486 till the year 1489, these two eminent men, Columbus and Behaim, of kindred tastes and pursuits, were in intimate intercourse and friendship; but no evidence other than the above quoted assertions of chroniclers exists, of what aid if any, that Martin Behaim during this period rendered to the theory of Columbus.

In 1491 Behaim returned home to Nüremberghh; and there, at the request of the principal magistrates of the city, he commenced, and in August, 1492, completed his celebrated terrestrial globe.

In 1493 he returned to Portugal and Fayal, and after one short and adventurous voyage, died in Lisbon, in 1506. I will close my extracts with but two sentences from the memoir of M. Otto. Speaking of his having made his terrestrial globe, he says: "The track of his discoveries may there be seen under the name of 'Western Lands,' and from their situation it cannot be doubted that they are the present coasts of Brazil, and the environs of the Straits of Magellan. This globe was made in the same year, that Columbus set out on his expedition, from whence it is not possible that Behaim could have profited by the works of this navigator, who besides went a much more northerly course."

This prefatory summary of his life, and the theories that have been attached to his fame, will find its best apology for a length which may seem tedious, in the interest which it may throw about the final and chief monument of his life,—his terrestrial globe. No other person has, as far as I am informed, given in print a description of this globe: and it is much to be regretted that Mr. Irving did not close his digest of the chief events in the life of "Martin Behem," in the Appendix to the 3d volume of his history of Columbus, by something more than a mere allusion, arising probably from his lack of opportunity of inspection.* It may well happen that the Augsburg rail road may bring many a traveller to quiet Nürembergh, whose appreciation would be highly gratified by a sight of the globe; but it is not in the catalogue of the lions of the town, which the valet is prepared to show the traveller; who, unless favored by personal friends resident there, may very likely depart from Nürembergh, without even the knowledge of its existence and preservation.

In the New York Literary World for the twenty-second day of January, 1848, I find an article entitled "Nürembergh;" whose preparation, beguiled some weary hours of my quarantine at Malta, in the previous November; containing a sketch of the present state and appearance of that city, and among other matters a description of Behaim's terrestrial globe.

* I am in this favored by the confirmation of Mr. Irving himself, that he had never visited Nürembergh, or seen this globe.

I ask your permission, to extract therefrom such brief statement of facts as may be material to our present purpose.

"There is one other object of interest which is worth notice, before bidding adieu to Nürembergh. The family of Behaim here, possess a globe made by their ancestor, Martin Behaim, in the year 1492, while Columbus was yet at sea. It is in the mansion adjoining the Lindauer gallery. It is said to be the earliest in existence; and tradition says that its artist was an early patron, by his wealth and influence of the enterprise of Columbus. It is in perfect preservation, although dingy enough by the lapse of centuries. About two feet in diameter, it is suspended in a brass circle marked with the courses of the winds, with the names, and after the notions of classical geographers. The Equinoctial and Zodiac are defined, but there is an utter absence of latitude and longitude. America, North or South, is not there; the ocean flows over that side of the earth which afterwards belonged to the Western World; and the fancy of the artist has depicted some whales spouting in the locality of the United States; and some Spanish Caravals are sailing in unknown directions over Mexico. A few mermaids are combing their locks somewhere near modern Greenland, and in old German, he has inscribed underneath, the intelligence that many of these peculiar animals are to be met with thereabouts. The configuration of Europe is certainly singular; a certain wavy line answers for all coasts; England is about the size of Malta; Germany of modern Russia; Spain about double the size of France; the Mediterranean dwindles to a small lake; a vast region protrudes into the sea beyond the Indies, and is described as the domain of the famous Kaiser Prester John, in the words, 'hier wohnt der sehr berühmter Kaiser Prester Johan.' The Antilles are small obscure islands, near the west coast of Africa. The Red Sea is a huge ocean, colored *red;* and Palestine is of the size of modern Turkey. The geographer evidently proportions the countries according to their relative importance. The whole surface is studded with droll figures, as specimens of the inhabitants, productions and distinctive features of the countries, with continual inscriptions in German, of their names, character, discovery, etc.; forming a diligent abstract of the works of the travellers and geographers whose names are quoted as authorities, and thus giving a very complete idea and resumé of the state of geographical knowledge of the time.

"This rarity, although amusing enough to us, is evidently the work of a man of much reading; and it certainly has an additional interest as showing the state of geographical knowledge existing in Europe at that period, when the great discoverer of a Western World had at last set forth on the voyage of achievement of the long settled purposes and convictions of his mind. Looking at this relic, one readily sees what vast obstacles were in his path; the causes of the deeply settled unbelief which met him on every appeal for assistance to his project, and how strangely it must have sounded to their ears, when he reasoned of the actual existence of a mighty continent in that waste of waters, which their fancy peopled with mermaids and other denizens of the deep. The Globe bears the autograph of the maker, and the date of its construction or completion, August, 1492, and is of course above all price to the family who still possess it. A few years since the French Academy of Sciences, caused a beautiful fac-simile in papier mache to be made of it, and one of the copies was presented to the family. The two globes stand together, and are open to examination of any one on application to the family."

In conclusion, I may be pardoned for adding a few words—a mere historic glimpse of Behaim's native city—Nürembergh; being an extract from the same review article, in a notice of the antiquity of families there.

The princes of Nürembergh were a burgher aristocracy in their origin; wealthy merchants, who either for a timely loan, or for some equally important ministry to the necessities of the great lord or neighboring kings, were raised to the rank of the noblesse, and the chronicles of the city are filled with records of numerous charters of freedoms and privileges of commerce granted to the city itself on similar considerations. The oldest of such charters still existing in the city archives, dated in twelve hundred and nineteen,* the gift or concession of the Emperor Frederick II., creates it a free city of the Empire, exempting it from taxes or service to other feudal lords, providing imperial courts of justice, and endowing it with rights of markets, fairs, coinage and many other commercial privileges. With this and many other similar and subsequent charters, the city grew rich and prosperous, its artisans were famous, its markets crowded with their own fabrics, and with the luxuries of the East; for according to its chronicles, the North and West of Europe were supplied by the merchant princes of Nürembergh. Instead of being as now a comparatively inferior city of some forty thousand inhabitants, its archives tell us of the days when a great portion of the commerce of Northern Europe and the Indian trade were in its hands; when there were more than one hundred thousand busy citizens here, when the merchants of Northern and Central Europe came in great numbers to its fairs and markets, and its burgher noblesse were the friends and equals of princes. All this has long since changed. The discovery of the passage of the Cape of Good Hôpe naturally diverted a large portion of its commerce, and it fell into a decline from which it has not yet fully recovered. So when the stranger now walks its quiet streets, he must in a great degree, content himself with the vestiges of its past greatness and its departed commercial pre-eminence, though he must feel a certain sadness in seeing the immortal arts of Dürer, Visscher and Kraft, degenerated in the hands of their modern successors, to the manufacture of German toys, and to find the once northern Venice now-a-days famous mainly for bijouterie.

*This date is but fifteen years after the capture, plunder and occupation of Constantinople, by the Fourth Crusade. Its diadem was given to Baldwin, Count of Flanders, Henry II., and their successors, till A. D. 1260, when the Greek Empire was for a brief period restored. The Fourth Crusade as is well known, opened the wealth of the East to Europe, and its treasures we are told, began even then to ascend the Danube; whose waters have within the last thirty years, by the enterprise of the Hungarian Count Sczécheny, again become the pathway of oriental commerce, with Vienna and Western Europe.

TAH-GAH-JUTE OR LOGAN

AND

CAPTAIN MICHAEL CRESAP;

A DISCOURSE BY

BRANTZ MAYER;

DELIVERED IN BALTIMORE, BEFORE THE

MARYLAND HISTORICAL SOCIETY,

ON ITS SIXTH ANNIVERSARY.

9 MAY, 1851.

PRINTED FOR THE

MARYLAND HISTORICAL SOCIETY,

By JOHN MURPHY & CO.

BALTIMORE.

To my Brother

CHARLES FREDERICK MAYER,

This effort to delineate the border trials of our Pioneers, and to reverse the decree of history between an Indian and a meritorious Marylander, is affectionately inscribed.

Baltimore, 16th June, 1851.

NEARLY three hundred and sixty years have passed since this Western World was revealed to mankind by the discovery of Columbus, and though three centuries and a half afford ample time for the doing of many deeds, yet scarcely a year elapses without adding some new marvel to the influences of America upon the progressive civilization and comfort of the human race.

If we look on the map, at the portion of this Continent occupied by us at present, we are amazed at the vast expansion of our territorial limits within much less than one-third of this time. In the middle of the last century the British dominions in America were but a fringe upon the Atlantic shores. Beginning in the Bay of Fundy their outline ran south-westwardly skirting the eastern shore of Lake Ontario, until it touched the northern spurs of the Alleghanies, and then, descending along the slopes of those mountains, it struck the northernmost angle of Florida, and finally terminated on the Atlantic at the mouth of the Alatamaha. The average breadth of this scant region was not more than five degrees. West and north-west lay the vast primeval forests, the gigantic lakes and rivers, claimed by the French as Canada and the Province of Louisiana; while south, on the Gulf of Mexico and the Atlantic, stretched the romantic shores of Florida, under the dominion of Spain. It was not until the epoch of the Indian troubles, of which I am about to speak, and on the eve of our Revolutionary war, that the Ohio became the recognized boundary between the White and the Red man; and he who now entering

2

one of those floating palaces of the western waters at Brownsville, and descending the Ohio to the Mississippi, and the Mississippi to the Gulf, can hardly believe that within less than eighty years, the whole of this magnificent region, where the progress of trade has not effaced all traces of romantic nature, was still a dreary and dangerous wilderness, tenanted alone by the wild beast, or by human beings almost as savage. There are men still living who recollect the legends of Indian warfare or foray in Maryland, Pennsylvania, or Virginia, and can recount the escape or the death of some ancestor by the tomahawk and scalping knife. There are those amongst us, too, whose hair is still unsilvered, who may remember their sport as boys in watching the straggling Indians,—half beggars, half bandits,—who every winter thronged our streets, but whose only use of the bow and the arrow was to win the pennies we ventured in order to test the sureness of their aim.

But where, even now, is the "Far West," which in those days was spoken of as something mysteriously indefinite,—as something denoting perils of journey and Indian cruelty? It was then that we had still territorial boundaries to settle with Britain, and titles as well as rights to adjust with stubborn tribes. It was then that the far-seeing and comprehensive merchant, laid the foundation of his wealth, by tracking the beaver in its wildest haunts in Oregon. It was then that California was remembered as a field of romantic Missionary labor, cherished under Mexican Viceroys, but as a land of abandoned enterprize. It was then that our young and restless spirits sought the valleys of the Ohio and Mississippi as homes which were beginning to be fully redeemed from the hunter and the savage. That was the Far West of those days. But now, strange names salute our ears, sounding no more of Indian conquests, but commemorative monuments as long as language shall last of victories over civilized men. We have abandoned an Indian nomenclature and adopted the calendar of Christian saints. Santa Fé, the Rio Bravo del Norte,—the Colorado of the West,—the Pecos,—the Gila,—the Valleys of San Juan, and Santa Clara,—the Plains of the Sacramento and San Joaquin, and the upland Vale at the foot of Mount Shastl;—the Great Basin, around whose saline waters the Mormon enthusiasts have nestled, seeking refuge among the savages from the bigoted persecutions of civilization;—Monterey,—San Francisco,—San Diego,—Chrysopolæ or the Golden Gates,—and last of all, the Pacific, itself, for an acknowledged boundary, and the Isthmus for a highway! There is, no longer, a "Far West." States, now planting on the brink of the Pacific and washed by its surge, curb, in that direction, the utmost possible limit of our dominion. Gold, in apparently inexhaustible quantities, has magnetically attracted an immense population in the brief space of three years. The first great experiment of planting the Anglo-Saxon race on the Pacific, facing the Indies with a clear and short highway in front, is no longer a problem to be solved. The tide of emigration sets no more exclusively from East to West, but rapidly ebbs and surges backward, as China, Hindustan, the Australian colonies, the Pacific Islands, the Chilian, Peruvian, and Mexican states, pour their motley crowds of eager immigrants along the whole coast from the Gila to the Columbia. The icy tops of the Sierra Nevada are passed, and the Great upland Basin of Utah becomes the thoroughfare of traders, pilgrims, and caravans from the far East. Through the wilderness to Santa Fé, and thence along the Southern passes of the mountains, other crowds press each other, to and fro, on the path of the modern Ophir. And thus, in the progress of a few brief years, the swollen tides of humanity bursting the barriers of the Alleghanies from the East, and of the Nevada from the West, must at last meet and mingle in the great Valley of the Mississippi which is destined to become the central mart of our mighty Union.

In God's genial providence of gradually opening the resources of this world for the progress of mankind there is the most perfect accommodation to the enlarging wants and capacities of our race. Every thing is not disclosed at once. The good, the desirable, the necessary, are hidden away in the earth's secret places, and the task of laborious enterprize is imposed on man for their discovery and useful preparation. Yet, marvellous as are the modern developments of industry, of science, and, sometimes even, of apparent chance, there is no exhaustion in these resources, for new means of success seem to keep constant pace with each new labor and enterprize. Our Beneficent Parent works out his wonderful schemes by human agents, not by miracles. Humanity, with all its virtues and all its sins, is charged with the noble task of free *development*, and thus the results become the work of man and are made the trials and tests his of responsibility.

The Old World became crowded, and space was required in which the cramped and burdened millions might find room for industry and independence,—and a New Continent was suddenly disclosed for their occupation. The old political systems of Europe and of the Eastern nations decayed in consequence of the encroachments of individual power made despotic by corruption or force,—and a virgin country was forthwith opened as a refuge for the oppressed masses in which the principle of absolute political and religious freedom might be tried without any convulsive effort to cast off the fetters of feudalism. The labor of man, even in this new world began to strip commercial countries of their forests or made them too valuable for fuel,—and, suddenly, the heart of the earth is found to be veined with minerals which will save the lives of the majestic monarchs who shade and shelter the surface. Coal thus becomes the most potent agent in commercial development, for, without it, the seas could not be traversed with the rapidity and certainty that modern wants exact. The increasing industry and invention of the largely augmented populations of various countries, required, either a greater amount of capital to represent their productions, or a new standard of value for the precious metals already in circulation,—and, at once, apparently by mere accident, an adventurer discovered amid the frosts and forests of the Pacific, a golden region in which the fabled sands of Pactolus are realized. At last, even steam itself becomes too slow for mankind, and human skill, chaining magnetism to its purposes and lacing the earth with its wires, embroiders the whole world with the electricity of thought. But all these vast storehouses of invention, comfort and wealth, are not placed at our doors, in the midst of civilization, ready to be grasped, comprehended or used with equal ease by the dainty idler or the patient worker. Far away in distant regions they lie. Far away amid forests and perils. Far away in lands which are reached by dreary voyages. Far away,—requiring the renewal of hope in desponding hearts, and renewal of energies in broken men. There they lie—long concealed and wisely garnered temptations,—to be discovered at the appropriate moment in the world's progress, and to lead man thither as the founder of a new field of human industry.

In this genial development of our globe three classes of persons have always been needed:—the Discoverer, the Conqueror, and the Pioneer.

Emigration is the overflowing of a bitter cup. Men do not ordinarily leave their native lands and kindred for the perils of the wilderness, or for a country with which they have no community of laws, language, or present interest, unless poverty or bad government crowds them into the forest. When the Discoverer and the Conqueror have found the land and partly tamed the savage, the Pioneer advances into their field of relinquished enterprize, and his task partakes, in some degree, of the dangers incurred by both his predecessors. He is always a lover and seeker of independence, and generally pursues it with a laudable desire to improve his lot; yet the perfect exercise of this independence sometimes becomes selfishly exclusive. Its essence, in our country, is the complete self-reliance of the one man or the one family. This spirit of social, political, and industrial independence, occasionally becomes wild, impatient and uncontrollable. Its mildest exhibition under such circumstances, is in rude manners or wayward lawlessness, which outraged neighborhoods are wont summarily to redress. True civilized liberty does not countenance such mockers of justice within its pale, and thus there are multitudes who not only go voluntarily and wisely into new lands, but other heedless or scoffing crowds are scourged by society into the sombre forest. Slowly and surely are these elements of new States, gathered, purged, and crystalized around the centres of modern civilization.

Hope, ambition, misery, avarice, adventure, noble purpose, drive off impatient men who will not be satisfied with the slow, dripping, accretions of wealth in the old communities. They require fortune and position by a leap. Independence demands space for the gigantic inspirations of its vast lungs, and flies headlong to the forest. The wandering woodsman or hunter gathers his brothers in armed masses for protection amid this chaos of unorganized freedom, and they support each other cheerfully in seasons of danger or disease. But the social law of humanity vindicates itself against the eager spirit of perfect independence. Wherever man who has once either drained or sipped the cup of civilization, is found, there must he be fed and clothed, nor does he cease to yearn for the relinquished luxuries, amusements, or comforts of the home he abandoned beyond the eastern mountains. Wherever man goes, man's representative,—money,—pursues him; and secretly he longs for the pleasing results of that civilization which he feigns to despise. Thus the Pioneer may be said to bait the forest like a trap, for the Trader. Taking up the war with the Indian where the Conqueror left it, he at once subdues the soil and the savage. The Farmer, at length, plants himself on the land that the Ranger wrests from the Indian. The Merchant covers with his sails the seas that were scourged by the Pirate. The dollar dulls the edge of the bowie-knife. Where the Pioneer treads, the Missionary follows. Element by element, civilization drops in. Peace, like a cooling shadow, follows the blaze of war. Death closes the career of the primeval Forester, and the law of God, vindicating by its perfect ultimate success, the merit of Peace, whose triumphs are the only true ones, plants the Trader and the Farmer on his grave, and that which was wildly won is quietly and permanently enjoyed.

Our habitual and perhaps almost necessary devotion to *the Present* in a country where property is so little treasured or transmitted in families, and our prying anxiety to know the secrets of the future, have made us too heedless of the memory of the Past. Our law of history, like our law of property, not only prevents an entail of our accumulations, but the Past and the Present may be said to disinherit the Future, and to leave no legacies. Yet I have ventured to hope that it would not be uninteresting to Marylanders, if, on this occasion of our annual historic festival, I spoke to them of the days that are gone, and endeavored, by a glimpse of our "scant antiquity," to display the romantic story of some of our own people who were among the first in Lord Baltimore's Province to mark the Pioneer progress to the western wilds. Maryland, thrust geographically as a wedge between the great Provinces of Pennsylvania and Virginia, was among the earliest to furnish her quota of hardy foresters, who in their contests with the Indian, prepared themselves for the subsequent conflict with England in the war of Independence.

You will recollect that it was only a few years after Pontiac's war that small settlements of whites had crept westward through the defiles of the Alleghanies and along the principal paths, the northernmost of which converged at old Fort Du Quesne or Pitt, whilst the southernmost led to the fountains of the Holston and the Clinch. A town was laid out on the East bank of the Monongahela within two hundred yards of Fort Pitt, and, for seventy miles above it, a route had been cut through the wilderness to "Red-Stone Old Fort," near the mouth of Dunlap's Creek, now the site of Brownsville.

About the year 1774, Virginia still *claimed* by virtue of her charter, all the territory between the parallels of 36° 30′ and 39° 40′ North latitude, from the margin of the Atlantic due West to the Mississippi, and thus enclosed within her assumed limit, not only the region which at present is comprised in Kentucky, but also the Southern half of Illinois, one-third of Ohio, and an extensive part of Western Pennsylvania. Settlements had been planted upon most of the *eastern* branches of the Monongahela, the Youghiogeny, and on the small *eastern* tributaries of the upper Ohio, for one hundred and twenty miles below Pittsburgh, as well as on the sources of the Greenbrier, the little Kenhawa and Elk river, West of the Mountains,—embracing in these districts, the North-Western counties of Virginia and the South-Western of Pennsylvania as at present defined. Pittsburgh was claimed as a frontier town of Virginia, while the southern settlements, on the tributaries of the Monongahela, were held to belong to the same province. Yet the vast region South of the little Kenhawa and Westward thence to the Mississippi, with but slight exceptions, was a perfect wilderness held by savages. The lonely, isolated settlement of a few poor, ignorant French Colonists on the Wabash and Illinois rivers, had, it is true, fallen under British dominion, after the peace of Paris, but these immigrants were scarcely regarded as British subjects, and were held as outlying foreign military colonists, more than a thousand miles in advance of civilization, having but little interest or sympathy with the Pioneers who penetrated the wilderness from Virginia, Pennsylvania or Maryland.

The French and Indian Wars and the true pioneer spirit which characterized so many Americans at that day, had sprinkled this region of woods, mountains and rivers, with bold, enterprizing woodsmen, traders, hunters, and agriculturists, and with lion hearted women who were proper mates for men stamped with so much energy and fortitude in the iron mintage of border trial. The majority of this enterprizing class was hardy and virtuous, though, as in all such frontier communities, the honest and daring were followed by miscreants who were willing either to shelter themselves from law in the wilderness, or to encounter the risks of a wild life without caring for ultimate results. But the pioneer was a liberal and hospitable being, for he appreciated the loneliness and discomforts of his own perilous lot, and was prompt to ameliorate the condition of all who ventured beyond the Alleghanies. His fringed and fanciful hunting shirt, which may still be found among the mountains of our own Cumberland,—his deer-skin leggins,—his gaily embroidered moccasins—his tomahawk and scalping-knife,—his bullet pouch, powder horn, and ready rifle,—made up his personal equipments of comfort and defence. He was a picturesque being as he was beheld descending the slopes of the mountains or relieved against the blue sky or the dark shadows of the forest. In his lonely region no mechanics were to be hired, and every Pioneer was obliged to do his own work or to possess within his family the necessary elements of labor in the field or at the plough, the loom, and the anvil. His gun was in constant use against the Indian as well as the bear and the deer. Yet never was he an ungenerous neighbor when a new cabin was to be erected for an immigrant, or a crop to be gathered for the friend who inhabited his district. The "husking match" and the "log rolling" are distinctly recorded among the kindly and helping memorials of early settlements, in those days, when the genuine "cabin," made without nails, mortar or bricks, was the home of many an ancestry that has given rulers to our Union. A common danger cemented these forest settlements in a bond of mutual defence and interest. It was a life of incessant wariness or of peril to be encountered, and thus, mutual dependence and the fear of the savage, formed the best police of the pioneer, for it warned off weak and irresolute interlopers and permitted none but the hardy and true to abide in the forest.

Nor were these men so improvident as to omit strengthening themselves, not only by social acts of faith and friendship, but by supplying their bands with forts, block houses, and stations, constructed of massive logs and slabs, proof against bullets, and built around or near a never-failing spring. These defences, constructed at points easy of access as places of refuge to a whole neighborhood of agriculturists or hunters, were perfect safe guards against a foe who had no artillery, but were rarely tenanted unless at periods of general alarm, or when the Pioneers left their farms in the spring upon the announcement of some Indian murder in the vicinity.

These adopted children of the wilderness were, of course, not unskilled in wood craft. The stars, the sun, the bark of trees were their guides. The weather informed the settler whether he was to encounter his game for the day on the mountain tops, the hill sides or in the vallies; and when "the buck" was slain, skinned, and dressed, the early night was passed in glee and story around the fire of his joyous "hunting camp." Witchcraft was firmly believed by many of them, for strange sights and sounds, and a lonely life, gave play to the imagination or to the recollection of old superstitions learned in infancy. Singing, dancing, shooting the rifle, throwing the tomahawk, wrestling, and all athletic or manly sports, formed the constant diversions of the settlers when they were at leisure or on remembered holidays; while the most boisterous merriment prevailed at wedding frolics, or at the "house-warming" of the forest bride and her gallant groom. Lawyers and Judges were unknown in these rough and simple communities, yet a strong moral sense and the stern demands of duty, preserved rights and interests in regions were no man could afford to be idle. Debts were but little known. Laziness, dishonesty, and ill-fame roused the general public opinion of the settlement. Thieves were flogged. Personal disputes were settled by battles with fists, after which the parties became reconciled; and evil men, in the emphatic language of the day, were "hated out of the neighborhood."

The wants of these backwoodsmen required an annual visit to the east, and every autumn associations were formed for the yearly caravan, which, with its long trains of horses, bearing peltries and Indian ware, might be heard tinkling its bells in the forests or along the mountain defiles as it wound its way to Hagerstown, Old Town, Cumberland and Baltimore to exchange the products of the wilderness for salt, iron, lead and powder.[1]

With these brief sketches of the country and the men of that part of the North American wilderness which was most closely connected with Maryland just before the revolution, I shall proceed to delineate the deeds and career of some individuals whose names are linked with our State's story by romantic incidents which I believe have passed into history inaccurately, and are now transmitted from page to page by new writers as conceded facts.

While endeavoring to perform this duty to the memory of a meritorious fellow citizen, I may also be able to illustrate the value of historical societies, which, by devoting themselves to

[1] See Rev. Dr. Doddridge's Notes on the Settlement and the Indian Wars of the Western parts of Virginia and Pennsylvania, from 1763 to 1783, in Kercheval's History of the Valley of Va.

the minuter investigations of literature, are enabled to trace critically the pedigree of long recorded falsehoods, and thus to vindicate individuals if they do not always exculpate our race from motives or crimes that would forever degrade mankind.

COLONEL THOMAS CRESAP,—the parent of Captain Michael Cresap who has been scornfully portrayed as the instigator if not one of the chief actors in the alleged murder of the Indian Logan's family in the early part of 1774,—emigrated from Yorkshire, England, to America, when he was about fifteen years of age. We know nothing of his intervening career until fifteen years after, when he married a Miss Johnson, and settled either at or near Havre de Grace, on the shores of our beautiful Susquehannah. He was, emphatically, a "poor man;" so poor, indeed, according to the family legends, that being involved in debt to the extent of nine pounds, currency, he was obliged soon after his inopportune marriage, to depart for the south in order to improve his fortune! He left his young wife in Maryland, and hastening to Virginia, became acquainted with the Washington family, and rented from it a good farm with the intention of removing finally to the flourishing colony. But, on returning for his bride, he found that he had become a parent, and that the resolute matron was loth to quit the Susquehannah for the Potomac. Accordingly, like a docile husband, he submitted to her whim, and contriving to free himself from debt, removed still higher up on the river to Wright's ferry, opposite the town of Columbia, where he obtained a Maryland title for five hundred acres of land. Unfortunately, however, for the settler, this was disputed ground, and as it was soon claimed under a Pennsylvania title, a sort of border war occurred, in which Cresap espoused the cause of Lord Baltimore with as much zeal as the Pennsylvanians sustained that of Penn. His enemies regarding him as a powerful foe, seem to have resorted to the basest means to rid themselves of his presence. An Indian was hired to assassinate him in his own house; yet, won by his kindness and hospitality, the savage disclosed the plot and was pardoned for the meditated crime. At length, however, a regular battle took place between the factionists, and

Cresap's party having wounded several of Penn's partizans, kept the field and gained the day.

The Pennsylvania warriors, nevertheless, soon rallied their discomfited forces and besieged the fort in which the Maryland champion had entrenched himself. But the stalwart Cresap held out bravely against all comers, though he was singled as the special victim of the assailants. Nevertheless, in time, he deemed it advisable to demand aid from his neighbors; and as his eldest boy, Daniel, was at this time, about ten years old, he despatched the young forester in the night to obtain the required succor. The wild frontier stripling apt as he already was in the ways of the wilderness, could not, however, elude the vigilant besiegers, and being taken captive, endeavored to destroy the hostile clan while assembled around the fire, by casting therein its whole stock of powder which he found tied up in a handkerchief. Fortunately for the party, he was detected in time to escape the disastrous explosion.

If the young Cresap was unable to blow up his father's assailants, the elder was well nigh doomed to the fate his son had designed for the followers of Penn. The besiegers finding that they could not arouse or dislodge the stubborn Yorkshireman from his lair, determined to set fire to the roof and thus to "roast him out" of his fortress! No terms of capitulation were offered; and as Cresap disdained to ask his life at their hands, he rushed to the door, and wounding the sentinel, escaped to his boat. But here, surrounded by superior numbers, he was seized, overpowered, bound, and thrown into the skiff. Nevertheless as his captors were conveying him across the Susquehannah in the dark, he contrived, notwithstanding his ligatures, to elbow one of the guard into the water. The Pennites, in the darkness, mistaking their companion for Cresap, beset him, forthwith, with oars and poles, nor was it until the lusty cries and rich brogue of the unfortunate Irishman undeceived them, that he was relieved from the beating and the bath. Passing through Columbia to Lancaster, Cresap was heavily manacled; but even then, lifting his arms as soon as the work was done, he smote the smith on the head with his ironed hands and levelled him to the ground. Nevertheless, he was effectually a prisoner and was borne off in triumph to Philadelphia, where the streets, doors and windows were thronged with spectators to see the Maryland monster, who taunted the crowd by exclaiming half in earnest half in derision:—"why this is the finest city in the Province of *Maryland!*"

The Pennsylvanians at length became weary of their sturdy and audacious guest, yet he would not depart until released by order of the King, about October, 1737, after suffering nearly a year's confinement.[1] In the meantime, his family sought shelter in an Indian town on the Codorus, near York, where it was hospitably entertained by the savages until his return. Finding his old neighborhood too dangerous or disagreeable, he soon removed to a valuable farm at Antietam; and as it was a frontier post, in advance of white population, he built, over a beautiful spring, a stone house which was half dwelling and half fortress.

He seems to have possessed the deserved confidence of some of the most respectable families of Maryland; for in this new settlement, he commenced the business of a trader, partly on a borrowed capital of £500, which he obtained from Mr. Dulany. But unluckily his venture of skins and furs, sent to England, was lost in a ship which was captured by the French, and he was thus compelled to begin the world anew for the third time. Yet his honest heart did not fail under renewed misfortunes. He offered his land, consisting of about 1400 acres, to Dulany, in payment of his debt; and being thus stripped of nearly all his worldly possessions, he removed, about 1742 or 1743, to a spot,

[1] See Jacob's Life of Cresap, p. 25. The most complete details of these border difficulties, which I have not space even to sketch at present, will be found by the historical student in the MSS. and Records preserved at Annapolis in the State library; in Rupp's History of York County, Pa., p. 547 to 563; and in Hazard's Register of Pennsylvania, page 200 *et seq;* and page 209 *et seq;* of the 2d volume,—in a sketch of the boundary dispute and hostilities growing out of it from 1728 to 1737, betwixt Lord Baltimore and the Penns. Cresap was an ardent partizan of the Maryland Proprietor, and acted with great vigor in defence of his own and his Lord's rights or demands. See, also, Gordon's Hist. Penna. 221. Gordon and Day are brief, while Proud is silent. Cresap was released in consequence of an order of the King in council commanding both parties "to refrain from further violence, to drop all prosecutions, and to discharge their respective prisoners on bail."

in what is at present Alleghany county, Maryland, called Old-town, or as he delighted to name it,—"Skipton,"—after the place of his nativity, situated on the north fork, a few miles above the junction of the north and south branches of the Potomac.[1] Here, at length, after all his early trials, he established his permanent home, and finally acquired by industry and perseverance in the neighborhood, a large landed estate on both sides of the river in Maryland and Virginia.

About this epoch, he renewed his intimacy with the Washington family, who always reposed confidence in him; and being known as a bold and skilful woodsman, he was employed by the parties who formed in 1748 the celebrated Ohio company. This association, among whose members, we find Lawrence Washington, and his brother Augustine, received from the British King a grant of five hundred thousand acres, to be taken chiefly on the south side of the Ohio, between the Monongehela and Kenhawa rivers, west of the Alleghanies.[2] The object of the enterprize was to settle land, and to carry on the Indian trade on a large scale. But the French, alarmed by this threatened advance of English Pioneers, began immediately to extend a line of forts along the Mississippi and Ohio, passing through a vast extent of territory which was claimed by Great Britain. In spite of all opposition, the English grantees pursued their enterprize, and Col. Cresap's knowledge of the country and of pioneer life, was of great service to them, in tracing the very first path through the windings of the Alleghanies. As one of their agents in that region, he employed an Indian named Nemacolin, to mark the road by the well known trail of the tribes, and it is said he performed his duty so well, that the army pursued the same path when Braddock marched to the west to dislodge the French. Colonel Cresap, thus stationed on the extreme outposts of civilization, became an important pioneer in the early development of the west; nor

[1] See Colden's Hist. of the Five Nations, p. 3, and 84, edition 1755. See Philadelphia Treaty of 1742, and Canassateego's speech at the Lancaster Treaty, 1744.

[2] Washington's Writings, vol. 2, appendix vi, pages 478 and 479, and appendix vii.

did he cease many years afterwards, to devote his mind and hopes to those fine regions in which he saw the future grandeur of his country. When he had attained the patriarchal age of ninety, he conceived and digested a plan to explore as far west as the Pacific, and nothing but his advanced years prevented the accomplishment of an enterprize which he cherished with the enthusiasm of an early borderer.

The grants to the English Company not only caused the French to establish their line of forts, but, as is well known, resulted in a war which retarded the advance of civilization. The Indians were roused, and desolated the border. Cresap, on his extreme frontier settlement among the Alleghany mountains, held a most dangerous post; but it was an eagle's nest, fit for a bold spirit, and he would not willingly desert it. When hotly pressed by the savage foe he fought his way to Conococheague, and having placed his family in safety, did not remain an idle spectator while ruin threatened the infant settlements on the head waters of the Potomac. The country swarmed with the savage *guerrilleros* of those days, and the hardy woodsman, adopting the Indian fashion of the times, took "the war path" with his own band and children, and struck the foe on several occasions at the western feet of the Savage Mountain, where his son Thomas fell by an Indian ball, and at Negro Mountain where a gigantic African, who belonged to his party, bequeathed his name in death to the towering cliffs. In these fights Michael Cresap obtained his first lessons in Indian warfare.

After these early border conflicts were over,—although he was sometimes afterwards harassed by the savages,—the veteran pioneer reposed at his homestead, respected and honored, until quieter days. He was a man of vigorous mind and constitution, and although his early education had been neglected, there are testimonials of his skill both in composition, surveying, and even hand-writing, in the possession of our Society which would do honor to a man of loftier birth and opportunities.[1] At the

[1] In the GILMOR MSS. *Maryland Papers*, vol. 1, *Article* No. 8, in the possession of the Maryland Historical Society, is the following *original letter from Colonel* Cresap, in which we have an interesting account of one of the Indian raids in 1763. It is written in a firm and formal hand, and would do credit to

age of seventy he visited England; and, while in London, was commissioned by Lord Baltimore to run the Western line of Maryland, in order to ascertain which of the two branches of the Potomac was, in reality, the fountain head of the stream.

one of much more clerkly reputation. The letter is thus addressed on the outside:

"ON HIS LORDSHIP'S SERVICE:—
To
"*His Excellency* HORATIO SHARPE, *Esquire*,
in
ANNAPOLIS.

"*To be forwarded by Express.*"

and endorsed:

"*From Col. Cresap*, 15 *July*, 1763."

"OLD TOWN, July 15th, 1763.

"May it Please your Excellency

"I take this opportunity in the highth of Confusion to acquaint you with our unhappy and most wretched Situation at this time, being in Hourly Expectation of being massacred by our Barberous and Inhumane Enemy the Indians, we having been three days successivly attacked by them, Viz: the 13, 14 and this Instant. On the 13th as 6 men were shocking some wheat in the field 5 Indians firing on them as they came to do it and others Running to their assistance;—on the 14th 5 Indians crept up to and fired on about 16 men who were sitting and walking under a Tree at the Entrance of my Lane about 100 yards from my House, but on being fired at by the white men, who much wounded some of them, they Immediately Run off and were followed by the white men about a mile all which way was a great Quantity of Blood on the Ground. The white men got 3 of their Bundles, containing sundry Indian Implements and Goods. About 3 Hours after several guns were fired in the woods, on which a party went in Quest of them and found 3 Braves Killed by them. The Indians wounded one man at their first fire tho' but Slightly. On this Instant as Mr. Saml. Wilder was going to a house of his about 300 yards Distant from mine with 4 men and several women, the Indians rushed on them from a rising Ground, but they perceving them coming, Run towards my House hollowing, which being heard by those at my house, they run to their assistance and met them and the Indians at the Entrance of my lane, on which the Indians Immdiately fired on them to the amount of 18 or Twenty and Killed Mr. Wilder;—the party of white men Returned their fire and killed one of them dead on the Spot and wounded severall of the others as appeared by Considerable Quantity of Blood strewed on the Ground as they Run off, which they Immdiately did, and by their leaving behind them 3 Gunns, one pistole and Sundry other Emplements of warr &c. &c.

"I have Inclosed a List of the Desolate men, Women and Children who have fled to my house which is Inclosed by a small stockade for safety, by which you'll see what a number of poor Souls, destitute of Every necessary of Life are here penned up and likely to be Butchered without Immdiate Relief and

His map of this survey is in the possession of the Maryland Historical Society, and, together with his report, has been used by our legislature in the boundary discussions with Virginia.[1]

In 1770, after his return from England, George Washington visited Colonel Cresap at his "Old Town settlement," in order to learn the particulars of the Walpole grant on the Ohio; and, as the future general of our armies returned from his examination of lands on the rivers of the west, he again tarried for the night in the humble dwelling of the old pioneer.[2] He had, thus, acquired the respect and confidence, not only of the Lord Proprietor of this Province, and of the clear-minded Washington himself, but was generally known in Maryland, Virginia, and Pennsylvania, as an energetic, far-seeing and hospitable man. No deed of needless daring, or of cruelty is recorded against him;—even the Indians who knew his rifle well, esteemed him cordially. When Nemacolin departed from the mountains of Cumberland, he left his son in Cresap's care. The savages with whom he had dealt so fiercely when necessity demanded,

assistance, and can Expect none, unless from the province to which they Belong. I shall submitt to your wiser Judgment the Best and most Effectual method for Such Relief and shall Conclude with hoping we shall have it in time."

"I am Honorable Sir
your Obedt. serv
THOS. CRESAP"

"P. S. those Indians who attacked us this day
are part of that body which went southward by this way
——— spring which is known by one of the Gunns we got from them."

"The Maryland Gazette" of July 21, 1763, informs us that the Colonel was not yet cut off by the savages, though it is feared he will be if not quickly relieved. The above story is repeated. Subsequent statements show that ten men were sent to assist Cresap.

[1] In the Gilmor MSS. *Maryland Papers*, vol. 1, *Portfolio of "Surveys, letters, &c., connected with the running of the Division line between Maryland and Pennsylvania,"* is the *original autograph map* made by Col. Cresap, in the neat style of a good country surveyor, and sent by him to Governor Sharpe. It came to Mr. Gilmor's possession with many other of the "Ridout Papers," and is attested by Horatio Ridout, whose father was Sharpe's secretary. This was the *first* map ever made to show the course and fountains of the north and south branches of the Potomac river, in regard to which there has been so much controversy between Maryland and Virginia.

[2] Washington's Writings, vol. 2, pp. 516 and 533. Journal of Tour to the Ohio river.

as they went, during his latter years, past his house on their hunting expeditions, were always welcomed and entertained. He had a huge ladle and kettle prepared expressly to feast them with a whole ox, and they, in turn complimented his hospitality by bestowing on him the Indian title of the "BIG SPOON."[1]

At the age of eighty he married a second time. He visited the British possessions, near Nova Scotia, at 100, and died at the age of 106! Such was the father of CAPTAIN MICHAEL CRESAP, whose name has been doomed most unjustly to infamy by the hasty adoption of the falsehood contained in a miscalled Indian speech.

MICHAEL, the youngest son of the pioneer, whose biography I have sketched, was born in that part of Frederick, which is now comprised in Alleghany county in this state, on the 29th June, 1742. In those early days there were no seminaries of learning in that remote region; and Michael, his son, was sent to a school in Baltimore County, under the charge of the Rev. Mr. Craddock. A wild and daring mountain boy from the wilderness, he had, at first, but few friends among the eastern boys; yet, with the usual power of manly courage and generosity, he soon fought his way into the good graces of his schoolmates. But the restraints of school life were uncongenial to his

[1] Jacob's Life of Capt. Michael Cresap. Cumberland, Md., 1828.

The Rev. John J. Jacob, by whom this Biograghical sketch of the life of Captain Michael Cresap was written, entered the store and was engaged in the western trading concerns of Captain Cresap, from the age of fifteen. This was about the year 1772. He was entrusted with the management and settlement of valuable ventures sent by the Captain to Redstone Old Fort or Brownsville, during the Indian war of 1774. When the Revolutionary conflict broke out, and after Cresap's death on the 18th of October, 1775, Jacob remained for a while with the hero's family; but, in July, 1776, he entered the militia as an ensign, and subsequently obtained a lieutenant's commission in the regular army with which he continued during five campaigns, until the winter of 1781. In this year he married the widow of Capt. Michael Cresap, his old employer; and thus, becoming possessed of all his papers, and being intimate with his motives and history during an intimate personal intercourse, he was fully enabled, as well as entitled, to vindicate the memory of his departed friend.

Later in life he was known as an esteemed pastor of the Methodist Episcopal Church, who, for many years, resided, and finally died, as a local minister in Hampshire County, Virginia.

habits; and flying from his preceptor, he traversed alone the 140 miles which lay between him and his home. The old Colonel, however, did not sanction the restive demeanor of the truant, but believing in the virtue of the rod and the necessity of filial obedience as well as education, flogged him severely, and sent him back to his teacher, with whom he steadily remained until his studies were finished.

Soon after leaving school, he married a Miss Whitehead, of Philadelphia, and the happy pair, both almost children, departed to the mountains to enjoy, as the romantic striplings probably supposed, "love in a cottage" in a little frontier village near his father's dwelling among the hills. But the Colonel would not countenance a life of idleness, and established Michael at once as a merchant and trader. Trade, in those days and neighborhoods, was often a perilous business in the hands of inexperienced men. And young Cresap, who imported largely from London, and dealt with the utmost liberality, so often found his confidence misplaced, that in the course of a few years he became almost ruined. Notwithstanding his kindness and honorable deportment, he seems to have had enemies, or at least extremely cautious watchers of his acts. The agent of the London merchant from whom he received his goods in America, reported to his principal in England, that Michael was a suspicious character, and might probably remove to some part of the western wilds where he would be out of the reach of the law. The consequence of this report was the immediate withdrawal of the young trader's customary supplies; but, as soon as Michael was able to trace the slander to its source, he charged it home upon the London agent and the controversy ended in a violent personal conflict in a private room in Fredericktown.

Cresap was thus compelled, both by the blow which his credit had received and his bitter experience among his customers, to curtail his business. Yet hope did not desert him. The population which had gathered around this frontier settlement, began, under the temptations of the west to flow off towards the Ohio. His active temper and prompt mind soon decided him. "Urged by necessity, prompted by a laudable ambition, and allured by the rational and exhilarating prospect before him, he saw or thought he saw, in the rich bottoms of the Ohio, an ample fund, if he succeeded in obtaining a title to those lands, not only to redeem his credit and extricate him from difficulty, but also to afford a respectable competency for his rising family.

"Under this impression, and with every rational prospect of success, early in the year 1774, he engaged six or seven active young men, at the rate of £2.10 per month, and repairing to the wilderness of the Ohio, commenced the business of building houses and clearing lands; and, being one of first, or, among the first adventurers into this exposed and dangerous region, he was enabled to select some of the best and richest of the Ohio levels."[1]

After the Indian and French wars and the treaty made by Bouquet, the attention of the Maryland, Virginia and Pennsylvania settlers, had been attracted to the great trans-Alleghanian region watered by the Monongahela, the Ohio, the Kenhawa, the Scioto, the Cheat and their affluents. Companies had been formed and lands granted. The outposts, or scouts and pickets of civilization, were fixed along these streams. Fort Du Quesne had become Fort Pitt, under the British flag. Wheeling was a station; and, all along the river, there were spots where traders and farmers had settled, or neighborhoods gathered for mutual protection around block-houses, forts and stockades. In this society, laudably engaged in repairing his fortune and preparing that of his infant family, I shall leave Michael Cresap early in the year 1774, and endeavor to transport you in imagination for a short time to another and perhaps more romantic scene among the hills and valleys of the Susquehannah.

Indian history, and especially Indian Biography must always resemble the pictorial sketches of the Indians themselves, who, by a few rude etchings on a rock, a few bold dashes on the skin of a buffalo, or scratches on the bark of a birch-tree, record the outline memoranda which may serve to recall an event though they can only commemorate a character by inferences.

[1] Jacob's Life of Cresap, p. 41.

Their story is but a skeleton; and hard, indeed, is the task which attempts to clothe the dry and dusty bones with flesh, and to make the restored being move at least with the semblance of real life. Their theatre is the forest. Their home a camp. Their only architecture a cabin or a perishable tent. Their only permanent and consecrated resting place—the grave! A wild, solitary and dangerous people,—almost without a record,—they flit like shadows through the wilderness of wood, prairie and mountain;—now here, now gone in the dim recesses of the valleys;—free as the deer, or transient as phantoms of mingled romance and horror; but, most generally, inscribing their wild red marks in the memory of white men by deeds of cruelty and blood alone!

In the early days of Pennsylvania the Valley of the Susquehannah was assigned by the Six Nations as a hunting ground for the Shawanese, Conoys, Nanticokes, Monseys, and Mohicans; and SHIKELLAMY, or as he was called by the Moravians, SHIKELLEMUS, a celebrated Cayuga Chief sent by those Nations to preside over a tribe, dwelt at Shamokin, an Indian village of about fifty houses and nearly three hundred persons, built on the broad level banks of the Susquehannah, on a beautiful site, with high ranges of hills both above and below it, affording magnificent views of the picturesque valley in whose lap the modern Sunbury is quietly nestled.

When Count Zinzendorf, on the 28th of September, 1742, accompanied by Conrad Weiser, two Indians, brother Mack and his missionary wife, after a tedious transit through the wilderness on their journey of Christian love, entered this beautiful vale of Shamokin, Shikellamy was the first to step forth to welcome them, and, after the exchange of presents, to promise his aid as a chief in fostering the religion of Christ among the tribe.[2] But when David Brainerd visited the Indian village, three years after, he found that the seed dropped by the holy Moravians had fallen on barren places. He was kindly received and

[1] Compare Minutes of Council, Aug. 12, 1731, Brainerd's Journal—and Loskiel, part 2d, p. 10.

[2] Loskiel.

entertained by the Indians, yet neither his requests nor the illness of one of the tribe could induce them to forego their wild and noisy revels. "Alas!"—exclaims the Journalist,—"how desti- "tute of natural affection are these poor uncultivated pagans, "although they seem kind in their own way! Of a truth, the "dark corners of the earth are full of the habitations of cruelty. "* * * * * The Indians of this place are accounted the most "drunken, mischievous, and ruffian like fellows in these parts; "and Satan seems to have his seat in this town in an eminent "manner!" [1]

The Six Nations used Shamokin as a convenient tarrying place for their war parties against the southern Catawbas; and, soon after the missionaries visited them, were desirous to have a blacksmith from the white settlements, who would reside permanently in their village, and save their long journeys from the mountains to Tulpehocken or Philadelphia. The Governor of the Province allowed the request, provided the smith should continue only as long as the Indians remained friendly to the English; and the Moravians, availing themselves of the opportunity, despatched a staunch brother named Anthony Schmidt, from their mission at Bethlehem, who, doubtless, in the intervals of his business from repairing the savages' rifles, was enabled, as an antidote, to edify them with a sermon on the horrors of war. The blacksmith, however, opened the way for the establishment of a Moravian mission at Shamokin in 1747, under the charge of Brother Mack. Bishop Camerhoff and the pious Zeisberger, visited it in 1748; and, in the following year, Shikellamy—this apparently virtuous chief over so boisterous, drunken, and roystering a tribe,—a man who is reported to have performed many embassies between the government of Pennsylvania and the Six Nations, as well as attended important councils at Philadelphia, departed for the Indian "hunting grounds" which lie in the pleasant prairies of the "spirit land" beyond the grave.

[1] Brainerd's Journal. Day's Penn. Hist. Col. 525.

[2] Conrad Weiser, a chief officer in the Indian Department of Pennsylvania, and the Moravians seem to have had great confidence in Shikellamy, and probably he died a sincere friend of the whites and a tolerable Christian. For an

Of this personage,—thus reared in a sort of modified fear, love, or admiration of the whites, and *in the midst of excessively bad associates,* as described by Brainerd, was born a second son, celebrated in the annals of our country by the spicy rhetoric of a speech which first attracted the attention of Mr. Jefferson, and has since been repeated by every American school boy as a specimen of Indian eloquence and Indian wrongs.

After Braddock's defeat in 1755, the whole wilderness from the Juniata to Shamokin, and from the Ohio to Baltimore Town, was filled with hostile Indian parties,—murdering, scalping, destroying and burning. I have not time to notice the breaking up of the mission at Shamokin and slaughter of the inoffensive whites throughout the neighborhood, in which all those miscalled friendly tribes were concerned as soon as they were encouraged by the successes of the French and the disasters of of the English. Their former professed Christianity, or the forbearance of their chiefs, had, in all likelihood, been the effect of sudden superstition or of salutary fear.[1]

During this epoch the son of Shikellamy,—Logan,—who had been named it is said for the secretary of the province whom his father knew and loved,[2]—disappears from the scene. We have few historical or biographical anecdotes of his early life, nor does he in fact become the subject even of legend until seventeen or eighteen years after his father's death.[3]

The Juniata breaking through the wild gap of Jack's mountain, enters the south-western end of Mifflin county, Pennsyl-

account of his death and character, see Day's Penn. Hist. Col. 526. Loskiel. Rev. J. Heckwelder's statement, appendix No. IV to Jefferson's Notes on Virginia, p. 40.

[1] Voyage dans la Haute Pensylvanie, Tome 3, chapitre iv.

[2] James Logan, the secretary, died in 1751.

[3] Some early notices of the sons of Shikellamy and their deeds may be found in the following writers: Rupp's History of Dauphin, Cumberland, Franklin, &c., counties, Pa., pp. 65, 319, 84, 259, 100, 316. Also Rupp's History of Northumberland County, pp. 92, 119, 166. Rupp's History of Berks and Lebanon Counties, Pa., 213, 41, 39. Rupp's History of Northampton, Lehigh, &c., Counties, Pa., p. 103. Kercheval's Valley of Va., p. 127. Loudon's Narratives of Indian wars, vol. 2, p. 223; this passage describes Logan's personal appearance in 1765, and recounts an anecdote or two.

vania, and meandering through Lewistown valley, again strikes the mountains at the romantic gorge of the Long Narrows, between the Black Log and Shade mountains, at a cleft barely wide enough for the river to pass, and, at its end, the stream breaks through the rocky masses of Shade mountain. Kishicoquillas creek is a never failing flood in this romantic neighborhood, fed by the mountain springs surrounding a valley out of which it bursts at a deep ravine in Jack's mountain, and enters the Juniata at Lewistown. Early settlements had been made in this attractive region, but when the Indian troubles broke out, the inhabitants fled, nor was it until the years between 1765 and 1769, that they began to return, and, about that period, Judge Brown, Samuel Milliken, McNitt, James Reed and Samuel McClay, became the earliest dwellers in the charming vale of Kishicoquillas.

About a mile or two above the deep and tangled dell where the stream passes Jack's mountain, beside a beautiful limestone spring, at a spot which was as solitary as it was romantic, an Indian cabin had been built for many years. As William Brown and James Reed, two of the pioneers whom I have named as early occupants of this region, had wandered one day out of the valley in search of choice locations and springs, they suddenly started a bear, and, like all foresters, being provided with their rifles, immediately gave chase. A shot speedily wounded the brute, which retreating to the higher ground, led them onward in quest of their prey, until, suddenly, this beautiful spring, gushing from the hill-side, burst upon their sight. Exhausted by a long and tedious hunt, the woodsmen were more delighted to find the stream than the game, and immediately resting their rifles against trees, threw themselves on the ground to drink. But as Brown bent over the clear and mirroring water he beheld, on the opposide side, reflected in the limpid basin the tall shadow of a stately Indian! With instinctive energy he sprang to regain his weapon while the Indian yelled—whether for peace or war he was unable to determine;—but as he seized his rifle and faced the foe, the savage dashed open the pan of his gun, and scattering the powder, extended his open palm in token of friendship. Both weapons were instantly grounded, and the men who a moment before had looked on each other with distrust, shook hands and refreshed themselves from the gurgling brook. For a week they continued together examining lands, seeking springs, and cementing a friendship which had been so strangely commenced at a period when "whoever saw an Indian saw an enemy, and the only questions that were asked, on either side were, from the muzzles of their rifles."

The Indian vision of the spring was Logan—the son of Shikellamy,—the solitary Indian;—no chief, but a wanderer sojourning for a while on his way to the west.[1]

Logan is well remembered and favorably described in the legends of this valley, for he was often visited in his camp by the whites. Upon one occasion, when met by Mr. McClay at the spring which is even now known by his name, a match was made between the white and red man to shoot at a mark for a dollar a shot.[2] In the encounter, Logan lost four or five rounds, and acknowledged himself beaten. When the whites were leaving the dell, the Indian went to his cabin, and bringing as many deer skins as he had lost dollars, handed them to Mr. McClay, who refused the peltries, alleging that he and his friends had been Logan's guests, and would not rob him, for the match had merely been a friendly contest of skill and nerve. But the courteous waiver would not satisfy the savage. He drew himself up with great dignity, and said in broken English: "Me bet to make you shoot your best;—me gentleman, and me take your dollars if me beat!" So McClay was obliged to take the skins or affront his friend whose sense of honorable dealing would not allow him to receive even a horn of powder in return.[3]

Deer hunting, dressing their skins and selling them to the whites seem to have been the chief employments of Logan at this period, and the means of his livelihood. Upon one occasion he had sold a quantity to a certain tailor named De Yong,

[1] Day's Hist. Coll. of Penn. 464 et. seq. Pittsburgh Daily American, 1842. American Pioneer, vol. 1, p. 188.

[2] Day's Coll. ut supra, 466, for a description of the site of this spring.

[3] Letter of R. P. McClay in Pittsburgh Daily American of 1842, and in Penn. Hist. Coll. by Day, 467. American Pioneer, i, 114, 115, 188.

who dwelt in Furguson's valley below the gap. Buckskin small clothes were in those days in demand among the frontier men as well as among the soldiers or fops of the cities, and when silver or paper money was scarce, barter was the customary mode of trade in those simple communities. Logan, according to agreement, received his pay from the tailor in wheat, which, when taken to the mill, was found so worthless that the miller refused to grind it. But law and the ministers of justice, had already found their way into the secluded valley, and the Indian appealed to his friend Brown, who by this time had been honored with the commission of a magistrate. When the judge questioned him as to the character of the fraudulent grain, Logan sought in vain to find words to express the precise character of the material with which it was adulterated, but said it resembled the wheat itself. "It must have been *cheat*," said the Judge. "Yoh!" exclaimed the Indian, "that's very good name for him!" and forthwith a decision was given in Logan's favor and a writ presented for the constable, which, he was told, would produce the money for his buckskins. But the untutored Indian,—too uncivilized to be dishonest,—could not comprehend by what magic this fragment of paper would force the reluctant tailor, against his will, to pay for the skins. The Judge took down his commission emblazoned with the royal arms, and explained the first principles and operations of civil law, after which Logan appeared to be better satisfied with the gentle operation of judicial process, and departed to try its effect in his own behalf, exclaiming—"law *very* good if it make rogues pay!"

When one of Judge Brown's daughters was just beginning to walk, her mother expressed sorrow that she could not obtain a pair of shoes to give more firmness to her infant steps. Logan stood by but said nothing. Soon after he asked Mrs. Brown to allow the little girl to spend the day at his cabin near the spring. The cautious and yearning heart of the mother was somewhat alarmed by the proposal, yet she had learned to repose confidence in the Indian, and trusting in the delicacy of his feelings, assented to the proposal with apparent cheerfulness. The day wore slowly away, and it was near night when her little one had not returned. But just as the sun was setting the trusty savage was seen descending the path with his charge, and in a moment more the little one was in its mother's arms, proudly exhibiting on her tiny feet a pair of beautiful moccasins—the product of Logan's skill.[1]

I have dwelt, perhaps tediously, upon these simple incidents of Indian and frontier life because they are the only ones I have been able to glean from the brief records of Logan's career, that exhibit him to posterity in a favorable light. His lot was soon to be changed. The lonely—simple—and perhaps sentimental savage was shortly to come in violent conflict with the whites who were "extending the area of freedom,"—and the rest of his life was chequered with horrible crimes and maudlin regrets, dark enough to efface the gentle deeds of his early years. According to the statement of Judge Brown, Logan departed to the far west soon after the occurrences I have recounted, and he never saw him more; but, in the language of the cordial old pioneer, "he was the best specimen of humanity, white or red, he ever encountered."

For a while, again, the curtain drops on our Indian legend, and the savage disappears behind the leaves of the forest, nor do we find his trail once more until the Rev. Mr. Heckwelder, when living as a missionary at the Moravian town on the Beaver about the year 1772, four or five years after the events we have just narrated, was introduced by an Indian in that neighborhood to Logan as the son of the old Shikellamy, the friend of the white men and Moravians at Shamokin. The savage impressed the missionary as a person of talents superior to Indians generally. He exclaimed against the whites for the introduction of spirituous liquors among his people;—spoke of "*gentlemen*" and their true character, regretting that the tribes had unfortunately so few of this class for neighbors; declared his intention to settle on the Ohio below Big Beaver, where he might live in peace forever with the white men, *but* CONFESSED TO THE MISSIONARY HIS UNFORTUNATE FONDNESS FOR THE "FIRE-WATER." At that time Logan was encamped at the mouth of

[1] Narrative of Mrs. Norris, in Day's Penn. Hist. Coll. 467.

Beaver, and in 1773, when Heckwelder was journeying down the Ohio towards Muskingham he visited the Indian's settlement, and received every civility he could expect from the members of his family who were at home.[1]

It was about this time that another Missionary, the Rev. Dr. David McClure, during a visit to Fort Pitt and the neighboring regions of the Ohio, met our hero, and saw many other Indians who were in the habit of resorting to the settlements for the sake of a drunken frolic, staggering about the town.[2] At that time Logan was still remarkable for the grandeur of his personal appearance. TAH-GAH-JUTE[3] or "Short Dress," for such was his Indian name, stood several inches more than six feet in height; he was straight as an arrow; lithe, athletic, and symmetrical in figure; firm, resolute, and commanding in feature; but the brave, open, and manly countenance he possessed in his earlier years was now changed for one of martial ferocity.[4] After tarrying and preaching nearly three weeks at Fort Pitt, Dr. McClure, in the summer or autumn of 1772, set out for Muskingham accompanied by a Christian Indian as his interpreter. The second day after his departure, the wayfarers unexpectedly encountered Logan. Painted and equipped for war, and accompanied by another savage, he lurked a few rods from the path beneath a tree, leaning on his rifle; nor did the missionary notice him until apprized by the interpreter that Logan desired to speak with him. McClure immediately rode to the spot where the red man remained, and asked what he required. For a moment Logan stood pale and agitated before the preacher, and then, pointing to his breast, exclaimed:—"I "feel bad here. Wherever I go the evil Manethoes pursue "me. If I go into my cabin, my cabin is full of devils. If I "go into the woods, the trees and the air are full of devils. They

[1] Appendix No. IV to Jefferson's Notes on Virginia, 46.

[2] Wheelock's Narrative, 1772–73, p. 50.

[3] "The aged Seneca, Captain Decker, told me that Logan's Indian name was Tah-gah-jute or Short Dress, and added that 'he was a very bad Indian.'"—*Lyman C. Draper, MS. note.*

[4] Compare Loudon's Nar. Indian Wars, vol. 2, p. 223, and McClure and Parish's Memoirs of Rev. Dr. Eleazer Wheelock, *Newburyport*, 1811, p. 139. Loudon describes him about 1765,—McClure in 1772.

"haunt me by day and by night. They seem to want to catch "me, and throw me into a deep pit, full of fire!" In this moody strain of abrupt, maudlin musing,—with the unnatural pallor still pervading his skin,—he leant for awhile on his rifle, and continued to brood over the haunting devils. At length he broke forth with an earnest appeal to the missionary as to "what he should do?" Dr. McClure gave him sensible and friendly advice suggested by the occasion; counselled him to reflect on his past life; considered him as weighed down by remorse for the errors or cruelties of past years, and exhorted him to that sincere penitence and prayer which would drive from him the "evil Manethoes" forever.[1]

The holy man departed on his pious mission, nor did he ever hear of the Indian again until after the bloody deeds which will be hereafter recounted. The "fire-water" of the "white man" had begun to do its deadly work upon all the elements of a noble character in the heart and mind of the untutored savage.

I must again shift the scenery of our stage and return once more to our Maryland settler and his band who had gone out early in the spring of 1774, although it is unquestionable that in the performance of his duties as a pioneer trader, he had previously visited that region for the joint purposes of locating land and carrying on commerce.

On an elevated and commanding bank on the east side of the Monongahela about seventy miles above Pittsburgh, there were at that period the remains of one of those Ancient Works, which, in consequence of the military skill displayed in the selection of their site, and arrangement of their walls or parapets, have been regarded as Indian forts. They are among the evidences of the supposed civilization of the races who inhabited the western valleys, anterior to the present tribes, and of whom even the legends are lost. On the north-west of the one at present under consideration, the river Monongahela rushed along the base of the hill; on the north-east and south were deep

[1] Wheelock's Memoirs, ut antea, p. 139, &c. I am indebted for this reference and anecdote to my friend Lyman C. Draper, who has kindly furnished it to me in MS.

ravines, while, on the east, a flat was spread out across which an approach could easily be detected. Several acres were enclosed within the works, and hard by were springs of excellent water.

This is the site of the town of Brownsville, the head of the present steam navigation of the Mississippi valley, nearest the eastern mountains,—and the spot, even at that early day to which the main trail over the Alleghanies had been directed. It became an attractive place to the whites as it had evidently been to the savages, as we may judge from the ingenious works with which they fortified it. This post, known in border history as "Red-Stone Old Fort," became the rallying point of the pioneers and was familiar to many an early settler as his place of embarkation for the "dark and bloody ground." In the legends of the west Michael Cresap, whom we left, to sketch the biography of Logan, is connected with this Indian strong-hold. In those narratives Cresap is spoken of as remarkable for his brave, hardy, and adventurous disposition, and awarded credit for often rescuing the whites by a timely notice of the savages' approach, a knowledge of which he obtained by unceasing vigilance over their movements. This fort was frequently Cresap's rendezvous as a trader, and thither he resorted with his people either to interchange views and adopt plans for future action, or for repose in quieter times when the red men were lulled into inaction and the tomahawk and the scalping knife were temporarily buried. These were periods of great conviviality. The days were spent in athletic exercises; and, in the evening, the sturdy foresters, bivouacked around a fire of huge logs, recounted their hair-breadth adventures, or if, perchance, a violin or jewsharp was possessed by the foresters it was sometimes introduced and the monotony of the camp broken by a boisterous "*stag-dance*."

The scrutinizing mind of Cresap, discovered at that early day, that this location would become exceedingly valuable as emigrants flowed in and the country was gradually opened. Accordingly he took measures to secure a Virginia title to several hundred acres, embracing the fortification, by what, at that time, was called a "*tomahawk improvement*." Not content, however, with "girdling" a few trees and "blazing" others, he determined to ensure his purpose; and, in order that his act and intention might not be misconstrued, he built a house of *hewed logs* with a shingle roof *nailed* on, which is believed to have been the first edifice of this kind in that part of our great domain west of the mountains. We are not possessed of data to fix the precise year of this novel erection, but it is supposed to have occurred about the year 1770; and the title to the property was retained in the Cresap family for many years, but was finally disposed of to the brothers Thomas and Basil Brown who had emigrated from Maryland.[1]

We now approach the final scene of our dramatic sketch in the valley of the Ohio. Cresap, in his last expedition to the west, had departed from Maryland, as I have already related, early in 1774, in order to open farms on the river, and was acompanied by hired laborers. But an Indian war was soon to break out, which, in the history of the west, is sometimes known under the name of this Marylander, as "Cresap's war," and sometimes under that of the Earl of Dunmore, who was then Governor of Virginia. Yet, this savage conflict, in which the Earl commanded the Virginians, and Cornstalk, a Shawanese chief led the Indians, had probably a very different origin from that which we shall hereafter see was erroneously ascribed to it, and in which Michael Cresap was unjustly supposed to have acted so bloody a part.

During the ten years subsequent to the treaty made by Bouquet, the gradual advance of the whites to the west had been a constant source of alarm to the Indians. There was no acknowledged boundary between the races. Every year brought them nearer and nearer in mingling confusion. Collisions and violent disputes were the natural and necessary results. Crimination and recrimination followed. The white man introduced his "fire-water," and the Indian learned to love its wild delirium, nor did he regret the mad revels and even the murders in which he participated while under its terrible influence. The savage and the settler constantly encountered each other with

[1] MS. of James L. Bowman, published in the American Pioneer in 1843. And subsequently reprinted in Day's Penn. Hist. Coll. p. 342, et seq.

mutual distrust. The town and the farm were to rise and spread out over the "war path" and the "hunting ground." The slow, eager, resistless encroachments of civilization, brought the two uncongenial and incongruous races, face to face, in contact, and the slightest breath was sufficient to fan into conflagration the fire that smouldered in the hearts of each.

Besides this, there had been no scrupulous fulfilment of Bouquet's treaty on the part of the Indians; and I am informed by one of our ablest border historians and scholars, that during these ten years of nominal peace, but in truth, of *quasi* war, more lives were sacrificed along the western frontiers than during the whole outbreak of 1774, including the battle of Point Pleasant.[1]

In order that I may not be supposed to allege these Indian exasperations carelessly, I will state,—as I believe it to be unquestionable history,—that the Shawanese, failing to comply with the treaty of 1764, did not deliver their white captives, and barely acquiesced, sullenly, in some articles of the compact, by command of the six nations. The Red-Hawk, a Shawanese[2] chief, insulted Colonel Bouquet with impunity, and an Indian killed the Colonel's servant on the next day after peace was made. This wanton murder being passed unnoticed at the time, gave rise immediately to several daring outrages.

In the following year individuals were slain by the savages on New River, and soon after, some men employed in the service of Wharton's company were waylaid and killed on their journey to Illinois, while their goods were plundered and borne off by the robber band. Sometime after this outrage, a number of men employed in slaughtering cattle for Fort Chartres, were destroyed, and their rifles, blankets and accoutrements carried to the Indian villages. All these brutal wrongs were unredressed, and although the Shawanese are not supposed to have been the only perpetrators of the bloody cruelties, yet, unresisting submission to such enormities seems to have been a mistaken policy

[1] MS. letter from Lyman C. Draper.

[2] Les Indiens disent Shawanahaac; je l'ai fait répéter plusieurs fois à quelques uns d'entreux. Nos ancêtres par défaut d'attention, out écrit Shawanee, et leurs descendans out suivi cet example. *Récherches sur les Etats Unis*, 1788, *vol.* 4, *p.* 153, *note.*

in an age in which the law of revenge or of prompt, compulsory, obedient, dread was the only imperative code comprehended by the savages. Before our military power had become strong, and especially in its very dawn in the west, the tribes supposed all to be feeble and forcibly submissive who did not resist, and non-resistance, of course, produced mischief. They measured us by their only standard of savage morality—revenge,—a law bloody indeed, but which the honest historian is forced to regard in considering the early years of nations, especially when the Indian and the unprotected white man come in contact, and when perhaps the moral grade and the surrounding circumstances of both races are properly considered.

He who writes history, in order to judge justly, must endeavor to make himself a man of the times he describes. He is unfair, if he decides on the events of the eighteenth century by the standards of the nineteenth. It would no doubt be considered infamous in Massachusetts, at the present day, if an Indian were killed, yet it will scarcely be credited that, in the early part of the last century, the General Court of that Province offered a bounty of £100 for every Indian's scalp. The cruel murders almost daily committed by the barbarians upon the defenceless frontier inhabitants, originated and were held to justify this enactment; and in one of the bloody onslaughts of the Massachusetts men against the savages, forty white warriors returned to Boston with ten scalps extended on hoops in Indian style, and demanded the reward of £1000, which was promptly paid.

Nor were these expeditions against the Red Men unsanctified by prayer. Chaplains accompanied the doughty fighters. Early on the day of conflict these pastors of the church militant lifted up their voices, and declaring that they had "come out to meet the enemy, besought God that they might find him. They trusted Providence with their lives, and would rather die for their country, than return if they could, without seeing the foe, and be called cowards for their pains!"

It might be supposed that these valiant clergymen contented themselves with beseeching the "God of battles," and refrained from mingling in the fray. But this was not the case, for in the quaint old ballad of the Fight at Pequawket it is metrically narrated that

"Our worthy Captain Lovewell among them there did die;
"They killed Lieutenant Robbins, and wounded good young Frye
" *Who was our English Chaplain; he many Indians slew,*
"*And some of them he scalpèd when bullets round him flew!*"[1]

As his Britannic Majesty's troops on the Ohio, at the epoch of which I have been speaking, had perhaps neither the power nor spirit to punish or reclaim the Indians, and enforce the peace and the treaty,—mischief became familiar to the tribes when they found that they escaped with impunity.[2] And, thus, in truth, the Indian hatchet was never buried. The summer after Bouquet's treaty the savages killed a white man upon the Virginia frontiers; the next year, eight Virginians were butchered on the Cumberland, and their peltries brought to the Indian towns where they were sold to Pennsylvania traders. Sometime after, Martin, a Virginia trader with two companions, was killed by the Shawanese on the Hockhocking,—only, as it was alleged by Lord Dunmore, because they were Virginians, at the same time that the savages allowed a certain Ellis to pass, simply because he was a Pennsylvanian. In 1771, twenty Virginians and their party of friendly Indians were robbed by them of thirty-eight horses, as well as of weapons, clothes and trappings, which they delivered to Callender and Spears and certain other Pennsylvania traders in their towns. In the same year, within the jurisdiction of Virginia, the Indians killed two lonely settlers; and, in the following, Adam Stroud, another Virginian, with his wife and seven children, fell beneath their tomahawks and scalping knives on the waters of the Elk. In 1773, the savages were still engaged in their work of destruction. Richards fell on the Kenhawa; and a few months after, Russel, another Virginian, with five whites and two negroes, perished near the Cumberland Gap, while their horses and property were borne off by the Indians to the towns where they fell a prey to the

1 Drake's Book of the Indians, Book III, p. 128, 130, 133.

2 Maryland Gazette, Dec. 1, 1774. Am. Archives, IV series, vol 1, p. 1015, extract of a letter from Red Stone Fort dated October, 1774.

Pennsylvania traders. These and many other butcheries and robberies of a similar character, were committed in the savage raids and forays, anterior the year 1774, and long before a single drop of Shawanese blood was wantonly shed in retaliation by the irritated people.[1] A Dutch family was massacred on the Kenhawa in June of 1773, and the family of Mr. Hog, and three white men, on the Great Kenhawa, early in April, 1774.[2] On the 25th of April, 1774, the Earl of Dunmore, at Williamsburg his seat of Government in Virginia, issued his proclamation, which, as dates are of great importance in this narrative, we should regard as unveiling other causes of border difficulty, besides the Indian hostilities, which were then occurring.

It will be remembered, as I have already stated, that the territorial claim of Virginia covered at that time a large part of western Pennsylvania, and that a bitter controversy had arisen between the two provinces and their respective authorities, especially as to the domain commanding the navigable head waters on the line of frontier posts. There was great jealousy on both sides. The Virginia pioneer,—planter, hunter and agriculturist,—had met in conflict with the Pennsylvania trader. The Indians, as we have seen in the statement I gave of some of the murders during the ten years after Bouquet's peace, molested the Virginian forester, and appear to have spared the Pennsylvania trader. The allegations of Lord Dunmore in one of his speeches to the Indians, already referred to, exhibit the soreness of provincial feeling on this subject.[3] In his proclamation of the 25th of April, 1774,—before there could possibly have been a communication of any retaliatory murders on the Ohio, committed by the whites upon the Indians,—the

[1] Earl of Dunmore's Speech to the Delawares and Six Nation Chiefs, Am. Archives, IV Series, vol. 1, p. 873.

[2] Am. Archives, IV Series, vol. 1, p. 1015, and see also Lord Dunmore's answer, dated at Williamsburg, 29 May, 1774, to the speech of the Indians dated at Pittsburgh, May 7, 1774,—Am. Arch. ut supra, p. 482; but compare the alleged Indian statements contained in a letter dated 29 May, 1774, from Arthur St. Clair to Governor Penn, in the same vol. p. 286.—See also Withers's Chronicle of Border War.

[3] Am. Arch. ut supra, 482.

British Earl, then at Williamsburg, declares, that inasmuch as there is trouble within his jurisdiction at Pittsburgh, and the authorities in that place and its dependencies will endeavor to obstruct His Majesty's government thereof by illegal means; and, inasmuch as that "*settlement is in danger of annoyance from Indians, also*," he has thought proper, with the advice and consent of his Majesty's counsel, to require and authorize the militia officers of that district to embody a sufficient number of men to repel *any assault whatever*.[1] The events that caused the issuing of this proclamation, must necessarily have occurred both among the white and the red men, a considerable time before, so as to have allowed the messenger to cross the mountains prior to the 25th of April.

But even anterior to this, on the 24th March, 1774, there was a letter published in the Williamsburg Gazette, addressed to the Earl, and signed Virginius, warning him of an Indian war, and beseeching him to convoke the House of Burgesses in order to raise men and means for the defence of the frontier.[2] The first volume of the fourth series of the American Archives, published by Congress, is full of narratives and official correspondence or minutes, disclosing the acrimonious provincial animosities as to western jurisdiction between Pennsylvania and Virginia at this time, and one writer declares that "more is to be dreaded from the rancorous feeling between the settlers from the two states than from the barbarians." The same volume contains copious documents revealing the violent scenes that occurred in 1774, upon the arrival at Pittsburgh of John Connolly, who was regularly commissioned by Lord Dunmore, though a native of Lancaster county, in Pennsylvania, to represent his authority as a magistrate for West Augusta.[3]

It is not a little singular, even if nothing more than a coincidence, that Lord Dunmore should have chosen the epoch of a

[1] American Archives, 4th series, vol. 1, p. 283. Ld. Dunmore's proclamation.

[2] Id. id. id. id. p. 272 in the notes.

[3] See as to the causes of this war, in confirmation, Withers's Chronicles of Border Warfare, chapter vi.—He is decidedly of opinion that it was not caused by the murders at Captina Creek and opposite the mouth of Yellow Creek, which will be subsequently narrated.

menaced Indian war, and of a growing dispute with the mother country beyond the seas, to assert formidably the rights of Virginia, not only by issuing his proclamation, but by despatching to the scene of action a man like John Connolly, who was well known not only for his bold, restless and artful temper, but for his sagacity, his knowledge of the world and of Indian affairs, and his exceedingly lax morality.[1]

I have not time at present, nor is this properly the occasion, to discuss a border controversy between the two great provinces, which has never yet been fully chronicled, and, at best, could only be an episode in our history. Yet I have thought it right to show that it occurred, singularly enough, just at the epoch of

[1] Burk's Hist. Virginia, 3d vol. p. 374, and vol. 4, p. 74.—At the latter reference the reader will find a further development of Connolly's subsequent conduct and hostility to American interests, as disclosed in the plot formed by Lord Dunmore to bring the Indian tribes of the West into the Revolutionary conflict. Connolly, on his way to Detroit, was arrested near Fredericktown in Maryland, by the committee of safety; was examined and committed to close custody on the 23d Nov., 1775. He had been commissioned by the Earl, as a Lieut. Colonel Commandant. 4th Burk, Appendix 4.—The joint plans of these loyal Britons show the great probability that there was, in truth, a scheme in embryo to crush the American Revolution at its birth, by a union between the Indians, negroes and loyalists, and by the excitement of an Indian war on the frontier, which would compel the settlers to think of self-protection against savages, instead of demanding from England the security of rights and liberty, at the point of the sword or muzzle of the rifle. By a letter from Lord Dartmouth to Lord Dunmore, dated at Whitehall on the 2d August, 1775, it appears that, *in the previous May*, Dunmore had communicated to the home government his vile plan of raising the Indians and negroes to join the miscalled loyalists in an onslaught against the Americans.

See also Sabine's Loyalists:—Article:—John Connolly.

The original papers relative to the arrest of Connolly and his incendiary companions in Maryland in 1775 are recorded in the MS. "Journal of the Committee of Observation of the Middle District of Frederick County," under date of the 21 Nov., 1775, in the possession of the Maryland Historical Society. This record gives, 1st: the letter from John Connolly to John Gibson dated at Portsmouth, Aug. 9, 1775; 2d: A letter from Lord Dunmore to the Indian Capt. White Eyes. It contains a *loving* message to "*his brother*" The Cornstalk—(the same who had fought at Pt. Pleasant); 3d: Proposals to General Gage for raising an army to the Westward for the purpose of effectually obstructing a communication between the Southern and Northern governments." One of the chief proposals was to raise the Indians.

See Letters from Arthur St. Clair to Gov. Penn, Ligonier, 29 May, 1774, IVth Series Am. Arch. vol. i. p. 287.

the wars of 1774, and of the Revolution, and was probably considered as a means of exciting the enmity and disaffection betwixt Virginians and Pennsylvanians,—of loosening the links between two vast territorial empires,—and of weakening thus the sympathetic bond which should have bound all Americans at that interesting moment. The fatal quarrel with Great Britain was already begun, and all the chief provinces, from Massachusetts southward, were rallying in the general national cause with a firmness of resolve that betokened danger to the dominion of the parent state unless our liberties were left untouched.

But there is a third motive for this war which we admit is not altogether proved against the British Earl, although there are facts that strongly fortify the belief entertained on the subject by early American writers and soldiers who served in the campaign. Among all the authors and journalists of the war there is evidently a strong impression, amounting almost to positive conviction, that Connolly, as the tool of Dunmore, secretly fomented the war, with ulterior views, as a counter irritation against the menaced resistance to England. Those who lived nearest the scene of action, and especially the Virginians who had the best means of judging Dunmore's motives, believed from circumstances that transpired during the conflict, that the Indians were urged to war by the instigation of emissaries from Great Britain and by the Canadian traders. It was generally credited that Dunmore had received from England advices concerning the approaching contest, and that all his measures with the Indians had for their ultimate object an alliance *of foreign troops and loyalists* with the ferocious warriors against the Americans. Nothing, indeed, was more natural than for British politicians at home to suppose that the excitement of an Indian war, and the contemporary dissension between the people of two large provinces in America, would be the means of preventing a colonial coalition in opposition to parliamentary taxation.[1]

[1] Burk's Hist. Virg. vol. 3, p. 380; Withers's Chronicles, p. 107; Dr. Doddridge's account of Dunmore's war, in Kercheval, (edition of 1833) p. 157; Rev. Mr. Jacobs' Life of Cresap, pp. 47, 52, 53, 67; Col. Stuart's Memoir of the

But, fortunately for our liberties, the alarm of an Indian war neither palsied nor benumbed the masses. And although Pennsylvania did not contribute largely to its suppression, it was not until the military ardor and indignation of the people throughout Virginia blazed up in the colony and reacted on Dunmore, that he affected, at least, to feel a hectic glow of virtuous indignation and placed himself at the head of the troops that gathered from every glen and mountain to repel the savage.[1]

It will be perceived, therefore, that there were three probable causes or motives for the war which broke out in 1774, the leading events of which I shall narrate very briefly.

I. The hostility of the Indians had been constantly manifested in the most murderous and predatory manner ever since Bouquet's peace in 1764; and, at the same time, the gradual enlargement of the white settlements had brought, in perilous neighborhood, two races who were naturally hostile, while neither the savages of the one, nor the hardy woodsmen of the other, were prepared, by continued forbearance, to avoid conflict or to unite in a common tenure of the soil.

II. The Pennsylvania disputes with Virginia as to territorial limits and jurisdiction were unwisely fomented by the forcible acts of Dunmore and Connolly, and thus the comity and good

Indian Wars, printed by the Virginia Historical Society, pp. 41, 43, 49, 56; Howison's History Virginia, vol. 2, p. 72; Hildreth's History U. States, vol. 3, p. 49; Monette's History Valley of the Mississippi, vol. 1, p. 385; Virginia Historical Register, vol. 1, p. 32, in Col. Andrew Lewis' letter; Annals of the West; Ohio Historical Collections, by Howe, p. 408; Almon's Remembrancer, vol. 2, pp. 218, 330; Smyth's Travels in America, Dublin, 1784. As to Dunmore's supposed treachery see Am. Arch. vol. 3, pp. 1191, 1192, 4th series, for some strong suspicions on this point from facts that became known after the treaty of Camp Charlotte and the close of the campaign.

[1] Burk 3, p. 381.—The *Pennsylvania authorities* took precautions soon after the outbreak of troubles to signify to the Indians, by messengers, that the alleged outrages were *not committed by Pennsylvanians*, and that the government of *Pennsylvania disavowed and condemned them, and therefore were not proper objects of revenge*. This timely notice is probably the reason why the Indian war was not carried on against the frontier settlements of Pennsylvania, but was chiefly directed against those of Virginia, where all kinds of savage barbarities were inflicted. See Gordon's History of Pennsylvania, p. 475; Monette's Valley of the Mississippi, vol. 1, p. 371. See also Drake's Book of the Indians, Book v, p. 45, for some sound reasoning on Dunmore's conduct.

will between two of the most important colonies were fearfully endangered.

III. It was probably Lord Dunmore's desire to incite a war which would arouse and band the savages of the west, so that, in the anticipated struggle with the United Colonies, the British *home interest* might ultimately avail itself of these children of the forest as ferocious and formidable allies in the onslaught on the Americans. But, at all events, nothing, so well as an Indian border-war, would excite a counteraction in the land at this moment of peril, and absorb the colonists in the exclusive duty of self-protection against a foe that was more to be feared than parliamentary taxation.

From this brief view of the political field of the colonies in 1774, let us return to the scene of impending hostilities.

We left Michael Cresap,—the western frontier trader,—a man of broken fortunes, emigrating from his Maryland homestead, among the mountains of Cumberland, to the broad lands and pleasant valleys of the Ohio. His purpose unquestionably was not warlike; for, in the disastrous condition of his affairs and with a large family to maintain, peace was absolutely necessary for success in his new field of enterprize. Accordingly, early in 1774, we find him on the Ohio river, in the neighborhood of Pittsburgh and Wheeling, with laborers brought under contract of hire from Maryland, engaged in opening and locating farms. He was there, neither as a "speculator" nor a "land jobber," as many of the emigrants of those days were unjustly stigmatized. His purpose was peaceful settlement, and he is no more to be blamed for his manly progress into the wilderness in quest of land, than were Washington and many other distinguished Americans of those days who possessed themselves of property in the prolific valleys of the west.[1]

[1] Historians have been in the habit of stigmatizing all concerned in the outbreak of this war as "speculators and land jobbers" who were anxious to drive off the Indians.—I shall insert below an advertisement from the Maryland Gazette of May 26th, 1774, which shows the opinion, at least of Washington, at that time, and is surely calculated to prove the honesty of purpose

Cresap was engaged in these honest and laudable pursuits when he suddenly received a summons which terminated forever his communication with the west.

After this region had been explored in 1773, a resolution was formed by a band of hardy pioneers,—among whom was GEORGE ROGERS CLARK, who, afterwards, as a general officer, became so celebrated in the annals of Kentucky—to make a settlement during the following spring; and the mouth of the Little Kenhawa was appointed as the place of general rendezvous, whence the united party should descend the river. Early in 1774 the Indians had done some of their habitual mischief. Reports of further and perhaps meditated dangers were rife along the river, as coming from the Indian towns. Many of the promised settlers, alarmed by the news, remained at their homes, so that, at the appointed time, not more than eighty or ninety men assembled at the rendezvous.

In a few days the anticipated troubles with the savages commenced. A small party of hunters, encamped about ten miles below Clark's emigrants, were fired upon by the Indians; but the red men were repulsed and the hunters returned to camp. This hostile demonstration, coupled with the rumors already spoken of, satisfied the Americans that the savages were bent on war. Accordingly, the whole band was regularly enrolled for protection; yet it was resolved to adhere to the original project

with which far-seeing men took advantage of their opportunities to obtain titles and open farms in the region beyond the Alleghanies:—

"FAIRFAX COUNTY, VA., MAY 10, 1774.

"In the month of March last the subscriber sent out a number of carpenters and laborers, to build houses and clear and enclose lands on the Ohio, intending to divide the several tracts which he there holds, into convenient sized tenements and to give leases therefor for lives, or a term of years, renewable forever, under certain conditions which may be known either of him, or Mr. Valentine Crawford, who is now on the land.

"The situation and quality of these lands having been thoroughly described in a former advertisement, it is unnecessary to enlarge on them here; suffice it generally to observe, that there are no better in that country, and that the whole of them lay upon the banks either of the Ohio or Great Kanhawa, and are capable of receiving the highest improvement.

4w. "GEORGE WASHINGTON."

of settling in Kentucky, inasmuch as the camp was amply furnished with every thing needful for such an enterprize.

An Indian town, called the "Horse-head Bottom," on the Scioto, near its mouth, lay in the pioneers' way, and they forthwith resolved to cross the country and surprise it. But when the question arose as to who should command so perilous an adventure, it was found that, in the whole band, no one possessed sufficient experience in Indian warfare to be entrusted confidently with the fortunes of his companions. It was known, however, that MICHAEL CRESAP dwelt on the river about fifteen miles above the camp, engaged with certain laborers in settling a plantation, and that he had resolved to follow this band of pioneers to Kentucky as soon as he had established his people. His experience of frontier life was conceded. The eager settlers, with one voice, resolved to demand his services in the hour of danger, and messengers were forthwith despatched to seek him. In half an hour they returned with Michael, who, hearing of the unwise resolution to attack the Indian town, had set out to visit the pioneer camp. The emigrants at once thought their army,—as they called it,—complete, and the destruction of the savages certain. But a council was called, and to the surprise of all, the intended commander-in-chief, promptly dissuaded his companions from the meditated enterprize. He said that, in truth, appearances were very suspicious, yet that there was no certainty of war;—that if the pioneers attacked the savages he had no doubt of success, but that a war would be the unquestionable result, the blame of which would fall upon the assailants. If they determined to proceed, however, he promised to send to his camp for his people, and to share the fortunes of the adventurers.

This mild but resolute counsel struck the whole band forcibly, and it was immediately resolved, according to Cresap's advice, to return to Wheeling as a convenient post where further tidings might readily be obtained. A few weeks, he thought, would determine the impending issue; and, as it was still early in the spring, if the Indians were found to be indisposed for war, the immigrants would have ample time to descend the river to their proposed settlement in Kentucky.

In two hours the Pioneers had struck their tents and were on their way to Wheeling. As they ascended the river they met Killbuck, an Indian Chief, accompanied by a small party, and had a long but unsatisfactory interview with him as to the disposition of the tribes. It was observed that Cresap did not attend this conference, but remained on the opposite side of the river, declaring that he was afraid to trust himself with the Indians, especially as Killbuck had frequently attempted to waylay and murder his father in Maryland, and that if they met, his fortitude might forsake him and he might put the savage to death.[1] These anecdotes denote the caution and self-restraint, the prudence and vigilance with which Michael Cresap behaved and counseled during the whole of these opening scenes, and exhibit him in the true light of an immigrant who was anxious to maintain inviolate the peace of a region in which his fortunes had been cast.

On the party's arrival at Wheeling, around which there were many white settlements, all the inhabitants appeared to be alarmed. They flocked to the camp from every direction, and refused to leave the protecting wings of the Pioneers. Offers were made to cover their neighborhood with scouts, until further reliable information was received; but no counsel or promise of protection would avail. Every day brought fresh accessions of strength to the party. Farmers, hunters, woodsmen, flocked to the band of Kentucky Pioneers, until its numbers became formidable.

The arrival of these men at Wheeling was soon known at Pittsburgh, and the whole of that region, as I have stated, was, under the asserted jurisdiction of Virginia, controlled by Connolly, under Dunmore's commission for West Augusta. When Connolly heard of the Pioneers' approach to Wheeling he sent a message to the party, informing it that war was to be apprehended, and requesting that it would remain in position a short time inasmuch as messages had been sent to the Indians and a

[1] Killbuck—see Jacob's Life of Cresap, p. 31, for a ludicrous accident that happened to this Indian whilst engaged in the assault on Cresap and his friends at the Old Town affair heretofore narrated.—It was perhaps the first time that a savage was so singularly *wounded* by a woman!

few days would solve the doubt. Before a complying answer could reach Pittsburgh, however, a second express arrived from Connolly, *addressed to Captain Cresap,* as the most influential man in the band, apprizing him that the messengers had returned from the Indians,—that *war was inevitable,*—that the savages would strike as soon as the season permitted,—and begging him to use his influence with the party to cover the country with scouts until the inhabitants could fortify themselves.[1] This message reached Cresap about the 21st of April,[2] and its reception was the signal of open hostilities against the Indians. Such was the natural result on so exposed a frontier, *where the white man or the savage who obtained the first shot was the victor,* and where Indian assassination or "private war"—to give it the most civilized name,—was the only rule recognized by the red men when they were aroused against encroaching Americans.

A new post was immediately planted, a council called, and the letter read by Cresap not only to his armed party but to all the neighboring Indian traders who were summoned on so important an occasion. The result was a solemn and formal declaration of war on the 26th of April, and that very night two scalps were brought into the camp.[3]

Some days prior to this Mr. William Butler, who seems not to have heeded the earlier warnings, had sent off a canoe loaded with goods for the Shawanese towns, and on the 16th of April, it was attacked, forty miles below Pittsburg, by three Cherokees,

[1] Jacob's Life of Cresap, 54; 4th Series Am. Archives, vol. 1, 468; Gen. Rogers Clarke's letter in the Appendix No. 1 to this discourse. Dr. Wheelar's testimony in Jacob, p. 110.

[2] The letter in the American Archives referred to above at p. 468, indicates the date of this letter or message from Connolly to have been on the *21st of April,* 1774. Devereux Smith writes to Dr. Smith from Pittsburgh under date of 10th June, 1774, as follows: "* * * * On the 21st of April Connolly wrote a letter to the inhabitants of Wheeling, telling them that he had been informed by good authority that the Shawanese were ill-disposed towards white men, and that he therefore required and commanded them to hold themselves in readiness to repel any insults that might be offered them." See also same vol. of Am. Arch. p. 287, where Connolly's "*circular* letter to the inhabitants on the Ohio" is spoken of. Jacob says he *once possessed it*: pp. 53, 54, 110, 113.

[3] McKee's MS. Journal, London Documents, Albany, N. Y. Am. Arch., IVth Series, 1st vol., p. 345.

who waylaid it on the river. They killed one white man, wounded another, while a third made his escape, and the savages plundercd the canoe of the most valuable part of the cargo.

The day after the declaration of war by Cresap and his men, under the warning authority of Connolly's message, some canoes of Indians were descried on the river keeping under the cover of an island to screen themselves from the party's sight. The skiffs were immediately chased for fifteen miles down the river, and driven on shore. A battle ensued, in which an Indian was taken prisoner, a few were wounded on both sides, and perhaps one slain. On examining the canoes they were found to contain a considerable quantity of ammunition and other warlike stores.[1]

In the deliberations of the camp on the night after the party's return, it was determined that a band should march on the following morning about thirty miles up the river in order to attack the settlement of Logan; but the band had not advanced more than five miles, when, halting for refreshment, Cresap asserted the gross impropriety of executing so dastardly an enterprize against a party composed of men, women and children, and who were known to cherish no hostile intentions but to be solely engaged in hunting. These facts were familiar to the pioneers, many of whom had visited the Indian camp during the preceding March, as they descended the Ohio to their original rendezvous.

Cresap's counsel immediately prevailed, and every man seemed disgusted with the project which, a short time before, he had so heedlessly and shamefully cherished. The party returned to camp in the evening, and speedly took the road to Red-Stone Old Fort.[2]

Thus, Cresap and his men were gone; but unfortunately, his prudent and friendly advice as to the luckless settlement of Logan was not heeded by others on the river. In May, 1774,

[1] See Alex. McKee's MS. Journal, London Documents, Albany, and Article in American Journal of Science for October, 1846, p. 10; and compare with the letter in Appendix No. 1, to this discourse.

[2] See General Clark's letter; Appendix No. 1.

and probably on the first day of that month, it was cruelly destroyed by others.[1]

The Indian camp was about thirty miles above Wheeling, close to the mouth of Yellow creek, while on the opposite side of the Ohio, near the river bank, was the cabin of a certain Baker, who sold rum to the Indians, and of course received frequent visits from the savages. This man had been particularly desired by Cresap to remove his liquors, and seems to have prepared to take them away at the time of the murder.

Towards the close of April, 1774, a certain Michael Myers,—a venerable man, who still lived on the Ohio a few miles above Steubenville, in February, 1850,—resided on Pigeon creek, which, according to the maps lies about forty miles from Yellow creek. A day or two before the following events, two land-hunters came to Myers's settlement and induced him to accompany them across the stream and down the banks of this Yellow creek in order to examine the country. Proceeding along the western shore of the creek for some miles, the travellers bivouacked for the night, and "hobbled" the only horse they had with them so as to prevent his straying from the camp. The animal, nevertheless, rambled off about three hundred yards out of sight, over a rising ground; and, soon after, hearing the beast's bell rattle violently, the woodsmen seized their guns and started to discover the cause. On reaching the top of the ridge Myers beheld, near forty yards below, an Indian in the act of loosening the horse which seemed restive and anxious to break from the savage, whose gun lay on the ground beside him. Myers, crouching behind the hillock, instantly levelled his rifle and shot the Indian without consulting his companions. It was now a little after sunset, and soon, another Indian, attracted by the

[1] See Gen. Clark's letter, Appendix No. 1.—Benjamin Tomlinson, in his testimony in Jacob's life of Cresap, p. 107, fixes the time on the "third or fourth of May; but John Sappington's statement in the 4th Appendix to Jefferson's Notes on Va., p. 52, dates it on the 24th" of May. From an examination of McKee's MS. Journal, London Documents, Albany; Clark's letter; the Penna. Packet of 23d May, 1774, and Mr. L. C. Draper's MSS., I am satisfied the massacre occurred on the 1st day of May, and that Sappington's date of the 24th May, *given from memory, after a lapse of twenty-six years*, is inaccurate.

crack of the weapon, approached rapidly armed with his rifle, but halted abruptly in astonishment as soon as he beheld his prostrate fellow. In the meanwhile Myers had reloaded his rifle, and before the savage could recover from his surprise, he too, fell before the forester's fatal aim. In the distance the camp of the clan, spread with deer and bear-skins, was visible, and as prompt succor was at hand, the Americans did not pause to see whether the Indian's wounds were deadly, but flying from the spot, recrossed the river for safety, and hastened to the neighborhood of Baker's cabin.[1]

The evening or night, before the tragedy which I am now about to narrate was committed at this cabin, a squaw came over to Baker's and aroused the attention of the inmates by her tears and manifest distress. For a long time she refused to disclose the cause of her sorrow, but at last, when left alone with Baker's wife, confessed that the Indians had resolved to kill the white woman and her family the next day, but, as she loved her and did not wish to see her slain, she had crossed the river to divulge the plot so as to enable her friend to escape. The savages had most probably been roused to revenge by the unfortunate rencounter of Myers with their slain or wounded clansmen!

In consequence of this astounding information, and in dread of the meditated assassination, Baker summoned twenty-one of his neighbors, who all reached his house before morning, when it was resolved that the strangers should conceal themselves in a back apartment, whence the assailing Indians might be watched. It was also determined that if they demeaned themselves peaceably, they should not be molested; but if

[1] MS. narrative sent to me by Mr. L. C. Draper who visited Myers in 1850, and received the account from his lips. Mr. D. thinks that the narrator *may* have confounded in his memory the events of another period; but as Myers *positively asserts that this affair led the hostile parties of Indians to go over next day to Baker's; as it gives the plausible pretext for the story of the squaw who visited Mrs. Baker; and as it is the same account that Myers has constantly told his neighbors*, I am inclined to rely in its accuracy. Mr. Myers has always sustained a good character; in early times was a Captain, and served as a Justice of the Peace for many years.—Myers admits that he took part in firing on the Indians who crossed in canoes on the day of the massacre.

hostility was manifested, they should show themselves and act accordingly.[1]

Early in the morning a party of seven Indians, composed of three squaws, with an infant, and four unarmed men, one of whom was Logan's brother, crossed the river to Baker's cabin, where all but Logan's brother obtained liquor and became excessively drunk. No whites, except Baker and two of his companions, appeared in the cabin. After some time, Logan's relative took down a coat and hat belonging to Baker's brother-in-law, and putting them on, set his arms akimbo, strutted about the apartment, and at length coming up abruptly to one of the men, addressed him with the most offensive epithets and attempted to strike him.[2] The white man,—Sappington,[3]—who was thus assailed by language and gesture, for some time kept out of his way; but, becoming irritated, seized his gun and shot the Indian as he was rushing to the door still clad in the coat and hat. The men, who during the whole of this scene had remained hidden, now poured forth, and, without parley, mercilessly slaughtered the whole Indian party except the infant! Before this tragic event occurred, however, two canoes, one with two and the other with five Indians, *all naked, painted, and completely armed for war*, were descried stealing from the opposite shore where Logan's camp was situated. This was considered as confirmation of what the squaw had said the night before, and was afterwards alleged in justification of the murder of the unarmed party which had first arrived.

No sooner were the unresisting drunkards dead, than the infuriate whites rushed to the river bank and ranging themselves along the concealing fringe of underwood, prepared to receive the canoes. The first that arrived was the one containing two warriors, who were fired upon and killed. The other canoe

[1] Some writers declare that Greathouse visited the Indian camp the night before the massacre and "decoyed" the savages over to drink on the next day. McKee's MS. Journal, *ut antea.* Moravian Journal, Am. Arch. 1, 285.

[2] See Withers's Border Warfare, p. 113, for Col. Swearingen's testimony as to the provoking conduct of Logan's brother at Yellow creek, and as to the origin of this affair.

[3] See McKee's certificate, in Jefferson, at the end of Sappington's narrative.

immediately turned and fled; but, after this, two others containing eighteen warriors, *painted and prepared for conflict as the first had been*, started to assail the Americans. Advancing more cautiously than the former party, they endeavored to land below Baker's cabin, but being met by the rapid movements of the rangers before they could effect their purpose, they were put to flight with the loss of one man, although they returned the fire of the pioneers.

In this desperate and bloody massacre, which was hastily perpetrated it seems in *anticipation* of an Indian attack,—an anticipation which was probably confirmed by the opportune appearance of the armed and painted warriors,—there were several men by the name of Greathouse deeply and fearfully concerned. There are persons who charge the whole of the horrid but debateable scene upon these individuals, yet its details are too disgusting to be dwelt on more than is needed in characterizing a single event of those cruel times.[1] Mr. John Sappington, whose statement in the IVth Appendix to Jefferson's Notes on Virginia is the clearest, most circumstantial and consistent I have met, declares that he does not *believe* "Logan had any relations killed, except a brother; that none of the squaws who

[1]See and compare: John Sappington's statement in Jefferson's Notes on Virginia, Appendix No. IV. p. 51; James Chambers's deposition, id.—id., p. 39; Robinson's at p. 42; Gen. Clark's letter, Appendix No. 1 to this discourse. Sappington states that he was "intimately acquainted with all the circumstances respecting the destruction of Logan's family," though he does not admit, in his carefully drawn statement, that he was *present* at the scene of murder. Tomlinson in his testimony given in Jacob's Life of Cresap, p. 107, alleges that he believes "Logan's brother was killed by a man named Sappington." McKee in his certificate appended to Sappington's testimony in Jefferson's Notes, says that Sappington admitted he was the man who killed Logan's brother. See also the statement written by Mr. Jolly, published in the American Journal of Science and Art, vol. xxxi, p. 10, and republished in Howe's Ohio Hist. Coll., 266. See Drake's Book of the Indians.

It is important to recollect that all these statements and depositions positively prove that Captain Michael Cresap was neither present at nor countenanced the alleged murder of Logan's kin at the Yellow creek massacre. The fact that *Sappington's* statement was published *by Mr. Jefferson himself*, indicates the confidence he placed in it, especially as he inserts it as a sort of supplement to the other testimony on the subject which had been printed *before* its reception. Logan's mother, brother, and sister, (Gibson's Indian wife or squaw, in all likelihood,)—were, probably, all of the relatives of Logan killed there.

were slain was his wife; that two of them were old women, while the third, whose infant was spared, was the wife of General Gibson," who, at that period was an Indian trader, and subsequently took care of the child as if it had been his own.

The war soon raged with savage fury. This act seems to have roused the Indians to immediate hostility. A letter from Arthur St. Clair to Governor Penn, dated at Ligonier, on the 22d of June, states that Logan is returned with one prisoner and thirteen scalps.[1] The blood of his kindred cried for vengeance and he had already trod the "war-path."

On the 12th of July, as William Robinson, Thomas Hellen and Coleman Brown, were gathering flax in a field, on the west fork of the Monongahela, they were surprised by a party of eight Indians, led by Logan. The savages stole upon them and fired before they were perceived. Brown fell, pierced by several balls, but Hellen and Robinson sought safety in flight. The former of these was too old to avoid capture; yet Robinson, with the agility of youth, and urged by his love of life and liberty, would have escaped but for an untoward accident. Believing that he was outstripping his pursuers in the race, he hastily turned to ascertain the fact, but while glancing over his shoulder, he ran with such violence against a tree as to be thrown stunned and powerless on the ground. The savages at once secured him with cords, and when revived, he was taken back to the spot where the lifeless and bleeding body of Brown was laid and where Hellen was already secured. Taking with them a horse belonging to the latter, the Indians immediately departed for their towns with the prisoners.

As they approached the Indian camp Logan gave the scalp halloo, and, immediately, several warriors came forth to meet them. The unfortunate captives were now compelled to run the gauntlet for their lives. Logan had manifested a kindly feeling to Robinson from the moment of his seizure, and previously instructed him as to the way by which he might reach the Council House of the clan without danger. But

[1] 4th Series Am. Archives, vol. 1, p. 475.

the decrepit Hellen, ignorant of the place of refuge, was sadly beaten before he arrived; and when, at length, he had come almost within the asylum, he was prostrated with a war club before he could enter. "After he had fallen, the savages continued to beat him with such unmerciful severity that he would assuredly have died under their barbarous usage, had not Robinson, at some peril to his own safety for the interference, stretched forth his hand and dragged him within the sanctuary. When he recovered from the violent beating he was relieved from the apprehension of further suffering by adoption into an Indian family."

A council was next convoked to decide the fate of Robinson. Logan assured him that he should not be sacrificed; but the council appeared resolved on his death, and accordingly he was tied to the stake. His captor, at once, appealed to the warriors with great vehemence; insisted that Robinson should be spared; and poured forth a torrent of vehement eloquence, which, nevertheless, did not avail to avert his stern and dreadful doom. At length, enraged at the pertinacity with which the life of Robinson, his own captive, was refused him, and heedless of consequences, Logan drew the tomahawk from his belt, and cleaving the cords which bound the victim to the stake, hurried him to the wigwam of an ancient squaw by whom he was at once adopted as a member of her family. He was to fill the place of a warrior who had been slain in the Yellow creek massacre.[1]

About three days after this occurrence, Logan suddenly brought to Robinson a piece of paper, and making a black fluid with water and gunpowder, commanded him to write a note which we shall see was soon used in one of the brutal raids of the detached parties that scoured the country and laid waste to every scattered or isolated settlement within a day's march of the Ohio. Men, women, children—and even cattle—were all indiscriminately scalped and butchered. The females were stripped and shamefully outraged. The men were slain, and knives, tomahawks or axes left in the breasts they had cleft asunder.

[1] Withers's Border Warfare, 118, et seq.; Robinson's narrative in Jefferson's IVth Appendix, p. 41; Howe's Ohio Hist. Coll., p. 267.

The brains of infants were beaten out, and the carcases left a prey to the beasts of the forest. [1]

When Judge Innes happened to be at the residence of Colonel Preston's family, in the fall of 1774, an express was sent to the Colonel as Lieutenant of the county, requesting a guard of militia to be ordered out for the protection of the residents on the lower portions of the north fork of the Holston. Every member of the family of a settler named John Roberts,[2] had been cruelly cut off by the savages, and the perpetrator of the assassination was traced by "the card" which he left as a bloody memorial of his visit! A war club was deposited in the house of the murdered forester, and, attached to it, was the following note—the identical one which Logan had forced Robinson to write with his gunpowder ink:

"CAPTAIN CRESAP,

"What did you kill my people on Yellow creek for? The white people killed my kin at Conestoga, a great while ago, and I thought nothing of that. But you killed my kin again on Yellow creek, and took my cousin prisoner. Then I thought I must kill too; and I have been three times to war since;—but the Indians are not angry—only myself.

"CAPTAIN JOHN LOGAN.

"*July* 21*st*, 1774."

This is a document savagely circumstantial and circumstanally savage;—cool, deliberate, and bloody, even to the date,—and left as this sentimental Indian's apology,—not as his challenge,—in the desolated dwelling and amid the reeking bodies he had butchered. It is the first deliberate charge made by Logan of the supposed murder of his relatives by Cresap at

[1] Md. Gazette, 30th June, 1774; Hite's account of the murder of Spier's family on the 3d or 4th of June.—See also same paper of 30th Nov. for letter from Col. Preston at Fincastle, 28th Sept., describing Indian murders and outrages.

[2] Among the MS. papers of Col. Wm. Preston in the possession of Mr. L. C. Draper, there is an original letter from Major Arthur Campbell, dated the 12th October, in which he enclosed the *original* missive from Logan and appended a copy. This is doubtless the one to which Innes alludes in Jefferson's Appendix. The correct name was Roberts.

Yellow creek, and I must promptly rebuke it by recalling to your minds all the facts of that occurrence, against which Cresap had protested to Clark's party, and from the theatre of which he had drawn off his men and departed.

While these events were transpiring, Michael Cresap had not only left the Ohio river, but had returned to his wife and interesting family in Maryland. Yet, soon finding his sympathies were excited for the forlorn inhabitants of the wilderness whom he had abandoned, and hearing constant reports of Indian cruelties, he speedily raised a company of volunteers and marched back to their assistance. Having reached "Catfish's Camp," on the spot where Washington, in Pennsylvania, now stands, his advance was stopped by a peremptory and insulting letter from Connolly, in which he was ordered to dismiss his men. It was no doubt written by its vile author in order to commence the systematic plan of charging the Indian difficulties of 1774 on Michael Cresap.

Ungrateful and offensive as was such a command to a person of Cresap's peculiar sensibility, he nevertheless obeyed, returned to his home, and dismissed his men with the determination to take no part in the Indian war, but to let the commandant at Pittsburgh fight it out as he best could. It seems, however, that the Earl of Dunmore and his lieutenant at Pittsburgh did not agree as to the value of Michael's services, for, when Cresap reached his Maryland home he found Lord Dunmore at his house, where he tarried some days in friendly intercourse or consultation with the young pioneer; and, notwithstanding his residence in Maryland, the British nobleman saw fit to send him forthwith a commission as Captain in the militia of Hampshire county, Virginia. This appointment, dated on the 10th of June, reached Cresap opportunely, and, carrying with it, as an unsolicited favor, a tacit expression of the Earl's approbation of his conduct, he resolved to accept it, especially as he was constantly appealed to by letters from his old companions beyond the mountains to hasten to their succor.[1]

[1] Jacob's life of Cresap, 56, 63, 65.

As soon as he raised his standard crowds flocked to it, and, indeed, so great was his popularity as a leader, that his own command overflowed with men and enabled him to fill up completely the company of his nephew, and partly also the company of Hancock Lee.[1] His forces were then united under the command of Major Angus McDonald, who had been, meanwhile, organizing the western people on the Youghiogeny and Monongahela for their own defence.

A campaign was also planned for the invasion of the Indian country west of the Ohio. "Orders were immediately sent to Colonel Andrew Lewis, of Botetourt county, to raise with all despatch, four regiments of militia and volunteers from the south-western counties, to rendezvous at Camp Union, in Greenbrier county. This was to be the southern division of the invading army, of which Lewis, a veteran of the French war, was made commander. He was ordered to march down the Great Kenhawa to the bank of the Ohio, and there to join the Earl in person. In the meantime Lord Dunmore was actively engaged in raising troops in the northern counties west of the Blue Ridge, to advance from Fort Cumberland by way of Red-Stone Old Fort, to the Ohio at Pittsburgh, whence he was to descend in boats to the Kenhawa. Such was the original plan of the campaign."[2]

McDonald, agreeably to Dunmore's orders, after a dreary march through the wilderness, had rendezvoused his four hundred men at Wheeling creek in June, and, from this place, it was resolved to invade the Indian territory on the head waters of the Muskingham, and to destroy the Wappatomica towns. The results of this expedition were not of remarkable value in the campaign, though the Indian towns were destroyed by the invaders after the savages had fled. McDonald and his men were harassed by the foe, and being short of provisions, returned with despatch to Wheeling.[3]

All the agricultural operations of the settlers on the river were of course broken up, and had I time, I would find great pleasure in narrating the campaign of the divisions under Lewis

[1] Jacob's life of Cresap, 57. [2] Monette, vol. 1, p. 374. [3] Id., p. 375.

and Dunmore. But that would require a volume rather than a discourse.[1]—I shall content myself therefore with stating, that the promised junction of Dunmore with Colonel Lewis was never effected. The earl changed his plan, and descending the Ohio from Fort Pitt with a fleet of one hundred canoes and several large boats to the mouth of the Hockhocking, erected a stockade which he called Fort Gower, and thence, ascended the Hockhocking to the Falls near the present town of Athens. From that spot he crossed the country westwardly to the Scioto, and, on its eastern side, on the margin of the Piqua plains, near Sippo Creek, entrenched himself in a regularly fortified camp, which, in honor of the British Queen, he named Camp Charlotte.

On the 10th of October the great and decisive battle of the campaign was fought by Lewis at "Point Pleasant," at the mouth of the Kenhawa, and it is regarded by most historians, as one of the most sanguinary and well fought conflicts in the annals of Indian warfare in the West. The Indians, under the celebrated Cornstalk chieftain, were repulsed with great slaughter, and fled precipitately across the Ohio to their towns, sixty miles up the Scioto. In the meantime, Dunmore had sent detachments from his head-quarters against different settlements on the neighboring waters, which were sacked and burned; and such had been the bloody character of the battle at Point Pleasant that the chiefs hastened to appeal for peace to Dunmore, before they could be again assailed by the relentless Lewis who was advancing in pursuit. After repeated overtures

[1]The following are the principal original authorities as to the campaigns and battles during the Dunmore war of 1774: I. Col. Stuart's narrative, in the Virginia Historical Soc. Publications, No. 1. II. Introduction to the Hist. of the Colony and Ancient Dominion of Va., by C. Campbell. III. Kercheval's Hist. of the Valley of Va. IV. Doddridge's Notes on the Settlement and Indian Wars of the W. part of Va. and Penna. V. A. S. Withers's Chronicles of Border Warfare. VI. 4th Series Am. Archives, vol. 1, especially p. 1016, et seq. VII. Howe's Hist. Coll. of Ohio. VIII. Day's Hist. Coll. of Penna IX. Howe's Hist. Coll. of Virginia. X. Chas. Whittlesey's Discourse before the Hist. and Phil. Soc. of Ohio, 1840. XI. Burk's Hist. of Va. XII. Drake's Book of the Indians, b. 5th, 42 et. seq. XIII. Map of the Ancient Shawanese towns on the Pickaway Plains, and of Camp Charlotte and Lewis's camp. Howe's Ohio Hist. Coll., 402.

and the destruction of several towns Dunmore consented to an armistice preparatory to a treaty. And finally, after the two divisions had nearly effected a junction the Council fire was lighted, the Council held, and peace resolved on.

But in the concluding scene of this bloody drama, the American and Indian chiefs could no where find one of its most daring and relentless actors,—a man whose name is not signalized any where *in open battle* in the records or legends of the time,—who was not in the conflict at Point Pleasant,[1]—but whose "war-path" and weapon were only traced along the bloody trail of private murder. Logan was absent. He was not satisfied. He had taken, perhaps, some thirty scalps,[2] but the ghosts of his murdered relatives were scarcely appeased in the "hunting fields" of the "spirit land." When the cause of his absence was demanded, it was replied that he was yet "like a mad dog; his bristles were up, and were not yet quite fallen; but the good talk, then going forward, might allay them." He said he was "a warrior, not a councillor, and would not come!"[3]

The continued withdrawal of Logan unquestionably filled the mind of Lord Dunmore with concern as to the stability of any peace which might be made with the Shawanese without the presence of a man who had shown such alacrity and bloodthirsty resolution in the cruel game of private war.

Accordingly, John Gibson, the alleged father[4] of the Indian woman's infant rescued at the Yellow creek massacre, was despatched by the Earl to seek for Logan. If, as is probable, the murdered squaw was Logan's sister, no messenger could have been more appropriately selected. He found him some miles off at a hut with several Indians; and, pretending, in the Indian fashion, that he had nothing in view, talked and drank with them until Logan touched his coat stealthily, and, beckoning him out of the house, led him into a solitary thicket, where sitting down on a log, he burst into tears and uttered some sentences of impassioned eloquence, which Gibson,—immediately

[1] Draper's MSS.
[2] Jolly's statement, American Journal of Art and Science, vol. xxxi, p. 10.
[3] Gen. Clark's letter, Appendix 1; Withers's Border Warfare, 136.
[4] See Sappington's testimony, Jeff: Appendix No. IV.

returning to the British camp—committed to paper.[1] As soon as the envoy had reduced the message to writing, it was read aloud in the council; heard by the soldiers; and proves to be neither a speech, a message, nor a pledge of peace:—

"I appeal to any white man to say if ever he entered Logan's cabin hungry and he gave him not meat; if ever he came cold and naked and he clothed him not? During the course of the last long and bloody war, Logan remained idle in his camp, an advocate for peace. Such was my love for the whites that my countrymen pointed as I passed and said: 'Logan is the friend of the white man!' I had even thought to have lived with you, but for the injuries of one man. Colonel Cresap, the last spring, in cold blood and unprovoked, murdered all the relations of Logan, not even sparing my women and children. There runs not a drop of my blood in the veins of any living creature. This called on me for revenge. I have sought it. I have killed many. I have fully glutted my vengeance. For my country, I rejoice at the beams of peace; but do not harbor a thought that mine is the joy of fear. Logan never felt fear. He will not turn on his heel to save his life. Who is there to mourn for Logan? Not one!"[2]

Thus the famous "speech of Logan" which has been so long celebrated as the finest specimen of Indian eloquence, dwindles into a reported conversation with, or message from, a cruel and blood-stained savage; excited perhaps when he delivered it as well by the cruelties he had committed as by liquor; false in its allegations as to Cresap; and, at last, after being conveyed to a camp about six miles distant,[3] in the memory of an Indian trader, written down, and read by proxy to the council of Lord Dunmore! Gibson, it is true, states in his testimony that he corrected Logan on the spot when he made the charge against Cresap, for he knew his innocence, but either the Indian

[1] MS. letter from my friend James Dunlap of Pittsburgh, and Gibson's testimony in Jeff. Appendix No. 4.

[2] See Appendix No. 2, for criticisms and commentaries on this speech and its history.

[3] See map of the Indian towns and British camps on the Pickaway plains—Ohio Hist. Coll. p. 403.

did not withdraw it or the messenger felt himself compelled to deliver it as originally framed.[1] When it was read in camp, the pioneer soldiers knew it to be false as to Michael Cresap; but it only produced a laugh in the crowd, which displeased the Maryland Captain. George Rogers Clark, who was near, exclaimed, that "he must be a very great man as the Indians palmed every thing that happened on his shoulders!" The Captain smiled and replied that "he had a great inclination to tomahawk Greathouse for the murder!"[2]

It is time to drop the curtain on these tragic scenes. The Indian fight was over;—peace was made with the savage Shawanese, but a more heartless war was about to occur with the christian Briton.

Cresap returned to his favorite Maryland, and spent the latter part of the autumn of 1774 and succeeding winter, in the repose of a domestic circle from which he had been so long estranged; but, in the early spring of 1775, he hired another band of young men, and repaired again to the Ohio to finish the work he commenced the year before. He did not stop at his old haunts, but descended to Kentucky, where he made many improvements. Being ill, however, he left his workmen and departed for his home over the mountains in order to rest and recover perfectly. On his way across the Alleghany mountain he was met by a faithful friend with a message stating that he had been appointed by the committee of safety at Frederick, a Captain to command one of the two rifle companies required from Maryland by a resolution of Congress. Experienced officers, and the very best men that could be procured, were demanded.

This was in July, 1775, and already on the 1st of August, in the same year, we find by the following extract from a letter to a gentleman in Philadelphia, dated at Fredericktown, Maryland, on that day, that the new revolutionary hero was prepared to take the field.

[1] See Gibson's testimony in Jefferson's 4th Appendix.

[2] See Clark's letter, Appendix 1. Clark was then a Captain by commission from Dunmore, dated May 2d, 1774.

"Notwithstanding the urgency of my business, I have been detained three days in this place by an occurrence truly agreeable. I have had the happiness of seeing Captain Michael Cresap marching at the head of a formidable company of upwards of one hundred and thirty men from the mountains and backwoods, painted like Indians, armed with tomahawks and rifles, dressed in hunting shirts and moccasins, and though some of them had travelled near eight hundred miles from the banks of the Ohio, they seemed to walk light and easy, and not with less spirit than at the first hour of their march. Health and vigor, after what they had undergone, declared them to be intimate with hardship and familiar with danger. Joy and satisfaction were visible in the crowd that met them. Had Lord North been present, and been assured that the brave leader could raise thousands of such like to defend his country, what think you, would not the hatchet and the block have intruded on his mind? I had an opportunity of attending the Captain during his stay in town, and watched the behaviour of his men, and the manner in which he treated them; for it seems that all who go out to war under him do not only pay the most willing obedience to him as their commander, but, in every instance of distress look up to him as their friend and father. A great part of his time was spent in listening to and relieving their wants, without any apparent sense of fatigue and trouble. When complaints were before him, he determined with kindness and spirit, and on every occasion condescended to please without losing his dignity.

"Yesterday the company were supplied with a small quantity of powder from the magazine, which wanted airing, and was not in good order for rifles; in the evening, however, they were drawn out to show the gentlemen of the town their dexterity at shooting. A clapboard with a mark the size of a dollar, was put up; they began to fire off-hand, and the bystanders were surprised, few shots being made that were not close to or in the paper. When they had shot for a time in this way, some lay on their backs, some on their breast or side, others ran twenty or thirty steps, and firing, appeared to be equally certain of the mark. With this performance the company were more than satisfied, when a young man took up the board in his hand, not by the end but by the side, and holding it up, his brother walked to the distance and very coolly shot into the white; laying down his rifle, he took the board and holding it as it was held before, the second brother shot as the first had done. By this exercise I was more astonished than pleased. But will you believe me when I tell you that one of the men took the board, and placing it between his legs, stood with his back to a tree while another drove the centre!

"What would a regular army of considerable strength in the forests of America do with one thousand of these men, who want nothing to preserve their health and courage but water from the spring, with a little parched corn, with what they may easily procure in hunting; and who, wrapped in their blankets, in the damp of night, would choose the shade of a tree for their covering and the earth for their bed."[1]

With this first company of riflemen, although in bad health, Captain Cresap proceeded to Boston, and joined the American army under the command of General Washington. Admonished, however, by continued illness, and feeling perhaps some dread forebodings of his fate, he endeavored again to reach his home among the mountains, but finding himself too sick to proceed he stopped in New York, where he died of fever on the 18th of October, 1775, at the early age of 33. On the following day his remains, attended by a vast concourse of people, were buried with military honors in Trinity church-yard. Let us deepen and not deface the meritorious inscription on his humble and forgotten grave![2]

It is needless to speculate upon what such a man might have become had he been spared during the war. Some of those who engaged in it as subordinates to him retired at its conclu-

[1]American Archives, vol. 3, p. 2, transferred from the Pennsylvania Gazette of Aug. 16, 1775.

[2]Compare Jacob's Life of Cresap, p. 98, and The Maryland Journal of Wednesday, Nov. 1, 1775. In the latter there is a letter from N. York, dated the 26th of October, giving an account of his death and burial.

sion with high commissions granted for services which no hardy warrior of the Revolution was more capable of yielding to the cause of his country than Michael Cresap.[1]

Let us turn once more for a moment to the Indian who has pursued the fame of our Marylander like a blighting shadow. We left him,—confessedly fond of the "fire-water," in his conversations with the Missionary Heckwelder, and tippling before he became eloquent with Gibson. His last years were melancholy indeed. He wandered from tribe to tribe, a solitary and lonely man. Dejected by the loss of friends and decay of his people, he resorted constantly to the stimulus of strong drink to drown his sorrow.

On the 25th of July, 1775, Captain James Wood having been sent with a single companion to invite the western Indians to a treaty at Fort Pitt, encountered Logan and several other Mingoes who had lately been prisoners at that post. He found them *all deeply intoxicated* and inquisitive as to his designs. To his appeal the savages made no definite reply, but represented the tribes as very angry. The wayfarers bivouacked near the Indian town, and about ten o'clock at night one of the savages stole into the camp and stamped upon the sleeper's head. Starting to his feet and arousing his companion, Wood and the interpreter found several Indians around them armed with knives and tomahawks. For a while the Americans seem to have pacified the red men, but as a friendly squaw apprized them that the savages meditated their death, they stole away for concealment in the recesses of the forest. When they returned again to the Indian town after daylight, Logan repeated the foul story of the murder of his "mother, sister, and all his relations" by the people of Virginia. By turns he wept and sang. Then he dwelt and gloated over the revenge he had taken for his wrongs; and finally, he told Wood that several of his fellows, who had long been prisoners at Fort Pitt, desired to kill the American messengers, and demanded if the forester was afraid? "No!" replied Wood, "we are but two lone men,

[1] McSherry's Hist. of Maryland, p. 186, and Jacob's Life, &c.

sent to deliver the message we have given to the tribes. We are in your power; we have no means of defence, and you may kill us if you think proper!" "Then," exclaimed Logan, apparently confounded by their coolness and courage, "you shall not be hurt!"—nor were they, for the ambassadors departed unmolested to visit the Wyandotte towns.[1]

We next hear of Logan in the autumn of 1778, when the famous Pioneer, SIMON KENTON, who was taken prisoner by the savages, spent two nights with his captors and Logan on the head waters of the Scioto.

"Well, young man," said Logan addressing Kenton, the night of his arrival, "these chaps seem very mad with you."— "Yes," replied Kenton, "they appear so—" "But don't be disheartened," interrupted Logan, "I am a great chief; you are to go to Sandusky; they talk of *burning* you there; but I will send two runners to-morrow to *speak good* for you!" And so he did, for on the morrow, having detained the hostile party, he despatched the promised envoys to Sandusky, though he made no report to Kenton of their success when they returned at nightfall. The runners, by Logan's orders, interceded with Captain Druyer, an influential British Indian-agent at Sandusky, who with great difficulty ransomed the prisoner and saved him from the brutal sacrifice of the stake.[2]

In the fall of 1779, Logan appears again to have cast aside his humanity, and is found at his old haunts on the Holston, engaged in the savage employment of scalping, or at least, of taking prisoners.[3] And, in June, 1780, when Captain Bird, of Detroit, with a large body of British regulars, Canadians and Indians, invaded Kentucky, captured Ruddell's and Martin's Stations, and carried off a large number of prisoners, Logan was one of the bloody and wanton marauders.[4]

[1] L. C. Draper's MSS. Journal of Captain James Wood. Jacob's Cresap, 85. IVth Am. Archives, vol. 3, p. 77. Mrs. W. C. Rives's Tales and Souvenirs, preface and p. 146.

[2] Draper's MSS. McDonald's memoir of Kenton; McClung's Sketches of Western Adventure.

[3] MS. letter in Mr. Draper's collection.

[4] American Pioneer, 1 vol. p. 359.

Our Indian hero must now have been well nigh fifty-five years of age,[1] and it may be supposed that so restless and fitful a life of fiery impetuosity and artificial stimulus, was drawing near a close from natural causes. But his chequered career of crime, passion, and bastard humanity, with all its finer features obliterated by the habitual use of intoxicating drinks, was doomed to end tragically.

It was not long after the inroad of Bird's British myrmidons and Indian allies in 1780, that Logan, at an Indian council held at Detroit, became wildly drunk, and, in the midst of delirious passion, prostrated his wife by a sudden blow. She fell before him apparently dead. In a moment, the horrid deed partly sobered the savage, who, thinking he had killed her, fled precipitately lest the stern Indian penalty of blood for blood might befall him at the hand of some relative of the murdered woman. While travelling alone, and still confused by liquor and the fear of vengeance, he was suddenly overtaken in the wilderness between Detroit and Sandusky, by a troop of Indians with their squaws and children, in the midst of whom he recognized his nephew or cousin Tod-kah-dohs. Bewildered as he was, he imagined that the lawful avenger pursued him in the form of his relative,—for the Indian rule permits a relation to perform the retributive act of revenge for murder,—and rashly bursting forth in frantic passion, he exclaimed that the whole party should fall beneath his weapons. Tod-kah-dohs, seeing their danger, and observing that Logan was well armed, told his companions that their only safety was in getting the advantage of the desperate man by prompt action. But Logan was quite as alert as his adversary;—yet, whilst leaping from his horse to execute his dreadful threat, Tod-kah-dohs levelled a shot gun within a few feet of the savage and killed him on the spot![2]

[1] Draper's MSS.

[2] Tod-kah-dohs or The Searcher, originally from Conestoga, and *probably* a son of Logan's sister residing there, died, about 1844, at the Cold Spring on the Alleghany Seneca Reservation, nearly 100 years old. He was better known as Captain Logan, and was either a *nephew* or *cousin* of the celebrated Indian. He left children, two of whom have been seen by Mr. Draper; so that, in spite of Logan's speech, *some* of his "blood" *still* "*runs*" in human veins, 77 years

When Mr. Jefferson wrote his Notes on Virginia in the years 1781 and 1782, he was anxious to disprove the theory of Buffon, Raynal and others, that animal nature,—whether in man or beast, native or adoptive, physical or moral,—degenerated in America. Whilst treating of the Aborigines, he desired to present a specimen of their intellectual powers, and, finding in a pocket book a memorandum, made in the year 1774, of the alleged "speech" of Logan, as taken down by him at that time from the lips of some one whom he did not recollect, he inserted it in his notes, accompanied by a slender narrative of the events that called it forth.[1] He spoke of Cresap as "a man infamous for the many murders he had committed on those much injured people," and charged the cold blooded murder of Logan's family upon the Marylander and his allies. In a future edition he modified but did not entirely withdraw this charge,[2] yet careless writers and historians, down to the present day, have continued to regard the Indian's remembered message as a genuine speech solemnly delivered in council, and reiterate its assertions as to the innocent Cresap! Poetry, even, has dwelt sweetly on

after the Yellow creek tragedy. The substance of this narrative was given me in MS. by Mr. Lyman C. Draper, who received it from Dah-gan-on-do or Captain Decker, as it was related to him by Tod-kah-dohs, who killed Logan. "Decker," says Mr. Draper, "was a venerable Seneca Indian, and the best Indian Chronicler I have met with. His narratives are generally sustained by other evidence, and never seem confused or improbable."—Logan's wife, who was a Shawanese, and had no children by him, did not die in consequence of her husband's blow, but recovered and returned to her people.—Compare Heckwelder's account, in Jefferson's Appendix. A different version of Logan's death is given, also, in Howe's Ohio Hist. Coll., p. 409, upon the authority of "Good Hunter," an aged Mingo, who is said to have been his familiar acquaintance. In this account he is represented to have been sitting before a camp fire near Detroit in Michigan, with his blanket drawn over his head, his elbows resting on his knees and his head upon his hands, buried perhaps in liquor or profound meditation, when an Indian, whom he had offended, stole behind him and buried a tomahawk in his brains!—See also, Vigne's Six Months in America, Philadelphia, edition 1833, p. 30, for another alleged version of his death from the hand of the same relative. Capt. Decker—Dah-gan-on-do—has lived all his eventful life of over one hundred years on the Alleghany, and knew Logan personally.—Draper MSS.

[1] Jeff. Notes on Va., Appendix IV, p. 30.

[2] Jeff. Notes on Va., Appendix IV. Stone's Life of Brant, vol. 1, p. 39.

the theme. Logan seems to have been the original whence Campbell derived the fine conception of his Outalissi,[1] and he has paraphrased in rhyme the passionate outburst:[2]

> " 'Gainst Brant himself I went to battle forth:—
> "Accursed Brant! he left of all my tribe
> "Nor man, nor child, nor thing of living birth!
> "No!—not the dog that watched my household hearth
> "Escaped that night of death upon our plains!
> "All perished—I, alone, am left on earth!
> "To whom nor relative, nor blood remains,—
> "NO! not a kindred drop that runs in human veins!"

Mr. Jefferson's illustration obtained greater fame and currency than he expected. It has become incorporated with our English literature. Indian error and obstinacy converted this Maryland *man* into a brutal monster; but I have striven to restore him to his original and meritorious manhood. Imagination transformed the savage into a romantic myth; yet it has been my task not only to reduce this myth to a man, but to paint him degraded by cruelties and intemperance even beneath the scale of an aboriginal birth-right. Indian instincts, rekindled by wrongs and the flame of the "fire-water," blighted a nature which at its dawn promised a noble and generous career. In his intercourse with white men LOGAN lost nothing but the virtues of a savage, while unfortunately he gained from civilization naught but its destructive vices.

[1] Graham's Hist. U. S., 4th vol., p. 341.

[2] Stone's Life of Brant, 2, p. 525; Gertrude of Wyoming, Part III, stanza xvii. In his notes Campbell repeats the old Logan and Cresap story, as usual; but, in later editions of his work retracts his errors *against Brant.* Brant's son, when in London, pointed out to the poet the slanders and injustice of his stanzas;—nevertheless he left them to posterity in the *text* of his poem though he qualified them in the *notes.* "The *name of Brant*, therefore," says Campbell, "remains in my poem, *a pure and declared character of fiction.*" Yet, a thousand persons read the poem while one only will peruse the antidote in the notes!—The fame of that dishonored Indian will descend to posterity with the taint of crime imputed by the poet, as the name of Cresap is disgraced from age to age by a mendacious morsel of Indian eloquence!

APPENDIX No. I.

General George Rogers Clark's Letter.

I must express my hearty thanks to my friend Mr. Lyman C. Draper for his kindness in sending to me valuable memoranda and extracts from papers which he has collected during many years of labor in gathering the materials for his history of the Western Pioneers. These documents have been cheerfully furnished me in the true spirit of a liberal man, who, as a historian, is anxious to ascertain or at least to approach the truth. In the marginal notes of my Discourse I have freely quoted from and credited these manuscript sources. I shall now present a copy of General George Rogers Clark's Letter, upon which Mr. Draper relies with great confidence as disclosing an accurate account of Cresap's conduct on the Ohio in 1774; but, before I offer it for the reader's consideration, I feel bound to mention that it appears to have been drawn forth in 1798, by a letter from the late Dr. Samuel Brown, (a friend of Mr. Jefferson,) of Lexington, Kentucky, who was for many years a distinguished professor in Transylvania University.

In 1839, the late Leonard Bliss, Jr., addressed to the Editor of the Louisville Literary News Letter the following note:—

"*To the Editor of the Louisville Literary News Letter:*

"Among the papers of Gen. George Rogers Clark, now in my possession, I have met with the following letter of his, detailing the circumstances connected with the murder of Logan's family, which induced the Mingo Chief, in his celebrated speech to Lord Dunmore, to charge the atrocity upon Captain Cresap, and also showing clearly, that Cresap was innocent of the crime alleged, and, so far from being the monster of cruelty represented by Mr. Jefferson, and by subsequent writers who have followed his authority, that he was a prudent and humane man, and 'an advocate of peace.' The error appears to have originated in a mistake with Logan, and to have been adopted by Mr. Jefferson, in his version of the story, from the Speech. The high authority of the 'Notes on Virginia,' and the fame of Logan's Speech, have immortalized the memory of Cresap; but it has thus far been an 'immortality of infamy,'—how ill-deserved, the following letter will show. And as the descendants of Cresap are still numerous in the United States, I beg you to publish it, with this note, in the

'Literary News Letter,' both as an act of justice to them, and to correct an historical error. The letter, of which this is a literal copy, is found in a Letter-Book of Gen. Clark, in his own hand-writing; and is, probably, the original draft. General Clark, at the date of the letter, resided in Louisville or its immediate vicinity.

"Very respectfully,

"Your obedient servant,

"LEONARD BLISS, Jr."

"Louisville College, *Jan.* 10, 1839."

When this letter appeared accompanied by Clark's, some doubt was expressed as to the authenticity of the latter, which, though asserted to have been found in Clark's hand-writing in his letter book, was not addressed to any one. Some time since many of the original MSS. and papers of Gen. Clark came into the possession of Mr. Draper, and among them he found the following from Dr. S. Brown, dated on the *15th of May*, 1798; and in all likelihood the reply of the General was given to it on the *17th of June in the same year*. The references in *both* letters to Mr. Thruston, prove that Clark's is an answer to *Brown's*:

Dr. Samuel Brown's Letter.

"Lexington, *May* 15*th*, 1798.

"Dear Sir:

"At the request of our mutual friend, Mr. Jefferson, I enclose you a letter of Mr. Luther Martin on the subject of the murder of Logan's family, together with a vindication of the account of that transaction as related in the Notes on Virginia. I am sorry that it has not been possible to procure, in this place, the Baltimore paper which contains Mr. Martin's first publication on this question. The charges there exhibited against Mr. Jefferson are much more specific and more virulent than they appear to be in the letter now forwarded to you. It is possible, however, that the whole of the correspondence may have come to your hands by some other route. At all events, I presume Mr. Jefferson's answer will sufficiently apprise you of the nature of the dispute, and bring to your recollection such facts and circumstances as will tend to elucidate the doubtful and obscure parts of that interesting story.

"I remember to have had some conversation with you respecting the affair when at your house, and although the variety and important nature of the events which your conversations suggested, have in some degree effaced from my memory that distinct recollection of this particular event which I ought to have, before I should attempt to communicate your account of it to Mr. Jefferson, yet still I am pretty certain that as you related the story, any mistakes that have crept into the Notes on Virginia are not attributable to Mr. Jefferson, but to Logan himself, or to those by whom his speech was originally published. I think you informed me that you were with Cresap at the time Logan's family was murdered, that Cresap was not the author of that massacre; that Logan actually delivered the speech as reported in the Notes on Virginia.

The Memoirs you have written of your own adventures, probably contain a full statement of the circumstances which gave rise to the dispute. A transcript from those Memoirs, or a statement of the business by you from memory, would be highly satisfactory to Mr. Jefferson and all his friends, and I am sure would be decisive evidence in the mind of every man of candor and liberality.

"I feel, and I am confident you must feel, sensibly hurt at a charge which can, in any degree, disturb the repose, or sully the reputation of that truly great and excellent man. I know you respect and esteem him, and I am really happy in assuring you that his respect and regard for you are equally cordial and sincere: of this, his last letter to me contains the most ample assurances. For myself, sensible that I have little which could entitle me to your friendship, I shall endeavor by my willingness to serve you, to convince you that I am truly thankful for those attentions I have received from you. And I shall consider myself singularly fortunate, if in any respect, I can be the means of rendering you and Mr. Jefferson mutually useful to each other. To your country you both have already been, and have it always in your power to be singularly useful.

"Mr. Thruston will do me the favor of carrying this letter, and I hope you will find leisure to prepare an account of Logan's speech before his return. I could wish to transmit it to Philadelphia before Congress rises, as it is possible the conveyance to Monticello will not be so safe.

"Do me the favor of presenting my most respectful compliments to the family, and be assured that I am,

"With sentiments of real respect,

"Yr. mo. obt.,

"SAM. BROWN."

GENL. GEORGE R. CLARK,
Jefferson County, Ky.

GENERAL GEORGE ROGERS CLARK'S LETTER.

"*June* 17, '98.

"DEAR SIR:

"Your letter of last month, honored by Mr. Thruston, was handed me by that gentleman. The matter contained in it and in the enclosed papers was new to me. I felt hurt that Mr. Jefferson should be attacked with so much virulence on account of an error, of which I know he was not the author. Except a few mistakes in names of persons, places, etc., the story of Logan, as related by Mr. Jefferson is substantially true. I was of the first and last of the active officers who bore the weight of that war; and on perusing some old papers of that date, I find some memoirs. But independent of them, I have a perfect recollection of every transaction relating to Logan's story. The conduct of Cresap I am perfectly acquainted with. He was not the author of that murder, but a family by the name of Greathouse;—though some transactions that happened under the command of Captain Cresap, a few days previous to the murder of Logan's family, gave him sufficient ground to suppose that it was Cresap that had done the injury.

"To enable you fully to understand the subject of your inquiries, I shall relate the incidents that gave rise to Logan's suspicion; and will enable Mr. Jefferson to do justice to himself and the Cresap family, by being made fully acquainted with the facts.

"This country was explored in 1773. A resolution was formed to make a settlement the spring following, and the mouth of the Little Kenaway appointed the place of general rendezvous, in order to descend the river from thence in a body. Early in the spring the Indians had done some mischief. Reports from their towns were alarming, which deterred many. About eighty or ninety men only met at the appointed rendezvous, where we lay some days.

"A small party of hunters, that lay about ten miles below us, were fired upon by the Indians, whom the hunters beat back, and returned to camp. This and many other circumstances led us to believe, that the Indians were determined on war. The whole party was enrolled, and determined to execute their project of forming a settlement in Kentucky, as we had every necessary store that could be thought of. An Indian town called the Horsehead Bottom, on the Scioto and near its mouth, lay nearly in our way. The determination was to cross the country and surprise it. Who was to command? was the question. There were but few among us that had experience in Indian warfare, and they were such that we did not choose to be commanded by. We knew of Captain Cresap being on the river about fifteen miles above us, with some hands, settling a plantation; and that he had concluded to follow us to Kentucky as soon as he had fixed there his people. We also knew that he had been experienced in a former war. He was proposed; and it was unanimously agreed to send for him to command the party. Messengers were despatched, and in half an hour returned with Cresap. He had heard of our resolution by some of his hunters, that had fallen in with ours, and had set out to come to us.

"We now thought our army, as we called it, complete, and the destruction of the Indians sure. A council was called, and, to our astonishment, our intended commander-in-chief was the person that dissuaded us from the enterprize. He said that appearances were very suspicious, but there was no certainty of a war. That if we made the attempt proposed, he had no doubt of our success, but a war would, at any rate, be the result, and that we should be blamed for it; and perhaps justly. But if we were determined to proceed, he would lay aside all considerations, send to his camp for his people, and share our fortunes. He was then asked what he would advise. His answer was, that we should return to Wheeling, as a convenient post, to hear what was going forward. That a few weeks would determine. As it was early in the spring, if we found the Indians were not disposed for war, we should have full time to return, and make our establishment in Kentucky. This was adopted; and in two hours the whole were under way. As we ascended the river, we met Killbuck, an Indian chief, with a small party. We had a long conference with him, but received little satisfaction as to the disposition of the Indians. It was observed that Cresap did not come to this conference, but kept on the opposite side of the river. He said that he was afraid to trust himself with the Indians. That Killbuck had frequently attempted to way-lay his father, to kill him. That if he crossed the river, perhaps his fortitude might fail him, and that he might put Killbuck to death. On our arrival at Wheeling (the country being pretty well settled thereabouts,) the whole of the inhabitants appeared to be alarmed. They flocked to our camp from every direction; and all that we could say could not keep them from under our wings. We offered to cover their neighborhood with our scouts, until further information, if they would return to their plantations; but nothing would prevail. By this time we had got to be a formidable party. All the hunters, men without families, etc., in that quarter, had joined our party.

"Our arrival at Wheeling was soon known at Pittsburgh. The whole of that country at that time, being under the jurisdiction of Virginia, Dr. Connolly had been appointed by Dunmore Captain Commandant of the District, which was called Waugusta.[1] He, learning of us, sent a message addressed to the party, letting us know that a war was to be apprehended; and requesting that we would keep our position for a few days; as messages had been sent to the Indians, and a few days would determine the doubt. The answer he got, was, that we had no inclination to quit our quarters for some time. That during our stay we should be careful that the enemy should not harass the neighborhood that we lay in. But before this answer could reach Pittsburgh, he sent a second express, addressed to Captain Cresap, as the most influential man amongst us; informing him that the messages had returned from the Indians, that war was inevitable, and begging him to use his influence with the party, to get them to cover the country by scouts until the inhabitants could fortify themselves. The reception of this letter was the epoch of open hostilities with the Indians. A new post was planted, a council was called, and the letter read by Cresap, all the Indian traders being summoned on so important an occasion. Action was had, and war declared in the most solemn manner; and the same evening two scalps were brought into camp.

"The next day some canoes of Indians were discovered on the river, keeping the advantage of an island to cover themselves from our view. They were chased fifteen miles down the river, and driven ashore. A battle ensued; a few were wounded on both sides; one Indian only taken prisoner. On examining their canoes, we found a considerable quantity of ammunition and other war-like stores. On our return to camp, a resolution was adopted, to march the next day, and attack Logan's camp on the Ohio about thirty miles above us. We did march about five miles, and then halted to take some refreshment. Here the impropriety of executing the projected enterprize was argued. The conversation was brought forward by Cresap himself. It was generally agreed that those Indians had no hostile intentions—as they were hunting, and their party was composed of men, women, and children, with all their stuff with them. This we knew; as I myself and others present had been in their camp about four weeks past, on our descending the river from Pittsburgh. In short, every person seemed to detest the resolution we had set out with. We returned in the evening, decamped, and took the road to Red-Stone.

"It was two days after this that Logan's family were killed. And from the manner in which it was done, it was viewed as a horrid murder. From Logan's hearing of Cresap being at the head of this party on the river, it is no wonder that he supposed he had a hand in the destruction of his family.

"Since the reception of your letter, I have procured the 'Notes on Virginia.' They are now before me. The act was more barbarous than there related by

[1] West Augusta.—L. C. D.

Mr. Jefferson. Those Indians used to visit, and to return visits, with the neighboring whites, on the opposite side of the river. They were on a visit to a family of the name of Greathouse, at the time they were murdered by them and their associates.

"The war now raged in all its savage fury until the fall, when a treaty of peace was held at Camp Charlotte, within four miles of Chillicothe, the Indian capital of the Ohio. Logan did not appear. I was acquainted with him, and wished to know the reason. The answer was 'that he was like a mad dog: his bristles had been up, and were not yet quite fallen; but the good talk now going forward might allay them.' Logan's Speech to Dunmore now came forward, as related by Mr. Jefferson. It was thought to be clever; though the army knew it to be wrong as to Cresap. But it only produced a laugh in camp: I saw it displeased Captain Cresap, and told him, 'that he must be a very great man; that the Indians palmed every thing that happened on his shoulders.' He smiled and said 'that he had an inclination to tomahawk Greathouse for the murder.'

"What I have related is fact. I was intimate with Cresap. Logan I was better acquainted with, at that time, than with any other Indian in the western country. I was perfectly acquainted with the conduct of both parties. Logan was the author of the Speech, as altered by Mr. Jefferson; and Cresap's conduct was as I have here related it.

"I am yours, &c.

"G. R. CLARK."

This correspondence shows that Mr. Jefferson was annoyed by the bitter strictures that were made by the Hon. Luther Martin *who had married Captain Michael Cresap's daughter*, and which were called forth in vindication of his father-in-law, by the original version of the Captain's conduct in 1744, as given on page 91 of the edition of the Notes on Virginia, published by Mathew Carey at Philadelphia, in 1794. About this time Mr. Jefferson was probably preparing his vindication from designed wrong to the dead, as will appear by the dates of Mr. Martin's communication to FENNELL on the 29th of March, 1797, and Jefferson's letters to JOHN GIBSON in February, 1798, and in March, 1800, (republished in the Olden Time Magazine for February, 1847,) and of the Appendix No. IV, together with the affidavits comprised in it as published in *a later* edition of his Notes on Virginia. General Clark's letter, was probably never received by the distinguished gentleman for whom it was designed or he would unquestionably have appended it to the documents in that edition.

I may properly add here that I have a MS. copy of an affidavit of John Caldwell, who resided near Wheeling in 1774, (also from among Mr. Draper's papers,) which fully exonerates Cresap from all participation in the murder of Logan's family. In this affidavit Caldwell states that many years before, he had given one to the same effect to a person whom he understood to be an agent or as acting under the direction of Mr. Jefferson; but as this is not contained in the IVth Appendix to the Notes, it is probable that, like Clark's letter, it never reached Mr. Jefferson's hands.

APPENDIX No. II.

Logan's Speech.

I have thought that it would be, at least, an entertaining and curious literary criticism, if I grouped together in an appendix the evidence that has been adduced both for and against Logan's message or speech, and, at the same time, presented, side by side, such exact copies of this document, as I have been enabled to discover from the earliest dates. Importance was given to the article, as we have already seen by the illustrative use made of it by Mr. Jefferson, as well as by its intrinsic merit. That he gave it to the world as he received it in 1774, and noted it in his memorandum book, no one can doubt; and if any sceptics still remain as to his sincerity, they may be referred to the IVth Appendix in his Notes on Virginia, for a vindication so far as the speech is concerned and the evidence was detailed at the epoch of his writing.

I shall place the most important pieces of evidence, *pro and con*, side by side:

FOR THE SPEECH.	AGAINST THE SPEECH.
The first piece of testimony in favor of the *message* from Logan, comes from John Gibson, and was sworn to and subscribed by him before J. Barker, at Pittsburgh, Pa., on the 4th of April, 1800, *twenty-six years* after the event occurred: * * * * * *	
I. "This deponent further saith that in the year 1774, he accompanied Lord Dunmore on the expedition against the Shawanese and other Indians on the Scioto; that on their arrival within *fifteen miles* of the towns they were met by a flag and a *white man* by the name of Elliot, who informed Lord Dunmore that the chiefs of the Shawanese had sent to request his lordship *to halt his army and send in* some person who understood their	I. See an argument on this subject written by the Hon. Luther Martin, son-in-law of Capt. Michael Cresap, and formerly a distinguished counsellor at law and Attorney General of the State of Maryland, in which he attempts to impugn this speech. It is dated the 29th March, 1797; and is addressed to Mr. James Fennell, who, in his public readings as an elocutionist, had given force and currency to the Logan speech.

language; that this deponent, *at the request of Lord Dunmore, and the whole of the officers with him*, went in; that on his arrival at the towns, Logan, the Indian, came to where this deponent was sitting with the Corn-stalk, and the other chiefs of the Shawanese, and asked him to walk out with him; that they went into a copse of wood when they sat down, when Logan, after shedding abundance of tears, delivered to him the speech, *nearly* as related by Mr. Jefferson in his Notes on the State of Virginia; that he the deponent, *told him then that it was not Colonel* CRESAP *who had murdered his relatives*, and although *his son*, Captain Michael Cresap, was *with* the party who had killed a *Shawanese* chief and *other* Indians, yet he was *not* present when HIS RELATIVES were killed at Baker's, near the mouth of Yellow creek, on the Ohio;—that this deponent, *on his return to camp*, delivered the speech to Lord Dunmore; and that the murders perpetrated as above *were considered* as ultimately the cause of the war of 1774, commonly called CRESAP'S WAR.

Signed JOHN GIBSON.

This letter republished in the Olden Time Magazine, vol. 2, p. 51, drew forth the evidence and reply, or vindication, contained in Mr. Jefferson's IVth Appendix to which so many references have been made in the course of this discourse.

II. GENL. GEORGE ROGERS CLARK says, in his letter of the 17th June, 1798, (ut antea,) *twenty-four years after the event*, that when the treaty was holding at Camp Charlotte, within *four* (?) miles of Chillicothe, the *Indian* capital of Ohio, Logan did not appear. "I was acquainted with him, and wished to know the reason. The answer was: 'that he was like a mad dog: his bristles had been up, and were not yet quite fallen; but the good talk now going forward might allay them.' *Logan's speech to Dunmore, as related by Mr. Jefferson, now came forward. It was thought clever; though the army knew it to be wrong as to Cresap.* But it only produced a laugh in

II. WITHERS in his Chronicles of Border Warfare, page 136, says,"—— *two interpreters* were sent to Logan by Lord Dunmore, requesting his attendance; but Logan replied, that "he was a warrior, not a counsellor, and would not come!'"

In a note on this passage, Mr. Withers adds:—"COLONEL BENJAMIN WILSON, SENR.," then an officer in Dunmore's army, says "that he conversed freely with one of the interpreters (Nicholson) in regard to the mission to Logan, and that neither from the interpreter, nor from any other one during the campaign, did he hear of the charge preferred in Logan's speech against Capt. Cresap as

the camp. I saw it displeased Capt. Cresap, and told him, 'that he must be a very great man; that the Indians had palmed every thing that happened on his shoulders.' He smiled, and said that he 'had an inclination to tomahawk Greathouse for the murder.'"

III. My learned and valued friend JAMES DUNLAP, Counsellor at Law, in Pittsburgh, writes me, under date of April 25th, 1851, as follows:

"I am well informed that Colonel Gibson, who was an uncle of Chief Justice Gibson, has frequently repeated here the story of Logan's delivering the speech to him. He used to say that at the treaty Lord Dunmore was about to hold with the Shawanese, he was uneasy at the absence of so distinguished a chieftain as Logan, and being indisposed to proceed without his presence, sent Col. Gibson for him; that Col. Gibson found him some miles off at a hut with several other Indians; that pretending in the Indian way, that he had nothing in view, he walked about, talked, and drank with them until Logan pulled him quietly by the coat, and calling him out, took him some distance into a solitary thicket, where, sitting down on a log, the Indian burst into tears and broke out in the impassioned language which glows so eloquently in the speech. Gibson said that he *returned at once to his friends and wrote down* the language of Logan immediately, and delivered it to Lord Dunmore in Council.

being engaged in the affair at Yellow creek. Capt. Cresap was an officer *in the division under Lord Dunmore;* and it would seem strange, indeed, if Logan's speech had been made public at Camp Charlotte, and neither he (who was so naturally interested in it, and could at once have proven the falsehood of the allegation it contained,) nor Colonel Wilson, (who was present during the whole conference between Lord Dunmore and the Indian chiefs, and at the time when the speeches were delivered, sat immediately behind and close to Dunmore,) *should have heard nothing of it until years after*"(!)

III. Mr. NEVILLE B. CRAIG, in the 2d vol. of his "Olden Time" Magazine, page 54, published at Pittsburgh in 1847,—when discussing the authenticity of the speech, says: "—we will state, that many years ago, Mr. James McKee, the brother of Alex. McKee, the deputy of Sir William Johnson, stated to us distinctly, *that he had seen the speech in the hand-writing of one of the Johnsons,* whether Sir William or his successor, Guy, we do not recollect, BEFORE IT WAS SEEN BY LOGAN!"

The reader will also find arguments by MR. CRAIG against the authenticity of the speech in this 2d vol. of the Olden Time Magazine, at pages 49 and 475.

IV. The message or speech was circulated freely at Williamsburgh immediately after Dunmore's return from his campaign in the winter of 1774, and was *published* then in the Virginia Gazette on the 4th February, 1775, and in New York on the 16th Feb., 1775, as will be seen hereafter.

V. WILLIAM MCKEE testifies in the IVth Appendix to Jefferson's Notes on Va., p. 42, that being in the camp on *the evening* of the treaty made by Dunmore with the Indians, he heard "*repeated conversations* concerning an *extraordinary speech made* at the treaty, *or sent* there by a chief-

IV. JACOB in his life of Cresap, gives the testimony of Mr. BENJAMIN TOMLINSON, on page 106 of his work. This testimony was prepared in Cumberland, Md., April 17, 1797, *twenty-three years* after the occurrence of the events.

The testimony is given by question and answer:—

"*Question 6th*: Was Logan at the treaty held by Dunmore with the Indians at Camp Charlotte, on Scioto? did he make a speech, and, if not, who made it for him?

"*Answer:* To this question I answer—Logan was not at the treaty. Perhaps Cornstalk, the chief of the Shawanese nation, mentioned among other grievances, the Indians killed on Yellow creek; but *I believe* neither Cresap nor any other person, were named as the perpetrators; and I perfectly recollect that I was that day officer of the guard, and stood near Dunmore's person, that consequently I saw and heard all that passed;—that, also, *two or three days before* the treaty, when I was on the out-guard, Simon Girty, who was passing by, stopped with me and conversed;—he said he was going after Logan, but he did not like the business, for he was a surly fellow;—he, however, proceeded on, and I saw him return on the day of the treaty, and Logan was not with him; at this time a circle was formed and the treaty begun; I saw John Gibson, on Girty's arrival, get up and go out of the circle and talk with Girty, after which he (Gibson) went into a tent, and soon after returning into the circle, drew out of his pocket a piece of clean new paper, on which was written in his own hand-writing—a speech for and in the name of Logan. This I heard read three times, once by Gibson, and twice by Dunmore the purport of which was that he, Logan,

tain of the Indians named Logan, and *heard several attempts at a rehearsal of it,*" &c. &c. See also Andrew Rodgers's certificate as to these facts in the same Appendix, p. 44.

was the white man's friend, that on his journey to Pittsburgh to brighten this friendship, or on his return thence, all his friends were killed at Yellow creek; that now when he died, who should bury him, for the blood of Logan was running in no creatures' veins; *but neither was the name of Cresap, or the name of any other person mentioned in this speech.*[1] But I recollect to see Dunmore put this speech among the other treaty papers."

From these parallel statements it will be seen that the chief evidence against the authenticity of the speech or message as detailed by John Gibson, is given by Col. Wilson and by Mr. Tomlinson, who was a citizen of our State, residing in Alleghany county, and admitted to be a person of the most respectable character for truth and intelligence. Testimony to this effect is adduced from high sources, and published in the 2d vol. of the Olden Time Magazine, page 476.

A sketch of Col. John Gibson will be found in T. J. Rogers's American Biographical Dictionary, 4th edition, Philadelphia, 1829. He has always been regarded as an honest and truthful person. He enjoyed the confidence of Washington who, in 1781 entrusted him with the command of the Western Military Department. In 1782, when Gen. Irvine had succeeded him, Col. Gibson was entrusted with the command during the General's absence, which continued for several months. Jefferson, Madison and Harrison respected him. He was a Major General of Militia, Secretary of Indian Territory under the administration of Jefferson and Madison; member of the Pennsylvania Convention in 1778; and an Associate Judge of the Court of Common Pleas of Alleghany Co., Pa. Chief Justice Gibson and General George Gibson, sons of Col. George Gibson who was mortally wounded at St. Clair's defeat, are his well known and esteemed nephews.

It will be observed that Mr. Tomlinson does not allege that Gibson did *not* go to Logan's village. He makes no statement in regard to him, until he saw him in the camp with Girty. And yet, it may have been perfectly consistent with the facts as they occurred that Gibson visited the Indian villages without Mr. Tomlinson being aware of his absence. Nothing was more likely to occur, I should think, in a frontier camp. It is very possible that Girty may have accompanied Gibson, as both had, many years before been Indian captives and were well acquainted with the Shawanese and Mingoes. Gibson says, according to Mr. Dunlap's statement, that Logan's message was not reduced to writing until his return to camp; and if Girty accompanied him, nothing was so probable as that they should unite and resort to a tent to commit it to paper. It is impossible for a man to know all that is going on in a camp. General Clark's letter seems to prove, conclusively, that Cresap's *name* was in the message when read in the camp, for he jeered him with his asserted importance in

[1] This would make it *correspond* with the Abbé Robin's copy which follows.

originating the war, whereupon Cresap broke forth in bitter invective against Greathouse;—and, moreover, it is evident that Logan had previously charged Cresap with the murder, as will be seen by reference to the note addressed to "*Captain Cresap*," which the Indian left in the house of Roberts, whose family he had murdered in 1774.

I think it may be fairly deduced from the preceding statements, that John Gibson, in his interview with Logan, heard from him an outburst of passionate sorrow, the purport of which *he subsequently reduced to writing after his return to the British camp from the Indian villages,—a distance of about six miles.*[1] When he reached camp, in all likelihood, he detailed the conversation with Logan to Lord Dunmore; and the Earl and the Indian trader, who were both anxious to make Logan participate in the treaty in some manner, committed the remembered language of the savage to paper, and caused it to be read forthwith to the army as a *speech or message* from Logan. The reader will not fail to remark, that *intrinsically, it does not pretend in its language to be a Message, a Speech or a pledge for the future; and, when critically examined, is nothing more than a savage expostulation or apology for cruelties committed by a man of strong feelings, but in which not a single note of personal grief or of submission is mingled!*

In all the versions of this paper which I am about to present, there is no *consent by Logan to the peace*, except in the copy given by the Abbé Robin; and if Dunmore wanted Logan's adhesion to the treaty, *that* speech would most probably have satisfied him. The *French copy* it will be observed, does not contain the name of Cresap!

SIX VERSIONS OF THE SPEECH.

I have diligently sought for the different copies of this celebrated document, which are known to exist in our country, and the following six are the fruits of my researches. The first is taken from a work which I found in the Baltimore Library Company's collection. It is entitled: "*Nouveau Voyage dans L'Amerique septentrionale, en l'Année* 1781*; et Campagne de l'Armée de M. le Comte de Rochambeau, par M. l'abbé Robin.*" The abbé was a chaplain in the army of our French auxiliaries:

I.

Original French of the Abbe Robin, published in Philadelphia and Paris in 1782.

"On a reproché aux Espagnols leurs cruautés contre ceux des pays dont ils se sont emparés: il paroit qu'on auroit aussi des reproches de ce genre à faire aux Colonies Angloises. Ce discours que m'a communiqué un

II.

Translation, Published at Philadelphia in 1783.

"The Spaniards have been reproached for exercising cruelties upon the inhabitants of the countries they conquered; but it appears that reproaches of this kind are no less well founded against the English. An Indian speech that was given me by a

[1] See Howe's Ohio Hist. collections, p. 402, for a Map of the Ancient Shawanese Towns on the Pickaway Plains, made by P. N. White, and containing the sites of Logan's cabin, Camp Charlotte (Dunmore's) and the position of Lewis's division when halted by the Earl This map shows that the distance between Logan's cabin and Dunmore's head-quarters *was fully six miles.*

professeur de Williamsburgh, dont voici la traduction, en est un monument. Il montre, en même temps, avec quelle mâle énergie ces sauvages savent s'exprimer:

"DISCOURS PRONONCE PAR LE SAUVAGE LONAN, DANS UNE ASSEMBLEE GENERALE, ENVOYE A M. le GOUVERNEUR DE VIRGINIE, LE 11 NET[1] 1754:

"LONAN ne s'opposera jamais à faire la paix qu'on propose avec les Hommes blancs. Vous savez qu'il ne connut jamais la crainte, et qu'il n'a jamais fui dans les combats. Personne n'aime plus que moi les Hommes blancs. La guerre que nous venons d'avoir avec eux, a été longue et cruelle des deux côtés. Des ruisseaux de sang ont coulé de toutes parts, sans qu'il en soit résulté aucun bien pour personne. Je le répete, faisons la paix avec ces hommes; j'oublie leurs injures, l'intérêt de mon pays l'exige: j'oublie encore que, naguere, le Major ———, fit massacrer impitoyablement, dans un bateau, ma femme, mes enfens, mon père, ma mère, et tous mes parens. L'on m'excita à la vengence—je fus cruel malgré moi. Je mourrai content si ma patrie est en paix: mais quand Lonan ne sera plus, qui est-ce qui versera pour lui une larme?"[2]

professor at Williamsburgh, a translation of which is subjoined is a proof of this. It discovers, at the same time, the bold and masculine energy these savages are taught by nature to express themselves:

"SPEECH PRONOUNCED BY THE SAVAGE LONAN, IN A GENERAL ASSEMBLY AS IT WAS SENT TO THE GOVERNOR OF VIRGINIA, ANNO 1754:]

[" LONAN will no] longer oppose making the proposed peace with the white man—you are sensible that he never knew what fear is—that he never turned his back in the day of battle—no one has more love for the white man than I have. The war we have had with them has been long and bloody on both sides—rivers of blood have run on all parts, and yet no good has resulted therefrom to any. I once more repeat it—let us be at peace with these men; I will forget our injuries, the interest of our country demands it—I will forget, but difficult indeed is the task—yes, I will forget, Major *Rogers cruelly and inhumanly murdered in their canoes, my wife, my children, my father, my mother, and all my kindred.* This roused me to deeds of vengeance—I was cruel in despight of myself—I will die content if my country is once more at peace: but when Lonan shall be no more who alas! will not drop a tear for him."[1]

The speech translated from the Abbé Robin's work is tolerably well rendered into English by the translator at Philadelphia in 1783, though it is not as accurate or elegant as it might be. The main facts however, are faithfully given, and we cannot doubt that it is the speech or message usually attributed to *Logan*, though it is assigned to *Lonan*, and that the date of 1754 for 1774 was a

1 Ce mot signifie apparament le mois Lunaire ou Solaire.

2 Nouveau voyage, &c., p. 147.

1 New Travels, &c., p. 67. Barton's Medical and Physical Journal, vol. 2, p. 148. See the latter for a full critical commentary on this speech, and for a *promise to disclose who Major Rogers was* in a future number of his journal—a promise which unfortunately was never fulfilled!

misprint or an inaccuracy either of the Professor at Williamsburgh, or of the Abbé in translating the original into French. The date, in the French copy of "11 *Nét*," is probably also a misprint for 11th November, inasmuch as the treaty having been made by Dunmore near the close of October, 1774, this copy of the speech may very probably have been committed to writing early in the following November. The general cast of thought in the speeches reported by Jefferson and the Abbé is the same; but they differ in force, elegance and eloquence. The essential points however, to which I desire to call the reader's attention are: that in the French edition the massacre is attributed, not to Cresap, but to a "Major ———;" in the English translation the blank is filled by the name of "Major *Rogers;*" and finally that Logan or Lonan asserts this blood thirsty commander murdered *his wife*, his *children*, his *father*, his *mother*, and *all his kindred*, IN THEIR CANOE!

Now, it will be recollected that Shikellamy, his father, died at Shamokin in 1749; so that he could not have been killed at Yellow creek in 1774; and, moreover, that Mr. Jefferson, in his notes on Virginia, (edition of 1794) says that "Col. Cresap, a man infamous for the many murders he had committed on these much injured people, collected a party and proceded *down the Kenhawa* in quest of vengeance. Unfortunately A CANOE *of women and children with one man only*, was seen coming from the opposite shore, unarmed and unsuspecting a hostile attack from the whites. Cresap and his party concealed themselves on the bank of the river, and the moment the canoe reached the shore, singled out their objects, and, at one fire, killed every person in it. This happened to be *the family of Logan* who had long been distinguished as a friend of the whites."

Here the story of the murder *in canoes*, and of the whole of Logan's family was repeated, and the geography of the scene is ascribed to the Kenhawa. This upon examination was found by Mr. Jefferson to be inaccurate, and in the edition of the Notes on Virginia, which he retained by him until his death, and in the IVth Appendix to more recent editions than that of 1794, he caused the paragraph above cited to be substituted by the following:

"Capt. Michael Cresap and a certain Daniel Greathouse, leading on these parties, surprized at different times, travelling and hunting parties of the Indians, having their women and children with them, and murdered many. Among these were unfortunately the family of Logan, a chief celebrated in peace and in war, and long distinguished as the friend of the whites."

This is certainly a mitigation of the charge against Capt. Cresap, but it leaves altogether indefinite the fact as to whether Greathouse and Cresap conjointly directed these parties, or which of the two murdered Logan's relatives. It relieves Cresap, however, altogether from the charge of murdering the Logan family *in canoes*, on the Kenhawa, a fact which seems to have been current at Williamsburgh, Va., when the Abbé Robin was there and received the speech of *Lonan* from the Williamsburgh professor!

It will be well for the reader to compare the speeches line by line as given by Mr. Jefferson and by the Abbé. The resemblances and the variances cannot fail to attract his critical notice.

This copy,—if we admit the date to be the 11th November, 1774, as we have stated it to have been most probably,—*is the eldest member of this family of speeches* I have been able to discover in tracing its pedigree. No manuscript copy of the time, has, to my knowledge, ever been found.

III.

My friend Mr. Thomas H. Ellis, of Richmond, Virginia, has kindly sent me the following authentic copy of the *message* of Logan, extracted from the "Virginia Gazette, No. 1226."

"WILLIAMSBURGH, *February* 4, 1775.

"The following is *said to be* a *message* from Captain Logan (an Indian warrior) to Gov. Dunmore, after the battle in which Col. Charles Lewis was slain, delivered at the treaty:

"I appeal to any white man to say that he ever entered Logan's cabin but I gave him meat; that he ever came naked but I clothed him. In the course of the last war Logan remained in his cabin an advocate for peace. I had such an affection for the white people that I was pointed at by the rest of my nation. I should have ever lived with them, had it not been for Colonel *Cressop*,[1] who *last year*, cut off in cold blood, all the relations of Logan not sparing women and children. There runs not a drop of my blood in the veins of any human creature. This called upon me for revenge; I have sought it, I have killed many, and fully glutted my revenge. I am glad that there is a prospect of peace on account of my nation; but I beg you will not entertain a thought that any thing I have said proceeds from fear! Logan disdains the thought! He will not turn on his heel to save his life! Who is there to mourn for Logan? . . . . No one."

IV.

From the IVth Series of American Archives, vol. 1, p. 1020, I extract the following:

"*New York*, February 16, 1775. Extract of a letter from Virginia: 'I make no doubt but the following specimen of *Indian* Eloquence and mistaken valour will please you; but must make allowance for the unskillfulness of the Interpreter:

"*The speech of* 'LOGAN—*a* SHAWANESE *Chief*—to Lord Dunmore:

"I appeal to any white man to say if ever he entered Logan's cabin hungry *and* I gave him not meat, if ever he came *cold or* naked and I *gave him not clothing. During the course of the last long and bloody war* Logan remained in his *tent* an advocate for peace; nay, such was my love for the whites, *that those of my own country pointed at me as they passed by, and said, 'Logan is the friend of white men!'* I had even thought to live with you, *but for the injuries of one man.* Colonel Cresap, *the last spring*, in *cool* blood *and unprovoked* cut off all the relations of Logan not even sparing my women and children. There runs not a drop of my blood in the veins of any human creature. This called *on* me for revenge. I have sought it—I have killed many—I have fully glutted my *vengeance. For my country I rejoice at the beams of peace; but do not harbour the thought that mine is the joy of fear. Logan never felt fear.* He will not turn on his heel to save his life. Who is there to mourn for Logan? *Not* one."

[1] He is here, in this message delivered in *October*, 1774, called *Colonel* Cressop, both title and name being inaccurately given. In the note left by Logan in the house in Virginia whose inhabitants he had murdered, dated 12th *July*, 1744, he styles him *Captain Cresap*. Thus he evidently knew his *proper* title *anterior* to the message in October, in which he miscalls him. That the title, if introduced at all, was assigned by Logan is unquestionable, for Gibson says so in his preceding testimony.

The comparison of these two copies is not a little singular; the one published on the 4th Feb., 1775, at Williamsburgh, Va., and the other only fourteen days after, in New York, on the 16th of the same month in the same year.

The Virginia announcement states it to be only a "*message*" which was "*said to have been*" sent by *Captain* Logan, (who was known to be a Mingo,) to Lord Dunmore. The New York copy, during the transit from Virginia, is magnified into a SPEECH, and dignifies the orator as a "SHAWANESE CHIEF!" Nor has the language of the document deteriorated by its travel northward. The Indian abruptness and directness has been softened by the journey, and the reader will particularly note the variances which we have endeavored to point out by causing the chief passages to be printed in italics.

The next member of this eloquent lineage blooms in mature perfection, in the pages of Mr. Jefferson's Notes on Virginia; and, with its translation into French, in the year 1788, I shall close my analysis of the genealogy.

Mr. Jefferson says in his IVth Appendix: "——— the speech itself" was "so fine a morsel of eloquence that it became the theme of every conversation, in Williamsburgh, particularly, and generally indeed, wheresoever any of the officers resided or resorted. I learned *it* in Williamsburgh; I believe at Lord Dunmore's, and I find in *my pocket book* of that year, (1774,) an entry of the narrative as taken *from the mouth of some person, whose name, however, is not noted, nor recollected, precisely in the words stated in the Notes on Virginia:*

V.

"I appeal to any white man to say if ever he entered Logan's cabin hungry, and he gave him not meat; if ever he came cold and naked, and he clothed him not. During the course of the last long and bloody war, Logan remained idle in his cabin, an advocate for peace.—Such was my love for the whites that my countrymen pointed as they passed, and said:—'Logan is the friend of white men.' I had even thought to have lived with you, but for the injuries of one man. Colonel Cresap,[1] the last spring, in

Extract from "Recherches historiques et Politiques sur les Etats-Unis de l'Amerique Septentrionale," 1788, 4th vol. p. 154.

VI.

"Y-a-t'il un homme blanc qui puisse dire qu'il soit jamais entré ayant faim dans la cabane de Logan, et à qui *Logan* n'ait pas donné à manger, et que *Logan* n'ait pas revêtu! Durant le cours de la dernière longue et sanglante guerre, Logan est resté oisif dans sa cabane, exhortant *sans cesse ses compatriotes à la paix.* Telle étoit son amitié pour les blancs, que *ses frères*, le montrant au doigt en passant, disoient: 'Logan est l'ami des blancs.' *Il* vouloit même aller vivre *au milieu* de vous, avant qu'un homme,

[1] Cresap happened to be only a *Captain;* but the translated Robin edition makes the felon a *Major*, while Mr. Jefferson's elevates him into a *Colonel*, though Logan had called him simply *Captain* in his bloody *missive of the 21st July*, 1774!

cold blood, and unprovoked, murdered all the relations of Logan, not sparing even my women and children. There runs not a drop of my blood in the veins of any living creature. This called on me for revenge. I have sought it: I have killed many: I have fully glutted my vengeance. For my country, I rejoice at the beams of peace; but do not harbor a thought that mine is the joy of fear. Logan never felt fear. He will not turn on his heel to save his life. Who is there to mourn for Logan?—Not one."[1]

le Colonel Cresap, au printems dernier, de sang froid et sans provocation, eût assassiné tous les parens de Logan, sans épargner même *les* femmes et *les* enfens. Il ne coule plus maintenant *aucune* goutte de mon sang dans aucune créature vivante. J'ai voulu me venger; J'ai combattu: j'ai tué beaucoup *de blancs*. J'ai assouvi ma vengeance. Je me réjouis pour mon pays *des approches* de la paix; mais gardez vous de penser jamais que cette joie soìt celle de la crainte. Logan n'a jamais connu la crainte: *Il ne tournera jamais ses pieds* pour sauver sa vie. Qui reste-t'il *maintenant* pour pleurer Logan? Personne."

The slight variations in the translation are noted by italics.

[1] Jeff. Notes on Va. Ed. 1794, p. 91.

ERRATUM.—Page 8, eighth line from top, for *his of* read *of his*.

CATALOGUE

OF

PAINTINGS, ENGRAVINGS

&c. &c.

AT THE

PICTURE GALLERY

OF THE

Maryland Historical Society.

FOURTH EXHIBITION,

1853.

BALTIMORE:
JOHN D. TOY, PRINTER,
Corner of Market and St. Paul Streets.

Officers of the Society.

President.

J. SPEAR SMITH.

JOHN P. KENNEDY, Vice-President.
J. MORRISON HARRIS, Cor. Sec.
S. F. STREETER, Rec. Sec.
J. HANAN, Treasurer.
WM. HAMILTON, Librarian.

Committee on the Gallery.

J. H. B. LATROBE.
T. EDMONDSON, Jr.
S. W. SMITH.

CATALOGUE OF PAINTINGS.

The Pictures marked thus (*) are for sale—for prices apply at the door of the Gallery.

NO.	SUBJECT.	PROPRIETOR.	ARTIST.
1	Landscape,	S. W. Smith.	Harting
2	Portrait of a Boy,	A. J. Miller.	A. J. Miller
3	The Casket of Jewels,	C. J. Eaton.	Schopin
4	The Naughty Boys,	Cooper.	Ketz
5	The Toilet,	Ketz.	Ketz
6	Portrait of a Young Lady,	A. J. Miller.	A. J. Miller
7	Portrait of David Harris, Esq.	Jos. Sterrett.	Pyne
8	The Farrier from Landseer,	G. S. Oldfield.	Newell
9	The Dauphin, Louis 17th,	John P. Kennedy.	Madame Le Brun
10	St. Thomas of Villaneueva, giving alms at the door of his Cathedral, at Seville,	S. Wethered.	from Murillo
11	Landscape,*	J. Pawley.	in the style of Breughel
11½	Portrait—Gentleman in his Study,	E. Earle.	Rothermel
12	A Monk at his Devotions,	Weston.	Backolan
13	The Happy Family,	Thomas Sully.	T. Sully
14	Louis XV. and his Companions,	C. J. Eaton.	Hogarth
15	A Tale of the Revolution,	Thomas Sully.	T. Sully
16	Anaconda attacking a Horse and his Rider,	Earles Gallery.	James Ward, R. A.
17	A Nativity,	Charles Gilmor.	Carlo Maratti
18	Portrait of a Girl,	J. B. Norris.	after Greuze
19	The Broken Pitcher,	S. Owings Hoffman.	Barker
20	A Magdalene, from Titian,	H. S. Taylor.	Scardino
21	Worshipping the Golden Calf,	Mr. Cooper.	after Rubens
22	A Girl Blindfolded,	Mr. White.	
23	Mercury charming Argus to sleep whilst he steals the Cow Io,	Charles Gilmor,	Both
24	Taming the Shrew,	John P. Kennedy.	Stephanoff
25	Henri de Laroche Jaquelin,	John P. Kennedy.	Greuze

NO.	SUBJECT.	PROPRIETOR.	ARTIST.
26	A Subject from Heathen Mythology,*	J. Pawley.	from Rubens
27	Portrait of Archbishop Hughes,	Mr. Spalding.	Inman
28	Landscape,	Mr. Elder.	
29	Portrait of Alexander McClure,	Jarrett.	Peale
30	A Monk, an original sketch for his great picture of St. Anthony, of Padua, in the Cathedral of Seville,	E. M. Greenway.	Murillo
31	Cows,*	Thos. C. Ruckle.	
32	Landscape,	John C. Brune.	after Salvator Rosa
33	Christ disputing with the Doctors.*	Thos. C. Ruckle.	Thos. C. Ruckle
34	The Finding of Moses,	Mr. Cooper.	Italian School
35	Flower Piece,	F. Lucas, Jr.	Boschaert
36	Landscape,	John P. Kennedy,	Jos. Shaw
37	Martyrdom of St. Andrew,	G. W. Brown,	from Carlo Dolce
38	Jacob Wrestling with the Angel.	Dr. J. H. Thomas.	
39	The Good Shepherd,	Thos. C. Ruckle.	from Murillo
40	Bishop Atkinson,	A. J. Miller.	A. J. Miller
41	Cardinal Richelieu,	Mr. White.	
42	Suonatore di Violino,	J. C. Brune.	from Raphael
43	The Nativity, (Fesche Gallery,)	Henry S. Taylor.	Panini
44	Interior of a Cathedral,	Charles Gilmor.	Van Vliet
45	Landscape,	O. A. Gill.	G. L. Brown
46	Boors Regaling,	S. W. Smith.	from Teniers
47	Adam and Eve expelled from Paradise,	S. O. Hoffman.	Poelemberg
48	A Subject from the Decameron of Boccacio,	F. Sullivan.	
49	Misers Receiving Jewelry as Pawns,	J. B. Morris.	Detouche
50	Marine,	Jos. Reynolds.	Stanfield
51	A Lady,	G. Van Arden.	Newell
52	Landscape,*	Thos. C. Ruckle.	
53	The Misers,	C. J. Eaton.	from Quentin Matsys
54	A Winter Scene,	Mr. Cooper.	Molanier
55	Moonlight,	J. W. Barroll.	Barrett
56	Interior of the Studio of Van Ostade,	C. J. Eaton.	Herbertstoffen
57	Judith,	Pennsylvania Academy of the Fine Arts.	C. Jacobs

"Then Judith, standing by his bed, said in her heart, O Lord God of all power, look at this present upon the work of my hands for the exaltation of Jerusalem. For now is the time to help thy inheritance, and to execute mine enterprizes, to the destruction of the enemies which have risen against us.

"Then she came to the pillar of the bed, which was at Holofernes' head, and took down his falchion from thence, and approached to his bed, and took hold of the hair of his head and said, Strengthen me, O Lord God of Israel, this day.

"And she smote twice upon his neck with all her might, and she took away his head from him."—*Apocrypha, Book of Judith, xiii.* 4, 8.

NO.	SUBJECT.	PROPRIETOR.	ARTIST.
58	Virgin and Child, (after Cignani,)	Henry S. Taylor.	Piani
59	Architectural Ruins, (Fesche Gallery,)	Henry S. Taylor.	Panini
60	The Casket of Jewels,	Ernst Fischer.	Ernst Fischer
61	A Storm Approaching,	C. J. Eaton.	Ledieu
62	Cattle Piece,	J. H. McHenry.	Cartier
63	View in Venice,	Charles Carroll.	Canaletto
64	The Dreadnought Hospital Ship,	Alex. Turnbull.	Knell
65	The Descent from the Cross,	Mr. Elder.	from Vandyke
66	Sacred Heart,*	F. Sullivan.	
67	Homer Reciting his Poems,*	J. M. King.	
68	Confiance a L'Amour,	Wm. Woodville.	Schlesinger
69	The Notte of Corregio—The Holy Night, the adoration of the Shepherds,	Md. Hist. Soc.	after Corregio

"The Notte is celebrated for the striking effect of the light, which, in accordance with the old legend, proceeds from the new-born babe: the radiant infant and the mother who holds him, are lost in the splendor, which has guided the distant shepherds. A maiden on one side, and a beautiful youth on the other, who serve as a contrast to an old shepherd, receive the full light which seems to dazzle their eyes; while angels, hovering above, appear in a softened radiance. A little further back Joseph is employed with his ass, and in the back ground are more shepherds with their flocks. Morning breaks in the horizon, an ethereal light flows through the whole picture, and leaves only so much of the outline and substance of the forms apparent as is necessary to enable the eye to distinguish the objects."

NO.	SUBJECT.	PROPRIETOR.	ARTIST.
70	Barn Fowls,	C. J. Eaton.	Huard
71	A Horse and Pigs,	Earle's Gallery.	Morland
72	Cows.	" "	"
73	Arabs before their Tent,	J. H. McHenry.	Max Schmidt, M. S. 1851.
74	David and Prophet Nathan,*	Dr. Van Wyck.	Old Palma
75	Titians Bella Donna,	J. B. Morris.	Nichols
76	A Scene in Venice,		
77	Neapolitan Boatman,	Dr. Van Wyck.	Guisseppe Russo
78	Landscape, with Figures and Cattle,	S. Owings Hoffman.	P. Potter
79	A View in Venice,	Charles Carroll.	Canaletto
80	Landscape,	O. A. Gill.	G. L. Brown
81	Extracting a Tooth,	Mr. Weston.	
82	Sunset,	Wm. Woodville.	Andreas Achenbach.
83	Miser dancing to his Money Bags,	J. B. Morris.	Detouche
84	Rouget de Lisle,	Pennsylvania Academy of Fine Arts.	Godefroi Guffens.

"Rouget de Lisle was a young officer of Engineers at Strasburg. He was born at *Sous-le-Salnier*, in the *Puza*, a country of reverie and energy, as mountains commonly are. He relieved the tediousness of a garrison-life by writing verses and indulging a love of music. He was a frequent visitor at the house of the Baron de Diedrich, a noble Alsacien of the constitutional party, the Mayor of Strasburg. The family loved the young officer, and gave new inspiration to his heart, in its attachment to music and poetry, and the ladies were in the habit of assisting, by their performances, the early conceptions of his genius. A famine prevailed at Strasburg in the winter of 1792. The house of Diedrich was rich at the beginning of the revolution, but had now become poor under the calamities and sacrifices of the time. Its frugal table had always a hospitable place for Rouget de Lisle. He was there morning and evening as a son and a brother. One day, when only some slices of ham smoked upon the table, with a supply of camp bread, Diedrich said to De Lisle, with sad serenity, 'Plenty is not found at our meals. But no matter; enthusiasm is not wanting at our civic festivals, and our soldiers' hearts are full of courage. We have one more bottle of Rhenish wine in the cellar. Let us have it, and we'll drink to liberty and the country. Strasburg will soon have a patriotic fete and De Lisle must draw from these last drops one of his hymns, that will carry his own ardent feelings to the soul of the people.' The young ladies applauded the proposal. They brought the wine, and continued to fill the glasses of Diedrich and the young officer until the bottle was empty. The night was cold. De Lisle's head and heart were warm. He found his way to his lodgings, entered his solitary chamber, and sought for inspiration at one moment in the palpitations of his citizen's heart, and at another by touching, as an artist, the keys of his instrument, and striking out alternately portions of an air, and giving utterance to poetic thoughts. He did not himself know which came first; it was impossible for him to separate the poetry from the music, or the sentiment from the words in which it was clothed. He sang altogether, and wrote nothing. In this state of lofty inspiration, he went to sleep with his head upon the instrument. The chants of the night came upon him in the morning like the faint impressions of a dream. He wrote down the words, made the notes of the music, and ran to Diedrich's. He found him in the garden digging winter lettuces. The wife of the patriot mayor was not yet up. Diedrich awoke her. They called together some friends, who were, like themselves, passionately fond of music, and able to execute the compositions of De Lisle. One of the young ladies played, and Rouget sang. At the first stanza, the countenances of the company grew pale;—at the second, tears flowed abundantly,—at the last, a delirium of enthusiasm broke forth. Diedrich, his wife, and the young officer cast themselves into each other's arms. The hymn of the nation was found. Alas! it was destined to become a hymn of terror. The unhappy Diedrich, a few months afterwards, marched to the scaffold at the sound of the notes first uttered at his hearth from the heart of his friend and the voice of his wife.

"The new song, executed some days afterwards publicly at Strasburg, flew from town to town through all the orchestras. Marseilles adopted it to be sung at the opening and adjournment of the clubs. Hence it took the name of the *Marseillaise Hymn*. The old mother of De Lisle, a loyalist and a religious person, alarmed at the reverberation of her son's name, wrote to him—'What is the meaning of this revolutionary hymn, sung by hordes of robbers, who pass all over France, with which our name is mixed up?' De Lisle himself, proscribed as a federalist, heard it re-echo upon his ears as a threat of war, as he fled among the paths of Jura, 'What is this song called?' he inquired of his guide, 'The *Marseillaise*,' replied the peasant.

"The *Marseillaise* was the liquid fire of the revolution. It distilled into the senses and the soul of the people the phrenzy of battle. Glory and crime, victory and death, seemed interwoven in its strains. It was the song of patriotism, but it was the signal of fury. It accompanied warriors to the field and victims to the scaffold."

85	Portrait of Peter Hoffman,	S. Owings Hoffman.	T. Sully
86	Portrait of Wm. Hoffman,	Mrs. S. Hoffman.	from Lawrence by T. Sully.
87	The Holy Family,	C. J. Eaton.	Sebastian Bourdon
88	Madame de Pompadour,	J. P. Kennedy.	Francis Boucher
89	Children playing Doctor and sick Child,	Ernst Fischer.	Ernst Fischer

NO.	SUBJECT.	PROPRIETOR.	ARTIST.
90	A subject from the Decameron of Boccacio,	F. Sullivan.	
91	Marine Piece,	Charles Gilmor.	Backhuysen
92	Crûche Cassée,*	Geo. B. Coale.	from Greuze
93	A Harvest Scene,	Jas. W. Barroll.	Ruysdael
94	Hercules and the Hydra,	C. J. Eaton.	Le Blanc
95	A Family of Dogs.	J. B. Morris.	Burckhardt
96	A Gypsey Girl.	Hugh Gelston.	
97	Portrait of O. A. Gill,	O. A. Gill.	Elliott
98	Portrait of a Lady,	Mrs. Hoffman.	Inman
99	Heraclitus.	C. McCully.	
100	Landscape,	Charles Gilmor.	Salvator Rosa
101	A Scene at an Encampment,	Hugh Gelston.	from Wouvermans
102	A Winter Scene,	Anthony Kennedy.	
103	An Interior,	S. W. Smith.	from Jan Steen
104	Ducks Feeding,	J. B. Morris.	Burckhardt
105	Somerset House,*	Wiedenbach.	Wiedenbach
106	Mother and Child,	Wm. P. Preston.	
107	Fruit Piece,	Mr. Warder.	Campadoglio
107½	Portrait of Rubens,	J. C. Brune.	from Rubens
108	Martin Luther at Worms,*	W. B. Canfield.	Jacobs
109	Huss at Constance,*	W. B. Canfield.	Lessing
110	Adoration of the Kings,*	J. Pawley.	Rembrandt
111	Pont Vecchio in Florence,	J. B. Morris.	Burzione
112	The Boar Hunt,	Pennsylvania Academy of Fine Arts.	Snyders
113	Cupids with Garlands of Flowers.	J. H. McHenry.	
114	The Four Ages,*	J. M. King.	
114½	Dead Hare,	Wm. Warder.	H. Fyt
115	An Inn Yard,	Charles Gilmor.	Morland
116	A Winter Scene,	J. K. Spalding.	
117	Pheasants,	C. J. Eaton.	Huard
118	A Lady,	S. W. Smith.	Reynolds
119	Death on the Pale Horse.	Weston.	a copy by Dunlop from West.
120	Portrait of Henry Clay,	Anthony Kennedy.	Harding
121	Landscape,	S. O. Hoffman.	Houseman
122	Landscape,	Jos. Reynolds.	Creswick
123	Portrait of Alx. McClure,	Jos. Sterrett.	Peale
124	Portrait of Louis McLane,	Mr. Jarrett.	Peale
125	Vender of Apple Fritters,	G. W. Brown.	Gerard Douw
126	Tivoli,	Wm. Read.	Hottenroth
127	Landscape,*	J. Pawley.	Van Goyen

NO.	SUBJECT.	PROPRIETOR.	ARTIST.
128	Landscape,	S. Owings Hoffman.	from Berghem
129	An Interior,	Mr. Stickney.	
130	Fruit Piece,*	J. Pawley.	
131	A Boy attempting to light a Candle,	Mr. Weston.	Schalken
132	Marine Piece,	Alex. Turnbull.	Stanfield
133	The Glass of Wine,	Dr. Cherry.	from Ostade
134	River Scenery,	Mr. Stickney.	
135	Banditti Robbing a Monastery,	Mr. Cooper.	Rothermel
136	Peasant Girl in a Storm,	Mr. Stickney.	
137	The Marriage Supper at Cana,	Md. Hist. Soc.	Powell

"Paul Veronese painted four pictures on this subject, equally celebrated, of which this is the first and the largest of the four. It comprises one hundred and twenty figures, the greatest part portraits, of the most celebrated personages of the age, in which the painter lived. The first figure on the left is Alphonse D'Avalos, Marquis de Guast, by the side of him is Eleanor of Austria, and her husband Francis 1st, in a Venetian Cap. Afterwards, we see Mary, Queen of England, and Sultan Soliman the second. At the angle of the table, the person in profile and bald-headed, is the Emperor Charles V., bearing the insignia of the order of the Golden Fleece.

"Paul Veronese is seated in front playing the viol—Titian, the bass, near him Tintoret touches the violin, and Bassan the flute.

"This picture was painted for the dining-hall of St. George in Venice, the conquests of France caused it to be brought to Paris in 1798, where it was placed in the principal saloon of the Louvre. It has remained there ever since, the Italian Commissioners empowered to take back the pictures in 1815, having consented to leave this splendid work in France, and to take in exchange a St. Stephen painted by Charles Lebrun."

NO.	SUBJECT.	PROPRIETOR.	ARTIST.
138	Portrait of C. Carroll, of Carrollton,	Mr. Jarrett.	Peale
139	Portrait of Dr. De Butts,	Mr. Jarrett.	Peale
140	St. Catharine,*	Thos. C. Ruckle.	from Raphael
141	Portrait of T. Sully,	Mr. Jarrett.	Peale
142	Portrait of Max Godefroy,	Mr. Jarrett.	Peale
143	Portrait of Col. John E. Howard,	Mr. Jarrett.	Peale
144	Portrait of Gen. O. H. Williams,	Mr. Jarrett.	Peale
145	Harvest Scene in Bavaria,	I. C. Canfield.	Bernard Girchner
146	View near Rome,	Mr. Weston.	
147	Head Waters of the Delaware,	Mr. Weston.	Beaumont
148	Villa Architecture,	H. McKim.	
149	The Transfiguration,	Wm. Read.	from Raphael
150	The Old Mill,	Dr. Cherry.	Williams
151	Sympathy, from Jalabert,*	Van Arden.	Van Arden
152	Landscape,	Mr. White.	
153	Prayer,	C. J. Eaton.	Entylain
154	A Woman Holding a Candle,	Mr. Weston.	from Schalken
155	Landscape,	J. P. Kennedy.	Zucharelli
156	A Monk,	C. J. Eaton.	Granet
157	A Woman Cleaning a Brass Kettle,	H. S. Taylor.	after Netcher

NO.	SUBJECT.	PROPRIETOR.	ARTIST.
158	The Cat Concert,	Mr. Stickney.	
159	Scene in Wales,*	J. Pawley.	J. Shaw
160	A Scene in Holland,	Mr. White.	
161	A Street in Brussels,	C. J. Eaton.	Garneret
162	The Philosopher,	J. P. Kennedy.	
163	The Blind Fiddler,*	Miss McCann.	from Wilkie, by Miss McCann
164	The Fiddler and Monkey,	C. J. Eaton.	from Van Ostade
165	The Keeper of the Wine Cellar,	C. J. Eaton.	from Van Ostade
166	The Song, "Thou Art Gone,"	T. Parkin Scott.	H. Peters Gray
167	Portrait of Wm. Mayhew,	Wm. Mayhew.	E. Fischer
168	Magdalen,*	F. Sullivan.	from Carlo Dolci
169	The Rival Lovers,	Ernst Fischer.	Ernst Fischer
170	Portrait of J. M. Bonaparte,	J. M. Bonaparte.	R. Weir
171	Portrait of a Little Girl,	Mrs. Wilson.	Ernst Fischer
172	View of Antwerp,	S. W. Smith.	Stork
173	The Astronomer,	Capt. Grahame.	
174	Old Portrait,	Mr. White.	
175	Flower Piece,	S. W. Smith.	Dan Seghers
176	Hope,	Wm. Read.	
177	Suburban View, Fesche Gallery,	H. S. Taylor,	Unknown
178	Orpheus Playing to the Animals,	Mr. Cooper.	
179	Hope,	Wm. Read.	Angelica Kauffman
180	St. Thomas of Aquinas,	S. W. Smith.	Cabrera 1763
181	Landscape,	S. O. Hoffman.	Paul Potter
182	The Astrologer,	S. W. Smith.	Vanderbosch
183	Daniel Webster at Marshfield,	Thos. Cunningham.	A. J. Miller
184	Head of a Girl,	Capt. Grahame.	
185	La Fornarina from Raphael,	S. W. Smith.	M. A. Orsi
186	Edward Seymour, Duke of Somerset,	S. O. Hoffman.	Holbein
187	The Capitulation of Mantua,	C. J. Eaton.	Steuben
188	"Little Nell,"	Earle's Gallery.	T. Sully
189	Madonna after Sasso Ferrato,	H. S. Taylor.	Piani
190	Guardian Angel,	Wethered.	from Murillo
191	Landscape,	J. K. Spalding.	
192	Bishop of Boston,	J. K. Spalding.	
193	Corregio's Magdalen,	J. H. McHenry.	
194	The Bust,*	E. Kett.	E. Kett
195	Landscape,	Charles Gilmor.	Ruysdael
196	Landscape,	Charles Gilmor.	Ruysdael
197	Indian shooting a Panther,	A. J. Miller.	A. J. Miller
198	Holy Family,	J. C. Brune.	Unknown
199	Italian Seaport,	G. W. Brown.	Onofrio Crescenti
200	Sunset,	G. L. Brown.	G. L. Brown

NO.	SUBJECT.	PROPRIETOR.	ARTIST.
201	Landscape, (Bavaria)	I. E. Canfield.	Bernard Girchen
202	Landscape,	Mr. White.	
203	Children stealing Apples from an Old Man Sleeping,	Mr. Lanning.	Lanning
204	Children worrying a Hog,	Mr. Lanning.	Lanning
205	Interior of a Stable,	Mrs. J. McKim.	
206	Full Length Portrait,	Mr. Spalding.	Geo. Larresse
207	Portrait of Charles, 5th Lord Baltimore, from the original by Godfrey Kneller,	Md. Hist. Soc.	T. Sully
208	Portrait of Sir Joshua Reynolds,	C. J. Eaton.	Stuart
209	Interior of an Aviary,	Mr. Warder.	Boschip
210	Peasant's Singing,	H. McKim.	Hemskerk
211	Fruit Piece,*	J. Pawley.	
212	Portrait of Louis XIII.	A. Kennedy.	Largilliere
213	Soldiers before a Fountain,	Mr. Stickney.	H. Lecompte
214	Fete Champetre,	C. J. Eaton.	Henry Sieurac
215	The Young Moor,	J. H. McHenry.	C. Cretius
216	Landscape,	Mr. Elder.	
217	Landscape,	J. K. Spalding.	
218	A Village Scene,*	J. Pawley.	Droogsloot
218½	The Holy Family,	Charles Gilmor.	Albano
219	Peasant's Regaling,	Dr. Cherry.	Ostade
220	The Schoolmaster,	Dr. Cherry.	Mieris
221	A Man Singing,	Dr. Cherry.	Ostade
221½	Landscape,	J. B. Morris.	Robbe
222	Catching Flounders.*	J. Pawley.	Joshua Shaw
223	The Fortune Teller,	S. O. Hoffman.	Dillens
224	The Madonna of St. Sixtus,	Md. Hist. Society.	from Raphael

"Here the Madonna appears as the Queen of the Heavenly host, in a brilliant glory of countless angel heads, standing on the clouds, with the Eternal Son in her arms; St. Sixtus and St. Barbara kneel at the sides. Both of them seem to connect the picture with the real spectators. A curtain, drawn back, encloses the picture on each side: underneath is a light parapet, on which two beautiful boy-angels lean. The Madonna is one of the most wonderful creations of Raphael's pencil: she is at once the exalted and blessed woman of whom the Saviour was born, and the tender earthly Virgin, whose pure and humble nature was esteemed worthy of so great a destiny. There is something scarcely describable in her countenance; it expresses a timid astonishment at the miracle of her own elevation; and at the same time, the freedom and dignity resulting from the consciousness of her divine situation. The Child, enthroned in her arms, rests naturally, but not listlessly, and looks down upon the world with a serious expression. Never has the loveliness of childhood been blended so touchingly, with a deep-felt, solemn consciousness of the holiest calling, as in the features and countenance of this Child. The eye is with difficulty disenchanted from the deep impressions produced by these two figures; so as to rest upon the grandeur and dignity of the Pope, the lowly devotion of St. Barbara, and the cheerful innocence of the two angel children.

This is a rare example of a picture of Raphael's later time, executed entirely by his own hand. No design, no study of the subject, for the guidance of a scholar, no old engraving, after such a study, has ever come to light. The execution, itself, evidently shows that the picture was painted without any such preparation. Proofs are not wanting, even of alterations in the original design. The two angels, in the lower part, are very evidently a later addition by the master's hand. According to Vasari, Raphael painted this picture for the principal altar of St. Sixtus, at Piacenza—at least, it was there in his time, and was only removed to Dresden in the last century. It has been supposed, with great probability, that it had been intended for a procession picture. We can easily conceive the elevating impression that this glorified appearance must have produced as it was borne slowly along over the heads of adoring multitudes, accompanied by the lights, the incense and the sacred songs of the different orders."

NO.	SUBJECT.	PROPRIETOR.	ARTIST.
225	Ballad Singers,	C. J. Eaton.	Boulanger
226	Girl Mending a Net,	Wm. Woodville.	Hildebrand
227	Flowers,	Wm. Gilmor.	Seghers
228	Prayer,	S. W. Smith.	Hauff
229	The Guardian Angel in the Cathedral, at Seville,	E. M. Greenway.	from Murillo
230	From Correggion's Danæ,	M. Hist. Soc.	copy by A. J. Miller
231	Head of a Girl,	H. McKim.	from Greuze
232	Interior of a Kitchen	J. C. Brune.	Dutch School
233	Soldiers before a Tent,	H. McKim.	Dillens
234	Sir Walter Raleigh, and Queen Elizabeth,*	Mr. Bujac.	
235	The Assumption of the Virgin,	Charles Gilmor.	
236	Head of Francavilla,	J. C. Brune.	
237	The Plate of Eggs,	S. W. Smith.	Inncherie
238	Portrait of a Girl,	H. Newell.	Newell
239	Coast Scene,	J. K. Spalding.	Unknown
240	Sheep,	G. B. Coale.	Omeganck
241	Madonna and Child,	S. W. Smith.	G. H. Rizzi
242	Fete Champetre,	C. J. Eaton.	Godefroi
243	Fisherman,	Charles Gilmor.	
244	The Larder,	G. S. Oldfield.	H. Newell
245	Still Life,	C. J. Eaton.	H. Fyt
246	The Good Shepherd,	S. Wethered.	from Murillo
247	The Revellers,	S. W. Smith.	Breydell
248	The Miser Surprised,	John P. Kennedy.	L. Detouche
249	Mont Blanc, by Sunset,	J. H. McHenry.	Biermaun
250	Portrait of a Lady,	G. S. Oldfield.	Ernst Fischer
251	" " Boy,	C. Getz.	H. Newell
252	" " Girl,	C. Getz.	H. Newell
253	Self-Admiration,	Hugh Gelston.	
254	Charity,*	G. M. King.	
255	Holy Family,	J. K. Spalding.	

NO.	SUBJECT.	PROPRIETOR.	ARTIST.
256	An Interior,	J. K. Spalding.	
257	Portrait of Wm. Gwynn, Esq.	Baltimore Bar Library.	McCann
258	Cattle,	S. W. Smith.	Klomp
259	Italian Peasant Worshipping at his Shrine,	Dr. Van Wyck.	Guisseppe Russo
260	Angel Appearing to the Shepherds,	C. J. Eaton.	D. Vries
261	A Swiss Scene with Chamois,	J. B. Morris.	Burckhardt
262	Head of a Girl,	C. J. Eaton.	Pallaggo
263	A Girl Looking Out of a Window,	J. C. Brune.	Miss Peale
264	Hagar and Ishmael,	Wm. Read.	
265	Abraham Offering his Son Isaac,	Wm. Read.	
266	Gypsies,	C. J. Eaton.	Boulanger
267	Cupids with Garlands of Flowers,	J. H. McHenry.	
268	Portrait of a Lady,	Dr. Cherry.	H. Newell
269	" "	A. J. Miller.	A. J. Miller
270	" "		H. Newell
271	Joseph and Potiphar's Wife,	Md. Hist. Soc.	from Cignani

SMALL ROOM.

NO.	SUBJECT.	PROPRIETOR.	ARTIST.
272	Philosopher in his Study,	Dr. T. H. Buckler.	Chinese Painting
273	Portrait of a Chinese Lady,	Dr. T. H. Buckler.	" "
274	Girl with Garlands of Flowers,*	A. George.	Van Lerius
275	An Altar Piece,	J. K. Spalding.	
276	Morning, (Sculpture,)	Wm. Read.	
277	Holy Family, Do.	Wm. Read.	
278	Portraits of Two Children,	T. Sully.	T. Sully
279	Nature, (Sculpture,)	Hugh Gelston.	from Sir Thomas Lawrence.
280	Art, Do.	Hugh Gelston.	from Sir Joshua Reynolds.
281	Landscape,	A J. Miller.	A. J. Miller
282	Nymphs Clipping the Wings of Cupid.	S. W. Smith.	
283	Head of a Girl,	Mrs. S. Hoffman.	
284	Cleopatra,	J. H. McHenry.	

NO.	SUBJECT.	PROPRIETOR.	ARTIST.
285	The Crucifixion,	J. K. Spalding.	
286	Head of a Girl,	John B. Morris.	from Greuze
287	The Laboratory,	Dr. Cherry.	
288	Arkadischer Scheffer,	Mr. Weston.	from Rembrandt
289	Suburban View, (Fesche Gallery,)	H. S. Taylor.	Unknown
290	The Pilgrim,	F. Von Kapff.	H. Scheffer
291	Deer,*	Burckhardt.	Burckhardt
292	The Card Players, Enamel,*	A. Bujac.	from Burnet
293	Playing at Draughts,* "	A. Bujac.	from Burnet
294	Chinese Painting,* "	Mr. Finley.	
295	Chinese Painting,* "	Mr. Turner.	
296	Chinese Painting,* "	Mr. Turner.	
297	Chinese Painting,* "	Mr. Finley.	
298	Landscape,	A. J. Miller.	A. J. Miller
299	Portrait of Bishop Atkinson,	Dalmaine.	Dalmaine
300	Head of a Jester,*	F. B. Mayer.	F. B. Mayer
301	Raphael Sketching the Head of the Madonna della sedia,	Z. C. Lee.	Attributed by the Proprietor to Raphael.
302	Lucretia,	Mrs. A. Buckwalter,	Mrs. David Webster.
303	Madonna della Seggiola,	H. S. Taylor.	Piani
304	Portrait of a Colored Woman, (Pastel,)	Dalmaine.	Dalmaine
305	Teaching Music,	Wm. Woodville.	Voutier
306	Cupids,	J. H. McHenry.	
307	A Girl,	A. J. Miller.	A. J. Miller
308	A Girl Feeding Doves,	Wm. Woodville.	Seis
309	Water Color of two Children,	Ernst Fischer.	Ernst Fischer
309½	Battle of Ligny,	Wm. Woodville.	Camphausen
310	A Magdalene,	S. W. Smith.	Teniers
311	Madonna and Child,	John B. Morris.	from Murillo
312	Virgin,	Mrs. A. Buckwalter.	Mrs. David Webster
313	A Water Color Sketch,	C. J. Eaton.	
314	La Fornarina,	J. B. Morris.	from Raphael
315	Adoration of the Magi,	Dr. Cherry.	
316	Peasant Boy,	J. B. Morris.	
317	Cattle Piece,	J. B. Morris.	P. Potter
318	Portrait of a Lady,	Miss Shaw.	F. B. Mayer
319	Portrait of Judge Taney,	Judge Taney.	F. B. Mayer
320	Crayon drawing of a Young Gentleman,	Ernst Fischer.	Ernst Fischer
321	Portrait of Dr. Brown,	G. W. Brown.	Jarvis

NO.	SUBJECT.	PROPRIETOR.	ARTIST.
322	A Scene in the National Convention of France, May, 1794, (engraving,)	Md. Hist. Soc.	Vinchon

An insurrectionary mob broke into the hall of the National Convention, and after the commission of every horror, threatened, with savage yells, the life of its President, Boissy d' Anglas. He "continued calm and unshaken during this frightful transaction; bayonets and pikes still surrounded his head." "With the view of terrifying him, the wretches held up to him the bloody head of Feraud, a murdered deputy; he turned aside with horror; they again repeated it, and he bowed before the remains of the martyr; nor would he quit the chair, 'till compelled by the efforts of his friends; and the insurgents, awed with respect, allowed him to retire unmolested."

NO.	SUBJECT.	PROPRIETOR.	ARTIST.
323	Raphael sketching the Madonna della Sedia, Engraving,	Md. His. Soc.	H. Vernet
324	Portrait of an Old Lady,	Dalmaine.	Dalmaine
324½	Cordelia,	W. H. Brune.	C. Thompson, Rome.
325	A Flower Piece,	F. Lucas, Jr.	Boschaert
326	A View of Mr. Sterrett's Country Residence,	Jos. Sterrett.	Guy
327	Louis Phillippe and Queen Victoria,	Md. His. Soc.	Graeffle
328	Lake Windermere,	Mr. Finley.	Shaw
328½	Portrait of a Lady,	J. S. Smith.	J. K. Harley
329	Tinturn Abbey,	Mr. Finley.	Shaw

SUBJECTS IN BRONZE AND METAL.

NO.	SUBJECT.	PROPRIETOR.
330	Flora,*	I. E. Canfield,
331	Cupid,*	" "
332	Child and Bird,	" "
333	Dying Gladiator,	Mr. Brune,
334	Bachanalian Groups,	"
335	" "	"
336	Head of Byron,	Christhilf and Rigart.
337	Head of Washington,	" "
338	Lion,	" "
339	Crucifix	" "
340		Chas. Howard.
341	Head of Washington,*	Bujac.
342	Mare and Colt,	Mr. Reed.
343	Lion,*	Bujac.
344	Mare and Colt,*	Reed.
345	Huntsman,	"
346	Lion,*	Bujac.

NO.	SUBJECT.	PROPRIETOR.
347	Night,*	Bujac.
348	Italian Lazaroni,*	I. E. Canfield.
349	Female Figure,*	Bujac.
350	Bacchanalian Group,*	J. E. Cary.
351	Lord Byron,*	Bujac.
352	Head,*	"
353	Roman Horses,*	"
354	Stag Hunt,	Reed.
355	Mare and Colt,*	"
355½	Two Figures—Alarm,*	I. E. Canfield.
356	Bust of Hahnemann,*	W. H. Rhinehardt.
357	" Rev. Dr. Morris,*	" "
358	Reclining Figure—Faith,*	" "
359	Marble Bust of Buonaparte,	Hist. Society.

BALTIMORE:

OR

Long, Long Time Ago.

BY

W. B. B.

"TEMPUS EDAX RERUM."

—1853.—

Baltimore: Murphy & Co., Printers.

MURPHY & Co., PRINTERS,
178 *Market street, Baltimore.*

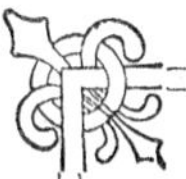

TO THE

MARYLAND HISTORICAL SOCIETY,

This humble effort to embody, in the idiom of the feelings, incidents and associations which, however worthy of commemoration, as appertaining to the social history of his native city, might appear trivial, in the graver phraseology which records its more important events,—is

RESPECTFULLY DEDICATED BY THE AUTHOR,

In the hope, that in "Friendship, as in Religion, the motive, not the value, of the offering propitiates its acceptance."

1853.

To

J. MORRISON HARRIS, Esq.,

Corresponding Secretary of the Maryland Historical Society.

Dear Sir:

If the accompanying jeu d'esprit, or of sentiment, or of a little, and very little of either, especially of the former, be not out of place, among the more serious and important contributions laid before the Maryland Historical Society; do me the favor to read it, at your next meeting; not as matter for its archives, but for the amusement, and in some instances, for the sensibilities of the members, among whom are doubtless some who remember Doctor Mann's corner, as the Jews of old remembered Zion; though they have not, in this case, a harp like David's to commemorate it, or the physical exile of the author of these lamentations, to hallow its reminiscence, as it is hallowed to him. But they have the moral separation, as well as himself. The alienation, of time, circumstance, and death, from early incidents and associations, which is, to the affections, what distance is to the body; nay, infinitely more, for material space may be overcome, and corporeal disunion have an end; but where is the Promethean fire to rekindle the loved and lost of by-gone days? Where, but in memories, such as these humble stanzas may excite, to melancholy, but not unpleasing action, the companions of our youth;—the events of a period, when to exist is to be happy; and when life is presented to us in côlors which, like those of the dawn, are as evanescent as they are gorgeous? Where? In the language of the Eastern Poet, well may echo, and experience answer, Where?

With sincere regard,

Yours,

W. B. B.

Ellendale, Va., *August*, 1852.

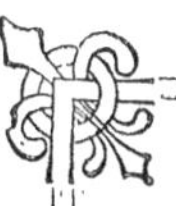

BALTIMORE:

OR

Long, Long Time Ago.

"TEMPUS EDAX RERUM."

I've been to our old haunts, dear Ned, I've been to Baltimore;
But it is'nt just the same old place, it was in days of yore;
Perhaps, because I'm changed myself, and could'nt play the Beau;
As you and I once did, my boy, a long, long time ago.

We've trod thro' thorny paths, Ned, we've culled but straggling flowers,
Since we quitted, for the wide, wide world, that early home of ours;
Then wonder not, tho' smiles be rife, that tears will sometimes flow,
As I lift the curtain of the Past, of long, long time ago.

It does'nt suit my rhyme, dear Ned, to give the years exact,
But thirty-five to forty-five, come near enough to fact,—
So I'll take the range between the two, and circumstance will show,
I'm telling of a by-gone age, of long, long time ago.

I stood by that old corner, Ned, where we've had lots of fun;
Whence "Docca Manna," cane in hand, would start us on the run;
But Mammon has a temple there; the Doctor's head is low,
And I did'nt see a brick to tell of long, long time ago.

So, I crossed the street, to Bigger's, but there a fabric rose
Before me, which they say is kept for concerts, and for shows;
While he at whose command old Time went either fast, or slow,
Had fallen 'neath his scythe himself, a long, long time ago.

That scythe mows down both great and small, for Little too, was gone,
Who, by some queer antithesis, held t'other corner-stone;—
And tho' a train-band Colonel, he would manfully bestow
His mind to march of clock and watch, a long, long time ago.

And Docca Manna's rival too, who made the square complete—
Four corners formed by Calvert intersecting Market Street—
With dandified Apotheca, kept less for use than show,
Had vanished from this classic ground of long, long time ago.

Such was, dear Ned, you know, the spot where boys
would congregate:
In after years, where Belles would pass, and Beaux
expectant wait;
Then marvel not its memories stirred my dormant feelings so,
The Present often was forgot in long, long time ago.

Then I strolled along *our* Market Street, determined
there to trace
Some ancient shop that bore its old familiar sign and face;
Lo! there but one, with rods and lines, arranged in
tempting show,
The same as taxed my boyish purse a long, long time ago.

Not oft on granite front appeared; on lettered architrave,
A name of old, long years had spared, from ruin, or the
grave;
But humbly nigh, a vestige left, as tho' designed to show
The triumph of progressive art, o'er long, long time ago.

Memorials of the Past were gone, or left, the wreck to tell,
The Little Darky, with his own, had rung their funeral
knell,
And saddened o'er, with mournful quest, 'mid monuments laid low,
I sought, where Nature once held sway, for long, long
time ago.

But all in vain.—Think not, dear Ned, proud oaks were
towering still,
To guide me, in my musing walk, to Belvidera hill;—

Alas! for Howard's sacred Park; for Dryads steeped in woe,
Stone, brick, and mortar leave no trace of long, long time ago.

Alas! for nutting boys, dear Ned, and sentimental girls;—
Above their wasted Tempé now, the smoke of chimneys curls;
And sights and sounds of busy life, proclaim the overthrow
Of sylvan sports, of young romance; of long, long time ago.

Or should we go where first we flashed our maiden swords abroad,
To Lindenberger's lot, you know, along the Pratt Street road;
We'd have to drill on house-tops now, no room for us below,
And not a haw-tree tells the pranks of long, long time ago.

I don't know where they find a place for our old troop's parade,
For even through McHenry's fields are streets and alleys laid;
And city cows; I can't conceive where they roam, to and fro,
For buildings cover all their range of long, long time ago.

The Basin stops these at its brink, but they are working round
To Whetstone Point, for grand reviews, so oft, of old, renowned;

And Federal Hill, of doubtful fame, in our young days, you know,
Is not the rowdy place it was, a long, long time ago.

I grew so tired of pavement, Ned, I thought it had no end,
For now to turnpike gates, of old, the city *airs* extend;
And houses all are strung along, in one continuous row,
Where we drove out, to breathe more free, a long, long time ago.

My strolls led not towards Potter's fields, or questions, much about;
But there, my boy, the dead, no doubt, are well nigh crowded out;
For the living walk the surface now, regardless that below,
Is mouldering many a cherished form of long, long time ago.

They've a place, they call it Green Mount, for graves, of modern years,
Where my eyes, all filled with wonder, could find no room for tears;
Perhaps, because they traced no names, to make the current flow,
As I read on moss-grown head-stones of long, long time ago.

I've told about the Old Town Clock; have sung the City Spring:
The Presbyterian Bell, and how I felt to hear its ring;

I thought of the old Court-house too, but this, dear Ned, you know,
Was reckoned of the things that were a long, long time ago.

I'd have to borrow ten more years, did I go back to this,
Its watch, bell, box, and pillory for such as did amiss;—
Besides, they'd make us out too old, if I should dare to show
That our Olympiads dated thence, some fifty years ago.

But no, I cannot quit thee thus, thou venerated seat
Of justice, and of school-boy sports, where such loved memories meet;
When "Court-house Boys," as well as men, their pleading faces show,
And claim their birth-right in the past, in long, long time ago.

The Court-house Boys! oh! were we once, so young and light of heart,
As imps who, at that magic name, to life, and gladness start?
Had we e'er sunny locks, and eyes, and cheeks of healthful glow,
As grace those called forth images, of long, long time ago?

Were we, dear Ned, of those who there, with plugging top in hand,
Or bandy, ready for the match, in anxious circle stand?
Or is it you and I, I see, on earth there, kneeling low,
To send the Marble to the ring of long, long time ago?

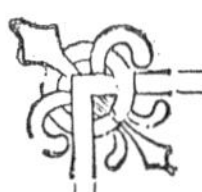

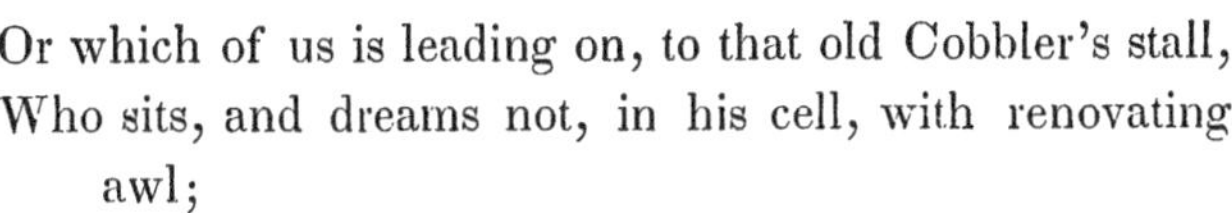

Or which of us is leading on, to that old Cobbler's stall,
Who sits, and dreams not, in his cell, with renovating
awl;
Of our wild freak, to hurl him down, shop, goods, and
all, below
The neighboring steep, though now filled up, of long,
long time ago.

And see! the laughing school girls' eyes that shine through
yonder panes,
Alas! I dare not ask my heart if but one pair remains
Of all that watched us, at our pranks, and home con-
spired, you know,
With us, to tease their pedagogue, a long, long time ago.

That kind old man, who, from his grave, if he could
rise, and trace
What time, and change, and grief have wrought on
school-hood's shining face,
Would think, no doubt, we'd paid him off, and cleared
the score we owe
For many a trick we played him once, a long, long time
ago.

And he, stern Captain of the watch, whose name I've
quite forgot,
But I see him hobbling in that pace we called one and
a dot;
The greatest man alive, we thought, when he his might
would throw
To that high bell, and pull the rope, of long, long time
ago.

The curfew-bell to our young sports, that sent us all to bed,
For nine o'clock, you know, was our retiring hour, dear Ned;
And if a rowdy, after that, but dared his face to show,
The watch-house lodged him for the night, a long, long time ago.

Beneath that awful frowning arch, the whipping-post behold,
For nine and thirty lashes, on the bare back, duly told;
Fine sport for us, but not for him, whose skin, at every blow,
Gave token of the law's effect, a long, long time ago.

Hard by, there stood another arm of awful warning, near,
Though seldom culprit hazarded a sentence to severe;
But when there did, 'twas glorious fun, eggs not too new, to throw
At him who dared transgress the rules of long, long time ago.

But Ned, dear Ned, those days have passed, their relics all are gone,
The Court is rased, from lofty spire, to firm foundation stone,
And, on its site a column stands, to those who met the foe,
And nobly fought, and bled, and died for long, long time ago.

They lie entombed, as valor should, in its maternal earth,
Their names aloft, recorded there; just tribute to their worth;

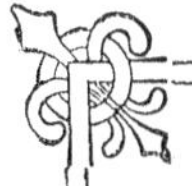

That boyhood's glance, and manhood's prayer, uplifted
from below,
May bless these martyrs to the homes of long, long
time ago.

Then I'd sit beside the window, in Barnum's grand hotel,
Swan's lot, what more need I, my boy, of its location tell?
And, looking on the passing forms that thronged the
street below,
Would, now and then, encounter one of long, long
time ago.

Ah! Ned, my friend, I did not dream I had so ancient
grown,
Till I read, on care-worn faces there, the wrinkles of
my own;
And ladies too, I sometimes met, divinities, you know,
But these had suffered mortal change since long, long
time ago.

But yet, my boy, in all these turns, tho' features had
grown old,
And heads were grey, and trembling hands stretched
out my own to hold;
I felt it there, all tingling still, the blood, in generous flow,
The welcome squeeze that told the pulse of long, long
time ago.

Yes, yes, the spirit still is there; tho' land-marks be
defaced,
And our old haunts, all dimly now, in modern changes
traced;

But all unchilled, all fervent yet, in hospitable glow,
Are kept alive the sacred fires of long, long time ago.

The sacred fires of heart, and hearth, oh! Ned, they burn as bright
As ever, in the dear old town where first we saw the light;
Then pledge me in this toast, my boy, let hearts and cups o'erflow,
To Baltimore as she is now, and was, long time ago.

W. B. B.

Ellendale, Va., *August*, 1852.

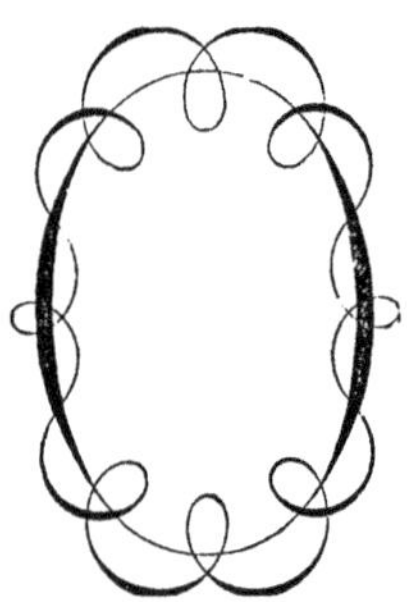

The Old Church Bell.

"SQUILLA DI LONTANO."

I'D rather hear that dear old Bell,
  In reckless discord, ring,
Than music's most harmonious swell,
  Though Mam'selle Lind should sing.

There is a language in its sound—
  A magic in its tone—
Calling bright images around—
  Restoring pleasures gone.

It falls on my long exiled ear,
  To make the dead alive,
Friends, kindred, early loves appear,
  And early hopes revive.

Not Orpheus, he whose fabled lyre
  Gave breath to stocks and stones;
Could half such wondrous life inspire,
  As that old Bell's loved tones.

A child, once more, in Sunday suit,
  I press my mother's side,
Holding my boyish prattle mute
  Lest God and she should chide.

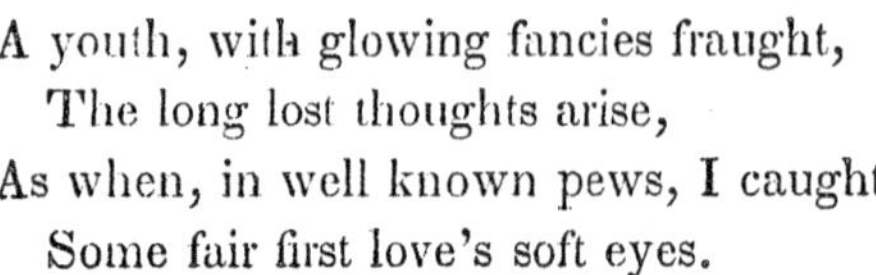

A youth, with glowing fancies fraught,
The long lost thoughts arise,
As when, in well known pews, I caught
Some fair first love's soft eyes.

A man, I look for aged worth;
The Fathers of the race;
And busy memory calls them forth
To take their honored place.

But Father, Mother, early love,
And early hopes are fled,
The friends, who now my heart-strings move,
Address me from the Dead.

And change has come on me, on all;
The very house of prayer
Has nought but thy familiar call
To tell me it is there.

Ring out old Bell,—thy noisy chime
Is music to my heart;
Ring, ring, and drown the voice of Time,
Lest dreams, and all depart.

The City Spring.

And art thou flowing still, old fount,
As when thy stream of yore
To its old barrel's brim would mount,
And sparkling there, run o'er?

Not thence, in marble channel, led,
With art's cramped arch on high,
Its course was nature's gravelled bed,
Its roof the boundless sky.

"Us boys" were not forbid to rove,
Or do as we might please;
For thou had'st then, no stately grove,
No fence, no walks, no trees:

No keeper's frown, no placard's threat
Repressed our sports and glee;
Though often, when we went home wet,
We'd rue our pranks with thee.

I'd love, if thou could'st speak, to hear
The tales thy tongue might tell;
They'd come as grateful to my ear,
As notes from that "Old Bell."

A thousand scrapes, ten thousand joys,
Thy chronicles contain;—
The old town, and the new town boys
Would live and fight again.

And pretty girls would gather round,
Who oft have dealt the prize
That fists, as well as lance, have found—
The light from Beauty's eyes.

Not Froissart's tales of war and love,
On which I am wont to pore,
Could so my yearning fancies move,
As thy collected lore.

They've hid from us, thy place of birth,
And now, thro' mouths of brass,
Thy formal streamlets, issuing forth,
To marble basins pass.

A ponderous ladle's by thy side
For all who seek thy brink;
And well dressed folk descend with pride
Thy marble steps, to drink.

Not thus, when all thy gifts were free,
Steps, ladle, pride, unknown;—
The homage then, of bended knee,
Made thy cool flood our own.

Thou'rt changed old friend, and so am I,
Since first our course began;

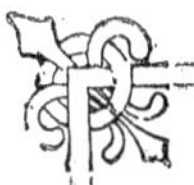

Thou'rt now a thing of majesty;
  And I an exiled man.

A temple rears o'er thee its crest,
  With column, frieze and dome,
A cottage, in the far, far West,
  Is now my humble home.

Well, be it so; I yet may fill
  This iron cup of thine,
Nor wish it Lethean; no, not 'till
  Some sterner lot is mine.

No—not while friends leave death's dull vale,
  And smiling meet my call;
And living loves my presence hail
  In home, in hearts, and hall.

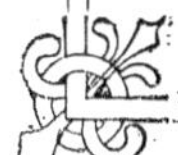

The Old Town-Clock.

Not silenced yet, thou babbling knave,
But taking still, delight,
To sound the hours, when gay larks crave
Admittance home at night?

Rousing mammas from needful nap,
Papas from happy snore,
As some sad truant's cautious rap
Tells of him at the door.

In vain the friendly night-lock there,
The gas-light, left to burn;
Some treacherous hinge, or creaking stair
Proclaims the late return.

E'en brides awake from slumbers fraught
With dreams, bright hope has cast;
Though long tried dowagers are taught
To sleep through all, at last.

I marvel thou'rt not voted down,
As all old things may be,
By thousands in this ancient town,
Who've cursed thy toll of *three*.

That awful hour, when pleasure's ranks
  Dismiss them for the night,
And, not less terrible, when banks
  Close on some hard run wight.

Ah! thou could'st tell another thing,
  Didst thou dare speak aloud,
Than old Church Bell, or City Spring,
  Howe'er with speech endowed.

But thou had'st best, perhaps, be mute,
  As what thou hast to tell,
Might now, not altogether suit
  The living age so well.

At least, I trust that, all the fuss
  May be when I'm away,
Should'st thou become but garrulous
  Of either night, or day.

Well! well! old friend, for thou art such,
  Albeit I rail at thee;
And in thy annals there is much
  Of pleasant thought to me;—

Thou'rt but the monitor of Time,
  And bound to sound the hours,
And if we're startled by their chime,
  The fault's not thine, but ours.

But we may yet redeem past hours,
  To wreathe with what are left,

And dress thy dial-plate with flowers
Whence all the thorns are reft:

That thus, when Life's last peal is rung,
From thy once dreaded bell,
A voice, responsive to thy tongue,
May whisper, all is well.

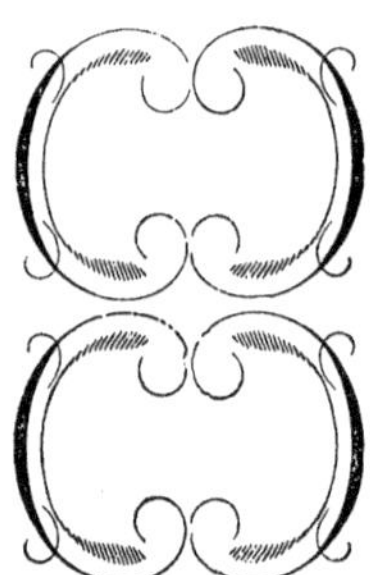

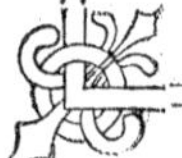

ORIGIN AND CAUSES

OF

DEMOCRACY IN AMERICA.

ORIGIN AND CAUSES

OF

DEMOCRACY IN AMERICA:

A DISCOURSE

BY

GEORGE W. BURNAP.

DELIVERED IN BALTIMORE,

BEFORE THE

MARYLAND HISTORICAL SOCIETY,

ON ITS

EIGHTH ANNIVERSARY CELEBRATION;

DECEMBER 20, 1853.

JOHN D. TOY, PRINTER.

ORIGIN AND CAUSES

OF

DEMOCRACY IN AMERICA.

MR. PRESIDENT AND GENTLEMEN:

The subject which I have chosen for your entertainment this evening, is THE ORIGIN AND CAUSES OF DEMOCRACY IN AMERICA. The United States have now taken rank among the most powerful nations of the globe. As such, we have begun to exert a wide influence in the affairs of nations, and to act no mean part in influencing the future destiny of the human race. It is evident, that that influence will be exerted in favor of popular liberty, the natural rights of man, in short, the universal government of the people.

Right or wrong, for good or for evil, this is the influence which we are destined to exert. We have a right to judge so from past experience. The impulse has already been felt throughout Europe, and throughout the world. Although in Europe it has suffered a temporary check, in the subjugation of Hungary, and the retrograde revolution in France, in the defeat of the Republican movement in Germany, and the suppression of the democratic demonstration in Italy, it may be emphatically said, that the cause, even there, is not dead but slumbering, to be revived at some future day with new energy, a profounder wisdom, and a more complete success. The existence and wonderful prosperity of this nation, are fixed facts, and the lesson they read is not likely to be lost upon the world.

Nations, like individuals, have their peculiar organic type, by which they are distinguished from each other. It is early manifested, and when once fixed, has the power of perpetuating itself through countless generations. Nationality seems to have a mysterious, creative, and transforming power. Like that vital energy, which determines the species of the trees of the forest, it has the power of assimilating all things to itself. The oak and the pine spring up, side by side, out of a common soil, and draw nourishment from the same elements, yet one converts those elements into the peculiar wood and foliage of the straight and lofty pine, the other into the low and gnarled oak. So nationality, operating upon the elements of a common humanity, assimilates it to its own type, transmits that type from age to age, and transforms to its own likeness whatever foreign element is thrown into it. What can be more different from each other, than the two nations which the British Channel separates? The Alps and the Pyrenees divide nations no less diverse from each other. It is not soil, it is not climate, for what more different than the ancient Roman and the modern Italian? What more dissimilar than the magnanimous soldiers of Alexander, and the cowering slaves who have so long kissed the footstool of the Ottoman throne?

We have existed long enough to develop and to exhibit our national characteristics. The most prominent of these, as I have already said, is Democracy. I mean, of course, in no sectarian or party sense. I mean a government constituted and administered by the people themselves. I mean a Democracy, in contradistinction to a Despotism, a Monarchy, an Aristocracy; and as equally distinguished from Anarchy, Agrarianism, and Socialism.

The formation of this great Republic in the western hemisphere, was a result wholly unforeseen and unpremeditated.

It was projected by no individual mind, nor was it the product of the consentaneous action of any number of minds, working together for a common object. The members of our confederacy had not a common origin. They were formed by different circumstances, yet when they at last came together to form a body politic, they were found completely homogeneous, they bore one type, and like the members of the human frame, they were found to coalesce into one consistent and symmetrical whole.

What were the origin and causes of this homogeneousness, this common element of Democracy, which pervaded each and all, and made their union into one nation so easy, so natural, and so perfect.

At the time of the discovery of America in 1492, nothing was more improbable than the formation of a vast Republic in North America, stretching from the Atlantic to the Pacific, and from either coast, sweeping the commerce of both oceans. There were then, in the nations of Europe, from which America was to be colonized, absolutely no materials from which such a product could be expected to spring. The Democratic element was no where developed; the government of the people was an idea which did not even enter the human mind. The nations were just emerging from the darkness and barbarism of the Middle Ages. So far from governing, in any part of Europe, the people were scarcely emancipated from slavery. They had been for ages bought and sold with the land they cultivated. There was but one nation, and that was England, in which they enjoyed representation in the national legislature, and there they had a voice merely to authorize and legalize taxation. There had been, in that country, a long and bloody struggle for power, but it had been between the kings and the feudal aristocracy, in which the people, who did the fighting, and endured the destruction of the wars, had no other interest than a change of tyrants. No one thought of vindicating their liberties, or improving their condition. They were the mere pawns upon the chess-board of political and national ambition; and they were used with no more feeling or sympathy than the ivory figures, which are stained red or left white, that they may not be confounded in the fight.

Spain had just been consolidated into one nation, under the government of Ferdinand and Isabella; and every energy had been strained to the utmost, in the struggle for the expulsion of the Moors. In the new monarchy which was established, the only representation which the people had in the government, was in the deputations from the cities; and in those deputations it was the wealth of cities, not the population, that was represented. Cities were tolerated in the States General from no respect for popular rights, but because the wheels of government could not move without money, and the mercantile wealth of cities alone could furnish this.

The people of Spain were then without education, without wealth, without power, without the knowledge even of their political rights. And, had the winds of heaven driven Columbus upon the coast of the United States, instead of the island of San Salvador, and North America been peopled from Spain instead of South, the territory we occupy would now have been what South America and Mexico are. So far from originating and enjoying a Republican government, its inhabitants would, like them, have been incapable of imitating one, when they had the model before their eyes.

The state of things was no better in France. There, at the period of which we speak, both king and nobles united to depress the people. They did not dare to trust them with arms, and chose rather to depend on foreign mercenaries for military defence, than to suffer the people to learn the secret of their strength. There was no effectual enfranchisement of the people in France, previous to the revolution of 1792, two hundred years after the discovery of America.

Louis the Fourteenth, with the rack of the inquisitor, and the soldier's sword, in the destruction of the Huguenots, had quenched out in blood, the first sparks of popular liberty, in France, before they kindled to a flame.

But France, just as she then was, tried her hand at colonizing the new world. Her ships, fortunately for us, wandered as far to the North as those of Spain had done to the South.

They sailed up the St. Lawrence, and laid the foundations of Montreal and Quebec. And there her colonies remain to the present day, unchanged and unimproved; a petrified specimen of what France was two centuries ago. So far are they from Republicanism, that few of them have intelligence enough to know the meaning of the word.

Venice and the Netherlands, were the only countries in Europe, in which there was even the shadow of popular liberty, and they were too happy, and too busy, in the enjoyment of the fruits of their trade and industry, to covet the possession of a howling wilderness.

And what was England herself, at that period, from which liberty finally went forth conquering and to conquer? Rather behind the rest of Europe than in advance of it. Her civilization had been arrested and delayed by a series of political calamities. Her energies had been exhausted in the ruinous endeavor to retain her continental possessions. Her best blood had flowed in the civil wars; her wealth had been wasted, and her soil almost depopulated, by the endless quarrel of a disputed succession. It was not until the claims of the rival houses of York and Lancaster were peacefully united in the Seventh and Eighth Henry, that England took her place in the march of nations towards the goal of freedom and happiness.

It was in the year 1497 that the continent of North America was first looked upon by English eyes. Henry the Seventh was then upon the throne. Had these shores been colonized then, even by Englishmen, what would have been the result? A little better, perhaps, than what took place in the Gulf of Mexico and on the banks of the St. Lawrence, but not much. The *people* of England then had no political existence. The only recognized symbol of their being, as well as the germ of their future power, appeared in the House of Commons. But so overwhelming was the landed interest, and so small was the mercantile and mechanical wealth of the country, that both king and nobility, so far from regarding it as a co-ordinate power, looked upon it as a convenient instrument of draining from the people their proportion of the public burdens; and of so little account was it as late as the reign of Henry the Eighth, that when that body hesitated to pass a bill at his order, he sent for the Speaker, and drawing his finger round his neck, declared, "If my bill is not passed to-morrow, this must come off." Queen Elizabeth, his daughter, reigned with a prerogative scarcely less despotic; and we may say, that during the dynasty of the house of Tudor, terminating in 1602, four years before the Virginia colony landed at Jamestown, the idea of a popular government, a government based on population and not on property or hereditary right, scarcely entered the mind of an Englishman, as within the bounds of possibility. And yet, from this very people, within a little more than a century and a half, sprang our glorious Republic, in perfect symmetry and beauty, like Minerva from the brain of Jove.

How was this wonderful result brought about? To develop this process is the theme of the present address.

From what I have already said, it will be readily inferred, that there was no design in the people of England, of founding a great Republic in this western world, nor did it enter into the minds of the Colonists themselves. With the exception of the Puritans, it was the height of their ambition to reproduce England and her institutions in America, just as she then was. They knew of nothing better; they could conceive of nothing more perfect. And after they arrived, they long continued to be Englishmen, though transplanted to a new world. Their idea of a perfect government was of a king, a nobility, and commons; but that the third estate was competent to subsist by itself, and discharge all the functions of government better by itself than in partnership with the others, never entered their conceptions, and was the slow revelation of experience.

The first Colonial Charter to Virginia, which dates in 1606, contained not a particle of the popular element. It was granted to two companies, one composed "of noblemen, gentlemen, and merchants of London;" the other, "of knights, gentlemen, and merchants, in the West." They were to have no representation in Parliament, and not even the power to make their own laws. They were to be governed, not by themselves, but by a "resident Council, appointed by the king, and removable at his pleasure." Legislation, even in the minutest affairs, was reserved to be exercised by the sovereign.

Scarcely, however, had a settlement been made on the banks of the James, when a revolution took place, symbolic of the future destiny of British colonization in the West. The government manufactured by royal hands in England, it was found, would not work in America. The Council, the offspring of European privilege and aristocracy, was found too feeble, spiritless, and inefficient for its new and untried position, and was compelled to give place to plain John Smith, one of nature's noblemen, who took command of the Colony by an authority more authentic and indisputable than earthly monarch could ever bestow, the authority of a commanding intellect, and an indomitable will.

The whole territory of Maryland was originally given away to a single nobleman. In providing for its government, Lord Baltimore took such views, and indulged such anticipations, as were natural to a nobleman of that age. The Charter, which was drawn up at his instance, and it is supposed according to his wishes, contemplates the transfer to America, whole and unchanged, of the feudal system, as it had existed in Europe ever since the overthrow of the Roman Empire. He secured to himself palatine, or royal jurisdiction, the highest privilege of the nobility in feudal times. The tenth section of his Charter confers on him the power of creating a titled aristocracy. In the language of the Charter, "We do give free and plenary power to the aforesaid, now baron of Baltimore, and to his heirs and assigns, to confer favors, rewards and honors upon such subjects, inhabiting within the province aforesaid, as shall be well deserving, and to adorn them with whatever titles and dignities they shall appoint, so that they be not such as are used in England."

The lands in Europe had then been held for ages, not by the people in fee simple, but by immense landed proprietors, and by them leased out to tenants from time to time. The same tenure of land was contemplated here. With these vast domains of the European aristocracy, certain rights of territorial jurisdiction were connected. The baron had power to organize and hold a court of his own, not subject to the control of the courts established by the nation at large. This independent jurisdiction was one of the greatest grievances of the feudal system. It was obnoxious to both king and people, but it was one which the feudal aristocracy retained with the greatest tenacity. This was to be conferred on the newly created American aristocracy. By the nineteenth section of the Charter, it is provided, "We also, by these presents, do give and grant license to the same baron of Baltimore, and to his heirs, to erect any parcels of land within the province aforesaid into manors, and in every of these manors, to have and to hold a court baron, and all things which to a court baron do belong."

It is needless to say, that these provisions remained a dead letter upon the parchment. Feudalism was found to be incapable of transportation across the Atlantic. It could not live for a day in the free atmosphere of America. The nobleman never came, himself, to give it effect. Emancipated from the prejudices, as well as the institutions of the old world, the emigrants to the new, resumed the original rights of man, and demanded the natural privileges of property and legislation.

In North Carolina, nearly the same experiment was tried over again. A Charter was there granted to eight noblemen instead of one. They were to be the proprietors of the soil. The dignity was to be hereditary, and in default of heirs, the deficiency was to be made up by the choice of the survivors. The territory was to be divided into counties. Two orders of nobility were to be created; one Earl and two Barons for each county. Legislation vested in the proprietors of the soil, and jurisdiction, or the distribution of justice, was handed over, likewise, to the hereditary nobility. To make the burden of legislation light, one of the greatest minds of that, or any other age, John Locke, was called in to exercise the function of lawgiver to the future oligarchy of Carolina.

These transactions date more than half a century after the Charter to Lord Baltimore. The insurrection of popular liberty, in England, had intervened, which was begun by the Puritans, and consummated by Cromwell and his Round Heads, and it is surprising that no greater progress was manifested in the appreciation of the rights and capabilities of the people. But Shaftsbury and Locke, the leading minds of that period, were neither of them enthusiasts in any thing, and they seem to have shared in the disappointment which was felt by the nation in the results of the so-called Commonwealth of England.

The Charter of Pennsylvania bears the date of 1681. And it shows the same features of feudalism with the Charter of Maryland. The whole State was made the property of one man, and powers nearly regal were conferred on the plain Quaker, William Penn. In fact, the whole State was made over to Penn, in discharge of a debt, owed to his father, by Charles the Second. In exercise of his regal rights, Penn proceeded to frame a government, and promulgate a code of laws, of his own device. But the principles of civil, as well as religious, freedom, which had been arrived at and promulgated by George Fox, here began to tell upon the world, and to be made practical in laying the foundations of a great Commonwealth. Penn, though bred up among the aristocracy of England, never sympathised with his associates, and was more at home in the ultra democracy of a Quaker meeting, than in the court of his Sovereign. The consequence was, that the Pennsylvania Colony soon took on the type of the new world. The power passed from the hands of the proprietors, and they finally were compelled to content themselves with a pecuniary compensation for the surrender of all feudal and royal prerogatives.

The first colonization of New York was nearly as aristocratic as that of the other States. The Hanse Towns, which first cast their eyes towards the magnificent country which now composes the Empire State, though in advance of the rest of Europe in the principles of civil freedom, knew as yet absolutely nothing of the government of the people. Grotius and Barnevelt, though the lights of their age, and finally the victims to their convictions as to the natural rights of man, never entertained the idea that a popular government was practicable.

In the Netherlands, power had long since passed from the hands of the feudal aristocracy, but it had not come into the hands of the people. It had been grasped and intercepted by the merchants, and the destinies of that land of industry and commerce, were in the hands of a moneyed, instead of landed, aristocracy.

The Colonies which were first sent out from the Netherlands, had for their object, not so much the establishment of a permanent settlement, as the immediate acquisition of wealth, which was to be gathered from the western wilderness, and enjoyed at home, amidst the luxury and repose of the Fatherland. The acquisition of territory was a secondary object. But though feudalism was become nearly obsolete at home, provision was made for its revival here. A Charter was obtained from the States General for the rising Colonies of the New World. In it, there is no trace of popular government. He, who within five years, should plant a Colony of fifty souls, became Lord of the Manor, or Patron, possessing, in absolute property, the lands he might colonize. Those lands "might extend sixteen miles in length, or if on a river, they might extend eight miles on each side, and so far into the interior as might be convenient." Such was the solid foundation laid by the freest people in Europe for a landed aristocracy, on the soil now constituting a most important part of the United States. Such was the beginning of a people who are now charged with being a democracy run mad. But it ought to be added that the traces of this landed aristocracy were not immediately obliterated. They remain to the present day, to be a cause of political uneasiness and discontent.

Thus it may be said, that every Colony South and West of the Hudson river, was aristocratic in its origin, and in the whole structure of its contemplated institutions. The fact was, that no other institutions were conceived of as possible.

No other idea was entertained, but of making America a repetition of Europe, as she then was; and had the intentions of the first projectors of the colonies taken effect, North America would have resembled England and the Netherlands as closely as Mexico and South America now resemble old Spain.

There was one exception to all this; the Puritans. The Colony of Plymouth was democratic from the beginning. The people who landed in 1620 in Massachusetts Bay, amid the cold and snows of December, had been exiles from England before they were emigrants to America. They left their country without her motherly blessing, and the latest recollections of their native home were associated with the bitterest and most relentless persecution. Monarchy, prelacy and aristocracy, were equally abominations in their sight. They came not therefore, forth like the other Colonies, under the patronage of titled wealth or noble families. They were the people themselves, going forth with strong hearts and toil worn hands, to fell the forest and create a world of their own. Their Democracy was organized on board the May-flower, before a Pilgrim had set foot upon the shore. The little Republic began to be, when forty-one signatures were affixed to the following document:

"In the name of God, amen. We whose names are under-written, the loyal subjects of our dread sovereign, King James, having undertaken, for the glory of God and the advancement of the Christian faith, and the honor of our king and country, a voyage to plant a Colony in the northern parts of Virginia, do by these presents, solemnly and mutually, in the presence of God, and one of another, covenant and combine ourselves together, into a civil body politic, for our better ordering and preservation and furtherance of the ends aforesaid, and by virtue hereof to create, constitute and frame such just and equal laws, ordinances, acts, constitutions and offices, from time to time, as shall be thought most convenient for the general good of the Colony. Unto which we promise all due submission and obedience."

Here, in this short document, is the essence, the substance, and almost the form, of all subsequent distinctive American institutions and legislation. It is a recurrence to first principles. It places the new society on the original ground of contract. It institutes a pure Democracy, the government of the people, for the people, and by the people.

The Puritans had been trained for more than half a century in the school of Democracy. During the struggle with King James, the Church and the Cavaliers, they had discovered and adopted the principle of congregational independence. They had maintained, that this was not only the original organization of the Church, but was in itself, the mode of administering Christianity most consistent with national justice, and the inalienable rights of man. This mode of government made every Church a little Republic by itself, and a seminary of Democracy. Here, too, men learned not only the theory, but the practice of self-government. They learned that a simple form of government was not only the best, but the cheapest; and that the immense sums which had been lavished on a splendid establishment, both in Church and State, was money worse than thrown away. James, with the true instinct of despotism, was not long in discovering the tendency of all these things, and he exclaimed, "No bishop, no king," and the Puritans, seeing the true issue, took up the challenge, and answered, "No bishop *and* no king."

But in carrying out their principles in their native land, they encountered obstacles absolutely insurmountable. There was the force of prescription, running against them with the accumulated strength of centuries; there was the feudal tenure of property; there was an hereditary aristocracy, to which the masses were accustomed to bow down, with a subserviency more mechanical and slavish, than that paid by the Spartan Helots to their masters. There was the Church establishment, which had grown up to such a massive strength as an outward institution, that it might live on as a body politic, long after the soul of religion had become utterly extinct.

Still worse was it for them, when they removed to the continent. There they found themselves foreigners, in the midst of a dense population, more than ordinarily obstinate in their prejudices, and fixed in their habits. Their hopes of propagating and perpetuating their principles in Holland, were about as desperate as to undertake to color the ocean with a single drop. They would not only have failed to propagate their principles, but have lost their nationality, and become absorbed and lost in the surrounding population. Their emigration to this country, desperate as might seem the undertaking, was the only salvation of themselves and their principles.

But Providence had reserved in North America a spot unoccupied, for the trial of the last great experiment of humanity. By crossing the ocean and landing on these desolate shores, they freed themselves, at one bound, of all the embarrassments which forbade the development of their principles in the Old World. The germ of popular liberty had room to expand itself in its simplicity, purity and perfection, until it has become a tree, overspreading a mighty continent, and the exiles and the oppressed of all nations, seek a refuge under the shadow of it.

But, as I have already said, New England was an exception. It was colonized by the people; and the people had sufficient resource in themselves, in their intelligence and moral control, to govern themselves. How was it that the same result followed every where else, under circumstances so different? How was it, that at the end of a century and a half, the more southern Colonies, beginning their existence under aristocratic auspices, and having a strong oligarchic bias at first, were found nearly abreast of Massachusetts in the career of democracy; and all the members of this vast Confederacy were found to be moulded, like the members of a human body, after one type, and ready to coalesce into one grand homogeneous nation?

The first cause, I shall mention, as having necessitated the universal establishment of Democracy in America, was *the cheapness of land and the dearness of labor*. A new country is the poor man's paradise. In crossing the Atlantic, the relations of capital and labor were completely reversed. The poor man's labor is his all. His consequence rises or sinks in precise proportion to the demand which exists for the only thing which he has to bring to market. In old and thickly peopled countries, like England and Holland, where labor of course was cheap and land was dear, the chance for a laborer to become a freeholder, was next to hopeless. He could not even emigrate without selling himself for a term of years into bondage. And it was in this way, that quite a large proportion of the first emigrants came over. When they arrived here, they found a totally different state of things. Here was a vast continent of land, but it was worth nothing until it was cleared and cultivated. The physical energies of the laborer alone could do this. The land owner became the dependent man, and the laborer dictated his own terms. When as yet there was no capital but land, the land owner was compelled to pay his laborer in land, and thus the laborer became a freeholder, as well as himself. The laborer too, was a capitalist, in the ownership of his own bones and sinews; and on the strength of his real consequence in the community, he demanded and obtained the right of suffrage; and when labor is represented, there is necessarily a Democracy.

In Europe, the recognition of popular rights was delayed for many ages by the universal prevalence of the feudal system. At the breaking up of the Roman Empire, the soil of Europe was appropriated, in large tracts, by military chieftains, who seized on every thing by right of conquest. Each landed proprietor built his castle in the midst of his domain, and reigned there with an absoluteness equalled only by Oriental despotism. There were no people, in our modern sense of the term. The population was divided into masters and slaves. The right of the one was to command, and the duty of the other was to obey. This system was hardly shaken when America began to be colonized. Neither party, the land holders nor tenants, conceived of any other state of things as possible.

A landed aristocracy, fortified by the usage of primogeniture, is one of the most lasting of all human institutions. Other property easily passes from hand to hand, and nothing is more shifting than mercantile wealth. During the Middle Ages, there was nothing to oppose to the power of the landed aristocracy. Mercantile wealth, the first power that made any stand against it, was almost unknown. That is the creation of civilization. In a state of barbarism, there are no manufactures; there is no consumption of luxuries; there is nothing to pay for luxuries; there is no commerce; no trade; nothing to buy or sell. There are no cities; for cities are merely the marts of exchange. A growing civilization created cities, and cities reacted on the progress of civilization. Cities and commerce transferred the sceptre from land to money, and the lordly castle became subordinated to the neighboring city. The last and final transition of power, is from property to persons, and city and castle become subordinated to the people, that great multitude whose power is irresistible, and their voice as the sound of many waters.

In Europe, at the time of the settlement of North America, this process of the transfer of power was going on. But every where its progress was gradual, tedious and unsteady. The first impulse was given by the Crusades. To win back the Holy Land and sepulchre of Christ from the Infidel, was the passion of Christendom for more than two centuries. Every thing was disturbed by this universal enthusiasm, and society was moved from its ancient foundations. Vast quantities of property changed owners. The nobles of Europe, in order to engage in those distant and expensive enterprizes, were obliged to have money. They had no ready money, and they were compelled to alienate their lands to procure it. The cities through which the Crusaders travelled, were enriched by their expenditures, or the fleets which bore them across the sea, brought large gains to their owners; and the wealth thus accumulated, laid the foundation of modern commerce, that most powerful agent in all the revolutions of the last five centuries. It was one of the steps towards the emancipation of the people, and their preparation to discharge the duties, as well as enjoy the privileges, of citizenship.

But, when the emigration to North America took place, all these intermediate steps were overleaped. The people came themselves, and unembarrassed by feudal rights and aristocratic usages, took the power into their own hands.

This leads me to speak of the next cause of the Democracy of the North American Colonies, which I shall mention—*their isolation.* Three thousand miles of ocean intervened between them and the old world. This circumstance was not without the most decisive and important effects. The people had their own way, because they could not be controlled by their old masters at the distance of three thousand miles. *Nobility never emigrated.* There was nothing to tempt it to quit its ancient home. It was a plant of such a peculiar structure, that it would not bear translation to another soil. Here it would have withered and died, amidst the rugged forests and stern climate of America. A nobleman is the creation of a local conventionalism. He flourishes only in an artificial atmosphere. He must be seen by gas light. He is at home only in courts and palaces.

The pomp of courts, and the splendor of palaces, are the contrivances, not more of human pride than of far-sighted policy. They are intended to impose on the imagination of the multitude; to lead them to associate with the condition of their superiors the ideas of providential and unattainable superiority, to which it is their destiny and their duty to submit. Take them away from the stage on which they choose to exhibit themselves; strip them of their dramatic costume; take away the overhanging chandelier and the glare of the foot lights, and let them mingle in the common crowd, and they become as other men, and the crowd begin to wonder how they could ever have looked up to them with so much reverence.

They gained likewise advantages from associating together. An English nobleman had a hereditary right to a seat in the House of Lords. He made a part of the national legislature. This privilege was independent of the popular will. It was real power, a possession so flattering to the pride of man. There was no reason therefore, why such a man should wish to leave his country. What could he find here congenial to his taste, or flattering to his pride, or tolerable to his habits of luxury and self-indulgence?

A rude village on the shore of the ocean, or on the banks of a stream, of a few log cabins, scattered here and there in the wilderness, was all the New World had to offer for many generations. Not many would emigrate to such a country, who had any thing to leave behind. Much less was it to be expected, that those would come here, who had drawn the highest prizes in life at home. They could not seek a new organization of the social condition, in which they had nothing to gain and every thing to lose. Here and there, there might be an adventurer of condition, who came to this country to improve his broken fortunes; but then it was, as in all new countries, with a hope of returning to enjoy his gains in a country and a state of society, where refined enjoyment was possible.

And after all, beyond a limited circle, America was, at that time, very little known and very little regarded by the people of England. And it is very much so to the present hour. The best informed people, strange as it may seem, know little more of the Geography of this country than they do of the interior of Africa; and thousands and thousands who move in respectable society, are ignorant whether we are white or copper colored, speak the English language or Choctaw.

America, then, grew up in neglect and by stealth. Unattractive to the higher classes, she drew to herself the people. Here came the people, the hard-handed and stout-hearted, and carved out a New World for themselves. They adapted their institutions to their wants, and before the Old World was aware, there had sprung up on this broad continent a gigantic Republic, ready to take her position among the nations of the earth.

The third cause of Democracy in America was *the progress and establishment of civil liberty in England*, contemporaneously with the colonization of this country and formation of its institutions.

The seventeenth century, from the year 1603, when the House of Stuart ascended the throne of England, three years before the settlement of Virginia, till the revolution in 1688, six years after the arrival of Penn in Pennsylvania, was the period when the people of England were emancipated from political vassalage, and obtained their just weight in the British Constitution. The main organ of this stupendous revolution, was the English House of Commons. It was there that popular liberty, after struggling in the world for ages almost in vain, made her first successful stand, obtained a hearing for her cause, and found a voice to address herself to the nations.

After the suppression of the Roman Republic by Julius Cæsar, forty-three years before the Christian era, there had been nothing in Europe for more than fifteen hundred years, which could be denominated a government of the people. He, himself, in his Gallic Wars, gives a description of the condition of the people of Gaul and Britain at that period. "Over all Gaul," says he, "there are only two orders of men in any degree of honor and esteem, for the common people are little better than slaves, attempt nothing of themselves, and have no share in public deliberations. As they are generally oppressed with debt, heavy tributes, or the exactions of their superiors, they make themselves vassals to the great, who exercise over them the same species of jurisdiction as masters do over slaves. The two orders of men with whom, as we have said, all authority and distinction are lodged, are the druids and nobles."

When these northern nations overran the Roman Empire, and were converted to Christianity, the only political change that took place, seems to have been the substitution of the Christian ecclesiastics in the place of the Pagan druids. The people remained just where they were before. Hence it is that the Bishops sit in the British House of Lords to the present hour.

The first dawn of modern freedom was in the establishment, as a permanent body, of the House of Commons in England. Besides the king, the nobility and clergy, as arts, commerce and industry revived, there was seen gradually to spring up, a third estate, the people. They acquired wealth, and consequently power. At any rate, it was necessary that they should bear a part of the public burdens. They were first summoned to take a part in legislation, merely to legitimate their own taxation, and so it continued for some generations.

But it was found, that the same hands which could grant, could withhold supplies, and both the monarch and the aristocracy discovered that the new power which they had called into existence, had already grown to an importance which could neither be dispensed with, nor controlled. With the acquisition of wealth, came as a natural consequence, education, intellectual development, literary culture. On these followed, as an inevitable result, social influence.

After a long struggle, the House of Commons obtained the liberty of free discussion, and then the principles of civil liberty grew apace. Words were spoken on the floor of the House of Commons, by Hampden and Prynne and their patriotic associates, which vibrated through the nation. Great principles of right, of law and humanity, which had had no articulate expression for more than fifteen hundred years, received a clear exposition and an able defence. In the meantime, literature was not idle. Milton, the sublimest genius that ever wore the vestments of mortality, took up the cause of mental freedom and civil liberty, with a force and an eloquence never surpassed. No right of man, no principle nor form of popular government, was left undiscussed.

The spread and growth of these principles were resisted by king and nobility, with the most obstinate perseverance. Inch by inch, the ground was contested. At every successive Parliament, the Commons rose in their demands, and required new guaranties for the rights of the people. The king became desperate, and for thirteen years attempted to govern without a Parliament. Failing in this, and yielding at last to the necessities of his condition, he again summoned the representatives of the people only to discover that the balance of power had passed over to the people, and the sceptre of absolute dominion had fallen forever from his hands. But so great a question as this, the balance of the British Constitution, could not be settled without the trial by battle. The sword was drawn, and Monarchy and Democracy fought hand to hand through many a bloody year.

This struggle was no common contest. It was not like the war of the roses, a matter of personality and partizanship—whether this or that branch of royalty should sit upon the throne; but whether Monarchy or Democracy should have the ascendency in the British Constitution; whether the king should govern, according to the will of the people, expressed by law, or after his own arbitrary will and pleasure.

Victory at length declared for the people, and monarchy and aristocracy were driven into banishment. And had Cromwell been thirty years old instead of fifty, they might never have returned, and England been at this time a representative Republic.

But the old obstacles were still in the way. The hereditary reverence for monarchy and aristocracy was still strong in the minds of the people, and the violent measures which Democracy was compelled to take, in order to establish and maintain its ascendency, became almost as odious to the nation as the ancient regime of legitimacy itself. The tree was too old to be bent into a new shape, and as soon as the pressure was taken off, it recoiled with violence into its ancient position.

All this took place in the presence of the civilized world; its bearings were considered and its merits discussed. The interest felt in it was intense. No where was it so deep as in the American Colonies, whose fathers and brothers were engaged in the great war of principles and opinions. And it is not difficult to conjecture on which side their sympathies would be most likely to be enlisted.

The people, for it was the people who had emigrated, would sympathize with the people's cause. The people at home were struggling for that which their American brethren possessed without a struggle, by virtue of their position, the right to govern themselves.

This grand lesson, at least, was taught them, that king and aristocracy were at all events a superfluity; that England flourished quite as well as a Commonwealth as it had done as a kingdom. And though Englishmen restored their monarch and House of Lords for old acquaintance sake, to a young community it seemed quite unnecessary to import or manufacture so expensive a luxury.

At any rate, the charm of Divine right was forever broken. It was shown by experiment, that a king is the executive of a nation's will, their chief magistrate, and nothing more. His authority comes up from the people, but does not come down from his ancestors by hereditary right. An elective magistracy then, if clothed with the power of the people, might be just as efficient, far more convenient, and far less dangerous, than royalty. They had seen the royal power too, gradually waning, and the will of the people becoming supreme, even under the forms of monarchy. A new power rose up, unknown in former ages, the power of public opinion, the MIND of the nation came forth and declared itself supreme.

Such were the changes which took place in the political condition of England, during the seventeenth century; the period during which that portion of North America which now constitutes the United States, was colonized, and took on its political type and complexion. It is easy to see what influences from the mother country were predominant, and what were most congenial to a young and growing country, standing apart from the monarchical and aristocratic institutions of the Old World.

The last cause to which I shall advert of the rise of democratic institutions in America, was *the general diffusion of knowledge and education, and the great improvement of the condition of the laboring classes.* The materials for a Republic are educated mind and personal independence. The price of labor determines whether these shall pervade all classes.

A high price of labor gives the poor man the means of educating his children and himself, and gives him a sense of personal independence. But low wages condemn the masses to ignorance, dependence and degradation. A starving population will always be deaf to the voice of reason, and its stern necessities will drive it beyond all other control than that of an iron despotism. It throws off monarchy, only to fall back again under the more stringent constraint of the bayonet. The suffrages of an ignorant multitude are worth nothing, and the direction of the course of public affairs might as well be decided by the cast of a die.

If the question were asked, why the government of the people did not come sooner in modern times, it must be answered in all honesty, that the people were not sooner prepared to govern. An Italian ecclesiastic has lately told the American people, that in that part of Italy where he was first called to minister, only one person out of five thousand could read. How is such a people as that prepared to be governed by universal suffrage? The people of France lately elected an absolute Emperor for life, and voluntarily surrendered the fruits of the struggles, the bloodshed and the sufferings of the last sixty years. Political power will always follow intelligence, for knowledge is power. From the sixth to the sixteenth century, the Church shared largely in the government of the world. And it is customary, in modern times, to censure her as an usurper, and to attribute the part she acted in civil affairs, to worldly ambition. Much of this censure is unjust. The Church governed the world, because she was the only educated body of men then extant.

It is in vain that you put political power into hands too ignorant to wield it. Mexico, in emulation of our happy experiment of Republican institutions, attempted the same. But it was only to demonstrate that she was wholly unprepared for the experiment. The right of suffrage was established with comparative ease. A President was chosen by the voice of the people, but there was not sufficient intelligence to perceive the necessity of performing the duty corresponding to the right of suffrage—that of submitting to the will of the majority, when expressed through the ballot box. The defeated candidate raised a civil war, and overturned the Constitution before it could be carried into effect. Our experiment would have ended in the same way, had not education been universally diffused.

In this country, from the very first, the people of the different Colonies were sufficiently intelligent to make and administer their own laws. A large proportion of them were capable of the duties of magistracy, and their constituency knew when their public functionaries served them with wisdom and fidelity. The art of printing had been in full exercise more than a century before the first Colony was planted. Not only was the power to read very generally diffused, but books were multiplied, and they went with the primitive settlers into the remotest forests, and the literary luminaries which rose one after another upon the Old World, sent their rays across the Atlantic, and trained up a new born people to intelligence, freedom and virtue.

The different Colonies had not been long established, before a certain national feeling began to spring up on this side the Atlantic, and young America began to have a literature of her own. Her Provincial Legislative Assemblies, allowing the largest liberty of speech, became the seminaries of democratic principles. Liberal education began to enlarge the minds of the rising generation, and no where, since the suppression of the ancient Republics, had the classics of Greece and Rome met a warmer welcome, or awakened a more congenial feeling, than in the young men of the New World. No where had men been placed in a situation so analogous to that of the great patriots and scholars of antiquity. As early as 1704, the newspaper press began its operations in the Metropolis of New England, by sending forth the "Boston News Letter;" and then and there was laid one of the corner stones of our nationality. Then and there the great American soul, already incarnate, began to breathe forth its inspiration, and carry vitality to the remotest members. Then and there American mind began to react upon itself, and fuse into one mass the various materials of which the Colonies were composed. The progeny of this patriarch of newspapers, who shall number; and what finite intellect shall calculate the influence they have exerted on the institutions and the destiny of the country!

It was they which helped to form and discipline and nationalize those great men who prompted, directed and carried through, the struggle of the Revolution, which gave us a being and a name among the nations of the earth.

That great struggle, with its blood and tears and toils and treasure, cemented and consolidated our nationality forever. The boldness of the undertaking, the doubtfulness of the issue, and the immediate sacrifices which it demanded, consecrated to the service of their country the true, the pure, the patriotic and the brave, while it appalled and kept aloof, the timid, the time-serving and the false. The very length and severity of the contest only made the object for which they fought so long and so desperately, the more dear to all hearts.

The labor and patience, the heroism and sacrifices, of that martyr age, set apart the most conspicuous actors in the scene, to an elevation in the estimation of mankind far above the level of ordinary humanity. It made them, as it were, the Apostles of modern Liberty, and sanctified their precious words as a sort of sacred testament to all posterity. Every American feels himself enriched by the share he inherits of their glorious memories, and to forfeit that inheritance by treason or secession, he would feel as the blackest disgrace, the sorest bereavement and the most dreadful calamity.

Their noble deeds, their glorious words, their wise admonitions, their far-sighted wisdom, have set the tone of American patriotism, and they remain to guard, as it were with a sword of flame, the institutions they founded. The young are taught to repeat them with their earliest breath, the middle aged catch anew their inspiration, and the old weep tears of joy, that their eyes are permitted to see, and their ears to hear, the glory which has burst in noon-tide radiance upon their country, but which the early confessors and martyrs were permitted to see but dimly and afar off.

Under the guidance of Providence, our patriot sires may be said to have fixed the type of our nationality forever. The impediments which once existed to the permanency of a vast Republic, are now happily done away. The national roads of the Roman Empire continued for ages to bind its distant members together, when there was no other real tie than a central government, despotic in form and rapacious in administration. Here, separate States and local municipalities, are a guaranty against a dangerous consolidation, and the rapidity of communication which modern science has achieved, has almost annihilated distance, and made our vast Republic vital in every part.

We have been tried to the very verge of disunion and disorganization, only to see patriotism rise triumphant over every interest and every passion; and the sad eclipse which has come over the brightest names as soon as they have ceased to be Americans and to go for their country and their whole country, will appal the heart of every recreant statesman, who shall for generations, conceive the profane idea of dividing what God has so manifestly joined together.

What changes may take place, when this continent shall become as thickly peopled as China, whether a democracy like ours will then be practicable, no finite mind can foresee.

But till that time, there is every reason to believe, that the type of our national character will be preserved; we shall go on as we have begun, the great example of the possibility, of the power, and of the happiness of democratic institutions.

ANNUAL REPORT

OF THE

PRESIDENT

OF THE

Maryland Historical Society,

AND

LIST OF ITS MEMBERS.

1854.

BALTIMORE:
PRINTED BY JOHN D. TOY,
Corner of Market and St. Paul-sts.

List of Officers.

President.
JOHN SPEAR SMITH.

Vice-President.
JOHN P. KENNEDY.

Corresponding Secretary.
J. MORRISON HARRIS.

Recording Secretary.
S. F. STREETER.

Treasurer.
JOHN HANAN.

Librarian.
WM. H. TRAVERS.

Library Committee.
BRANTZ MAYER,.....GEORGE WM. BROWN,.....M. COURTNEY JENKINS.

Committee on Honorary Membership.
WILLIAM A. TALBOTT,......JOHN I. DONALDSON,......JAMES GEORGE.

Committee of Finance.
JOHN HANAN,............B. U. CAMPBELL,............ENOCH PRATT.

Committee on the Gallery.
J. H. B. LATROBE,......DR. THOS. EDMONDSON,......SAM'L W. SMITH.

Trustees of the Athenæum.
JOHNS HOPKINS,............MOSES SHEPPARD,............WM. MCKIM.

Council of Government.
ROBERT LESLIE,..........J. SAURIN NORRIS.

REPORT OF THE PRESIDENT

OF THE

MARYLAND HISTORICAL SOCIETY,

AT THE

ANNUAL MEETING IN MAY, 1854.

GENTLEMEN:

THE condition of the Society, in all its branches, is eminently prosperous. Nor has any thing occurred to apprehend an interruption to its onward course. On the contrary, there is every reason to believe that its future, promises increased utility, independence of existence, and salutary progress. The laudable punctuality of our associates in their payment of the annual contributions, has not only liberated us from every claim, but has left a surplus in the treasury. This, in fulfilment of the endowment plan, adopted at a late meeting, will be placed in the Savings Bank, to the credit of the Society, for future permanent investment, by the Finance Committee. This plan holds out to us the most advantageous consequences. For, after liberally providing for every appropriate expenditure, it carefully stores away the surplus and its increase, to meet unforeseen contingencies. When this fund shall have amounted to ten thousand dollars, the sum which it is intended to accumulate, then its income will suffice to maintain the association, should the annual contributions be, from any cause, discontinued. It gives too, the very best assurance, that any pecuniary donation or bequest will be faithfully secured, and sacredly applied to the nurture of learning and art, as well as to the conservation of the muniments of history.

It is obvious that an institution like this, and depending altogether on voluntary subscription, can never be free from peril. If members become indifferent to the interests of the Society, or, from any other cause, discontinue their contributions, then the labor of years, with all its fruits, is utterly wasted, and irretrievably lost. To protect ourselves from such a calamity, and to place us beyond the reach of danger, the project for securing a permanent fund, has been matured and adopted. It is simple in its several propositions, and of easy accomplishment. All that it requires is, a proper economy, with the active support of members, and due diligence on the part of the committee. In order to bring this plan again to your attention, you *will* permit me, once more, to submit its details, and to invoke for them your most favorable consideration.

They are as follows :

1. All surpluses which may remain, after defraying the annual expenditures, shall be deposited in the Savings Bank, to the credit of the Society, as also, all bequests or donations.

2. Prior to the annual meeting in February, of each year, the President and other officers—the Library Committee and the Council of Government, shall deliver to the Treasurer, their requisitions, for the ensuing year, on which such specific appropriations, as the Society may authorize, shall be made, and no other, than said appropriations shall be paid, unless on a subsequent and distinct vote of the Society.

3. That each member be urged to collect a sum of not less than five dollars, and pay over the same to the Treasurer, for the endowment fund.

4. That a book shall be kept, in which the Treasurer shall register the names and donations of the contributors to the Fund.

5. That a Finance Committee of three, of which the Treasurer shall be one, be annually chosen, whose duty it shall be to make permanent investments of said deposites; to reinvest the income arising therefrom, and to submit to the Society, such recommendations for the increase of the Fund, or modifications of the foregoing, as they may deem advisable.

Since my last report, there has been no intermission in the presentation of the annual addresses, required by our rules. The fifth, in the order of these, was delivered by Geo. Wm. Brown, Esq. on the Origin and Growth of Civil Liberty in Maryland, and is as distinguished for its careful research, as for the profoundly interesting events with which it abounds.

The next in the series, is that of Brantz Mayer, Esq. with the title of Tah-gah-jute, or Logan and Captain Michael Cresap. It embraces the memorable Indian war of 1774, and that exciting incident, in our early border history, the unprovoked massacre of the whole family of the eloquent Logan. Many doubts and misrepresentations, had clouded the details of that signal atrocity, the perpetration of which had hastily, or rather, on false information, been fastened on Capt. Cresap. The obscurity which surrounded the subject, has now been effectually removed. The guilt has been unerringly traced, and with marked ability, to those, who were the actual culprits.

Maryland, Two Hundred Years Ago, being our seventh annual address, by S. F. Streeter, Esq. carries us back to the days of Charles the First, and leads us through the trials, adventures and persevering enterprise of the early colonists. The lucid narrative of incidents, so honorable to our progenitors, is alike accurate in detail, and grateful to the reader.

The Society is greatly indebted, for its eighth address, to the Rev. Geo. W. Burnap, D. D. who happily selected for his theme, the Origin and Causes of Democracy in America. To an essay of such high merit, it is saying but little, to add, that full justice is done to this attractive subject. The style is as remarkable for its purity, as are the deductions strictly logical, from the positions, so truthfully and justly assumed.

In addition to these essays there have, also, been published, several valuable papers. Amongst which, are Memorials of Columbus, by Robert Dodge, Esq. the Argentine Republic, by S. F. Streeter, Esq. and Early Currency in the Colonies, by the same gentleman. Besides these, a number of instructive productions, not yet published, have been read, by Dr. Wm. M. Wood, U. S. A.

Geo. L. L. Davis, and S. F. Streeter, Esqrs. All of these essays come mainly within the range of our designs, and supply acceptable additions to our collections.

From the commencement of the association, up to the present time, we have enrolled 466 members, of whom we have lost 19 by death, and 146 by resignation or removal from the city. But, at no period have our rolls been so well filled, as they are, at the present moment. In the month of May, of last year, they contained 250 names, whilst now they swell up to 301. No better evidence can be adduced, to prove the advancement as well as the abiding popularity of the Society.

Our correspondence and interchange of donations with other institutions, is maintained in a manner, that is every way useful and gratifying. Nor has there been any relaxation in the liberality of the Federal Government, our Senators in Congress, or of other gentlemen, towards us. Highly valuable acquisitions are daily made, from these sources, as well as from many of the State Governments, to our rich stores, whether in public documents, early history of the colonies, explorations, surveys, geography, ethnology, or in statistics. So likewise, in manuscripts, medals, coins, and mineralogy. It will not be out of place here, to recall to your attention, the state papers, recently printed, at great cost, by Massachusetts, New York and Pennsylvania, copies of which have courteously been presented to us. These commendable publications relate, for the most part, to original colonial documents, and are produced in a manner, every way worthy those great States.

Of the manuscripts presented to us, too much commendation can hardly be awarded to those received from Geo. Peabody, Esq. now of London. They disclose, for the first time, the contents of the large mass of original documents, relating to the colonial days of Maryland, and carefully preserved in the British State Paper Office. This acceptable gift from Mr. Peabody, consists of eleven volumes, admirably arranged, and beautifully executed. They comprise the whole of our colonial history, and any document we may desire to possess, is now placed within our reach. The grateful acknowledgments of the Society, so eminently due, have been proffered to the liberal donor, by the Corresponding Secretary. The same gentleman has also presented our thanks to Maj. Gen. Towson, U. S. A. for his magnificent donation of coins and medals, classified and arranged by that gallant officer, in nineteen appropriate cases. The mineralogical specimens, presented by Lewis Howell, Esq. have not yet been placed in an accessible condition, so requisite to render them available. It has been suggested, however, to raise a Committee on Natural History, to which they, with other similar objects, will be entrusted.

The Library now contains 2,123 volumes, relating chiefly, to historical, or to such other subjects, as are in strict accordance with our purposes. Of these, 605 volumes consist of U. S. congressional and executive documents, forming an invaluable and perfect series, which, together with our 307 volumes of Gazettes, furnish ample and highly useful sources of reference.

A very complete catalogue of the manuscripts has been made, and deposited in port folios, by the Assistant Librarian, under the direction of the Library Committee. They are thus rendered of easy access, an advantage, which they did not previously possess. He has also made a catalogue of all our other acquisitions, excepting the Library. It has been an arduous task, but was greatly needed, and has been well executed. I would recommend that it, with a list of the members, be now printed.

The Gallery of Fine Arts continues to flourish, and some highly appreciated additions have recently been made to the collection of paintings. There now remains scarce a doubt that, in a few years, we shall possess a Gallery, honorable to the city and creditable to the unwearied exertions of the committee, to which that department is confided. The last exhibition of paintings, compared well, if it did not surpass any of its predecessors in variety and excellence. It gave a signal manifestation of advancement in that taste, which guides the selection of those rare productions of art, which were so liberally contributed to the exhibition by our citizens. Though subjecting them to much inconvenience, yet they have not only borne it cheerfully, but have ever acceded to our requests. I feel assured that you will give your full acquiescence, in now presenting to them our sincere thanks, for their unvarying kindness.

The annual dinners and monthly soirees of the Society, have been well attended, and seem to have largely promoted its success, as well as a more intimate and social intercourse among its members. They tend also, to create a vivid and concerted movement of an association, linked together, by no pecuniary, or other tie, than that of a generous desire for the public good. As the cost of these re-unions is paid by those only who participate in them, they are, in no way, a charge on the general fund of the Treasury. And, in like manner, the Gallery sustains itself, and draws nothing from means, that are devoted exclusively to the support of the institution in its more appropriate functions.

The prosperity of the Society is undoubted, whilst it has more than come up to the most sanguine hopes of its friends, however ardent. A foundation too, has been prudently laid, to secure its future from casualty or decadence. From its origin to the present day, it has never met with a failure. In all that has been undertaken, it has succeeded, and a perseverance in the caution and energy, which have, invariably, characterised its course, cannot fail to ensure a continuance of its healthful progress.

With a surplus of means, to be invested, for future increment, and a roll of members, which is enlarged at each monthly meeting, you have a Gallery of Fine Arts, steadily advancing to its object. With an increasing Library, of the choicest works, you have a large array of manuscripts, alike essential to the historian or annalist. And, with an admirable collection of medals, coins, and minerals, you have the autographs and portraits of men, distinguished for virtue and patriotism. Such are the materials, for the maintenance of the Society; for the study of history and its evidences, or of general knowledge; and for the gratification, or improvement of taste, that you have secured. I think then, gentlemen, we have every reason to congratulate ourselves, on the elevated position, to which our labors have brought us.

J. SPEAR SMITH, *President.*

4th May, 1854.

LIST OF MEMBERS.

Geo. W. Andrews,
Wm. S. Appleton,
J. J. Atkinson,
R. H. Attwell,
Jas. W. Allnutt,
Geo. J. Appold,
Theodore R. Appold,
Wm. Meade Addison,
R. Snowden Andrews,
Jas. M. Buchanan,
Wm. Geo. Baker,
Geo. Brown,
Geo. Wm. Brown,
F. W. Brune,
F. W. Brune, Jr.
John C. Brune,
Wm. H. Brune,
John Buckler, M. D.
Thos. H. Buckler, M. D.
Robt. P. Brown,
Robt. D. Brown,
C. Bradenbaugh,
N. C. Brooks,
Robert D. Burns,
J. C. Backus, D. D.

James L. Bartol,
James Bordley,
Geo. W. Burnap, D. D.
Aug. W. Bradford,
Thos. E. Bond, Jr. M. D.
Thos. D. Baird,
Robert C. Barry,
Geo. S. Brown,
J. C. Baugher,
David R. Brown,
Wm. Bose,
Hugh Lennox Bond,
James H. Bevans,
Wm. M. Burwell,
John J. Baltzell,
Geo. W. Byrd,
Francis X. Brenan,
Wm. Brown,
Emanuel Baltzell,
Geo. B. Coale,
E. S. Courtney,
B. U Campbell,
James C. Coale,
Charles Carroll,
C. O. Cone, M. D.

J. Paul Cockey, M. D.
Chas. R. Carroll,
Allen A. Chapman,
Francis A. Crook,
Chas. Carroll, Jr.
J. A. Cunningham,
Wm. B. Canfield,
Ira Canfield,
David Cushing,
Mendes I. Cohen,
Andrew I. Cohen,
James Cortlan, Jr.
Thos. Corner,
A. F. Crane,
John I. Donaldson,
Samuel I. Donaldson,
Samuel C. Donaldson,
Thomas Donaldson,
Robt. A. Dobbin,
Jacob R. Drége,
John R. W. Dunbar, M. D.
Austin Dall,
W. H. Diffenderffer,
H. Diffenderffer,
Geo. L. L. Davis,
Henry Winter Davis,
Chas. H. Dupuy,
Isaac De Ford,
John M. Edgar,
Thos. Edmondson, M. D.
Basil T. Elder,
H. W. Ellicott,
James Ellicott,
W. Frederick Frick,
John Fonerden, M. D.
Robert Fulton, M. D.
Andrew Flanagan,
Wm. H. Gatchell,
John M. Gordon,
J. J. Graves, M. D.
Alexander B. Gordon,
Fred. B. Graff,
Chas. J. M. Gwinn,
Samuel K. George,
Geo. S. Gibson, M. D.
Geo. M. Gill,
Edward M. Greenway,
Levin Gale,
John P. Gunn, M. D.
Edward Gray,
James George,
Wm. H. Graham,
Chas. R. Gwynn,
Hugh Gelston,
Chas. E. Gardner,
J. Morrison Harris,
James Hall, M. D.
Wm. Hamilton,
John B. Howell,
Johns Hopkins,
Robert Hull,
Wm. G. Harrison,
Robert S. Hollins,
Henry Hardesty,
Lewis Howell,
John Hanan,
Samuel Hurlbut,
Henry R. Hazlehurst,
Wm. Harrison,
Cumberland D. Hollins,
Samuel O. Hoffman,
Alexander H. Hobbs,

Edward Hinckley,
Edmund A. Harrison,
Wm. R. Hodges,
Geo. C. Irwin,
M. Courtney Jenkins,
Austin Jenkins,
Reverdy Johnson,
Rev. J. R. Jarboe,
Hugh Jenkins,
John P. Kennedy,
Edward Kurtz,
J. T. Keys,
Robert R. Kirkland,
Wm. H. Keighler,
Anthony Kennedy,
Camillus Kidder,
Wm. Geo. Krebs,
Wm. M. Kemp, M. D.
John H. B. Latrobe,
Benjamin H. Latrobe,
Z. Collins Lee,
Robert Leslie,
Martin Lewis,
Wm. P. Lemmon,
Randolph B. Latimer,
J. C. Legrand,
S. S. Lee,
J. H. Luckett,
Henry B. Latrobe,
Francis B. Loney,
B. Rush Lloyd,
Edward Laroque,
John Lester,
Alonzo Lilly,
James Lucas,
Ferdinand C. Latrobe,

Brantz Mayer,
Chas. F. Mayer,
James H. McHenry,
Ramsay McHenry,
Wm. McKim,
Haslett McKim,
Robert M. McLane,
John V. L. McMahon,
John B. Morris,
John Murphy,
Thos. Murphy,
Wm. E. Mayhew,
Jonathan Meredith,
Leonard Mackall, M. D.
Wm. D. Miller,
Wm. E. Mayhew, Jr.
Henry Mankin,
Jos. C. Manning,
Robert Mickle,
Isaac Munroe,
Wm. M. Medcalfe,
G. W. Miltenberger, M. D.
Geo. H. Miles,
Samuel H. Martin, M. D.
J. G. Morris, D. D.
James Malcolm,
A. D. Miller,
Chas. T. Maddox,
Jos. Merefield,
M. W. Merryman, M. D.
J. G. Morris, Jr.
D. J. McKew, M. D.
Charles F. Mayer, of L.
Francis V. Moale,
Jos. H. Meredith,
Chas. C. McTavish,

Francis B. Mayer,
Geo. Maund,
Wm. Morrison,
Thos. Mackenzie,
J. Spear Nicholas,
Geo. Neilson,
J. C. Neilson,
J. Saurin Norris,
Wm. H. Owens,
C. Oliver O'Donnell,
Chas. H. Pitts,
Robert Purviance,
Robert Purviance, Jr.
Wm. P. Preston,
Enoch Pratt,
James R. Partridge,
Wm. A. Poor,
Wm. B. Perine,
John G. Proud,
Wm. S. Peterkin,
Benjamin C. Presstman,
Neilson Poe,
John F. Pickerell,
J. Hall Pleasants,
J. D. Pratt,
Edwin L. Parker,
Robert W. Pendleton,
Alexander Penn,
Lloyd N. Rogers,
Jos. Robinson,
Jos. Reynolds,
H. J. Rogers,
Wm. Reynolds,
Andrew Reid,
Chas. Reese,
A. Schumacher,
Wm. Schley,
S. F. Streeter,
John Spear Smith,
Samuel W. Smith,
Thos. W. Smith,
John S. Sumner,
B. R. Spalding,
Moses Sheppard,
J. H. Stickney,
Robert M. Smith,
Thos. Swann,
Wm. C. Shaw,
C. A. Schaefer,
P. H. Sullivan,
Nathan R. Smith, M. D.
Geo. H. Steuart,
Thomas M. Smith,
Lewis H. Steiner, M. D.
J. Hopkinson Smith,
J. Sellman Shipley,
J. Dean Smith,
Edward Slade,
Laurence Sangston,
J. Donnell Smith,
Henry F. Stickney,
James H. Stone,
Geo. E. Sangston,
Henry Stockbridge,
Henry C. Scott,
Thos. Sappington, M. D.
Wm. A. Talbott,
St. George W. Teackle,
J. Hanson Thomas, M. D.
John D. Toy,
Laurence Thomsen,
Isaac Tyson, Jr.

Wm. R. Travers,
Wm. H. Travers,
Alexander Turnbull,
Wm. G. Thomas,
John S. Tyson,
George Tiffany,
Geo. P. Tiffany,
Osmond Tiffany,
Luke Tiernan,
Jno. Jacob Thomsen,
Wm. W. Taylor,
Richard W. Tyson,
Frederick C. Von Kapff,
Herman Von Kapff,
Adalbert J. Volck,
P. G. Van Winkle,
B. C, Ward,
Geo. F. R. Waesche,
Samuel G. Wyman,
David S. Wilson,
Thomas Wilson,
James Winchester,
Wm. F. Worthington,
Ambrose A. White,
Henry Webster,
J. A. Weston,
Wm. Woodville,
J. O. Wharton, M. D.
Wm. Woodward,
O. H. Williams,
John H. Wyman,
Geo. W. Waters,
Geo. Warner, Jr.
Thos. Winans,
Geo. W. Ward,
Thos. H. Williams,
James H. Wood,
J. Thomas Wood,
Coleman Yellott,
Wm. H. Young.

HONORARY MEMBERS.

James M. Wayne,...........................	*Savannah, Geo.*
J. K. Tefft,..................................	" "
Geo. Folsom,...............................	*New York.*
Chas. Wilkes, U. S. N.....................	*Washington, D. C.*
Geo. Bancroft,............................	*Boston, Mass.*
Wm. H. Prescott,..........................	" "
Edward Everett,...........................	" "
Jared Sparks,..............................	*Cambridge, Mass.*
B. Silliman,...............................	*New Haven, Conn.*
David Hoffman,............................	*London.*
J. R. Bartlett,............................	*New York.*
Jas. Renwick,..............................	" "
Prof. Rafn,................................	*Copenhagen.*
Geo. S. Hilliard,..........................	*Boston, Mass.*
David Ridgely,............................	*Washington, D. C.*
Baron Fred. Von Baumer,................	*Berlin, Prussia.*
Lewis Cass,................................	*Detroit, Mich.*
Washington Irving,.......................	*New York.*
Robert Walsh,..............................	*Paris.*
J. McP. Berrien,...........................	*Georgia.*
W. Gilmore Simms,........................	*Charleston, S. C.*
Champolion Figeac,........................	*Paris.*
Count Leon de la Borde,..................	"
Gulian C. Verplanck,......................	*New York.*
Alexander Vattemare,.....................	*Paris.*
Peter Force,................................	*Washington, D. C.*
Prof. Jos. Henry,..........................	" "
Rev. Dr. Ryder,............................	*Georgetown, D. C.*
Pedro de Angelis,..........................	*Montevideo.*
Robert C. Winthrop,.......................	*Boston, Mass.*
James M. Gilliss, U. S. N.................	*Washington, D. C.*
Sir Henry Lytton Bulwer,.................	*England.*

A. Calderon de la Barca,................... *Spain.*
Thos. H. Benton,......................... *Missouri.*
Thos. Corwin,.............................. *Ohio.*
Alex. H. H. Stuart,........................ *Virginia.*
George Ticknor,........................... *Mass.*
George Peabody,........................... *London.*
Sir Edward Bulwer Lytton,................ *England.*
Martin Farquhar Tupper,.................. " "
Conway Robinson,......................... *Richmond, Va.*
Millard Fillmore,.......................... *Buffalo.*
Thomas Sully,.............................. *Philadelphia.*
Gen. J. N. Almonte,....................... *Mexico.*

CORRESPONDING MEMBERS.

Col. Jose Arĕnales,........................ *Buenos Ayres.*
J. Mora Moss,.............................. " "
John R. Baltzell,.......................... *Frederick, Md.*
James McSherry,........................... " "
Thos. G. Pratt,............................ *Annapolis, Md.*
Wm. F. Lynch, U. S. N..................... *Baltimore Co. Md.*
James A. Pearce,.......................... *Chestertown,* "
Wills de Hass,............................. *Wheeling.*
Anthony Kimmel,.......................... *Frederick Co. Md.*
Lieut. Col. Dixon S. Miles,................ *U. S. Army.*
Maj. Gen. Nathan Towson,................. " "
Wm. B. Buchanan,......................... *Wheeling.*
Wm. McCarty,.............................. *Sunbury, Pa.*
John B. Kerr,.............................. *Easton, Md.*
Jos. C. G. Kennedy,....................... *Washington, D. C.*

N. B. Shurtleff, M. D......................... *Boston, Mass.*
Edward D. Ingraham,........................ *Philadelphia.*
Job R. Tyson,.................................. " "
Nathan H. Wise,............................... *Maryland.*
J. Romeyn Broadhead,....................... *New York.*
Edward Armstrong,........................... *Philadelphia.*
John H. Rauch, M. D.......................... *Burlington, Iowa.*
George W. Curtis,............................. *New York.*
Frederic Kidder,............................... *Boston, Mass.*
Samuel G. Drake,.............................. " "
Geo. W. Brown,................................ *Ellsworth, Me.*
Lieut. Wm. Gibson,........................... *U. S. Navy.*
Josiah Curtis, M. D........................... *Boston, Mass.*
Peregrine Wroth, M. D....................... *Chestertown, Md.*
Gen. Tench Tilghman,........................ *Talbot Co.* "
Alexander Evans,.............................. *Cecil Co.* "
James Lowry Donaldson, U. S. A............. *Baltimore.*
James Lenox,................................... *New York.*
Robert Davidson, D. D........................ *Brunswick, N. J.*
Ephraim M. Wright,............................ *Boston, Mass.*
Isaac E. Heister,............................... *Pennsylvania.*

CATALOGUE

OF THE

MANUSCRIPTS, MAPS, MEDALS,

COINS,

STATUARY, PORTRAITS AND PICTURES;

AND AN

ACCOUNT OF THE LIBRARY

OF THE

Maryland Historical Society,

MADE IN 1854,

UNDER THE DIRECTION OF THE LIBRARY COMMITTEE AND PRESIDENT,

BY

LEWIS MAYER,

Assistant Librarian.

BALTIMORE:

PRINTED FOR THE SOCIETY BY JOHN D. TOY.

1854.

MANUSCRIPTS.

I. DOCUMENTS RELATING TO HISTORY OF MARYLAND.

Port Folio No. 1.

Contains all the Manuscripts, here mentioned, relating to the EARLY HISTORY OF MARYLAND.

1623—1681.

No. 1. Account of Sir George Calvert, pp. 11, and Charta Avaloniæ, pp. 25, copied from the originals among the Sloane MSS. in the British Museum.

2. Translation of the Charter for Avalon. MS. from British Museum.

3. A Relation of the Colony of the Lord Baron of Baltemore, in Maryland, near Virginia; a Narrative of the First Voyage to Maryland in 1633, by the REV. FATHER WHITE, and Sundry Reports from the Jesuit Fathers of the Colony, to the Superior General at Rome. Copied from the Archives of the Jesuits' College at Rome, and presented to the Maryland Historical Society, by Georgetown College, pp. 53, *MS. in Latin.*

4. Translation of the same into English, by Mr. N. C. Brooks.

5. Copy of "A Relation of the Successful Beginnings of the Lord Baltemore's Plantation, in Maryland," pp. 27, written in 1634.

6. A Relation of Maryland, by one of the first Settlers, published, London, 1635. Copied from an original in the Library of Harvard University and presented by Mr. J. R. Partridge, pp. 44.

7. Copies of Letters preserved in Georgetown College, from Members of the Society of Jesus, soliciting employment as Missionaries in Maryland, 1640, pp. 50. Presented by Mr. B. U. Campbell.

8. "The Answer to Tom Tell Troth, the Practise of Princes and the Lamentations of the Kirke. Written by the Lord Baltemore, late Secretary of State," pp. 108, London, printed, 1642.

9. "The Lord Baltemore's case, concerning the Province of Maryland, adjoining to Virginia, in America; with full and clear answers to all material objections, touching his Rights, Jurisdiction and Proceedings there," pp. 32, London, printed, 1653.

10. "An additional Brief Narrative of a late Bloody Design against the Protestants in Anne Arundel County and Severn, in Maryland, in the Country of Virginia, as also the extraordinary deliverance of these poor oppressed people. Set forth by Roger Heamans, commander of the ship Golden Lyon, an eye witness there," pp. 32. London, July 24, 1655.

11. A MS. tract entitled "Hammond *versus* Heamans, or an Answer to an audacious Pamphlet, published by an impudent and ridiculous fellow named Roger Heamans, &c. &c. &c." By John Hammond, a sufferer in those calamities. Printed at London for the use of the Author, pp. 38.

THE FOLLOWING DOCUMENTS ARE COPIES FROM THE ORIGINALS IN THE STATE PAPER OFFICE, LONDON.

12. Petition of James Clements and others, November, 1633.

13. A Law of Maryland concerning Religion.

14. Declaration shewing the Illegality of the Proceedings of the Patent of Maryland.

15. Letter from William Penn, Sept. 16, 1681, cautioning James Frisby, Edward Jones and others, in Maryland, not to pay taxes to Lord Baltimore.

MARYLAND PROPRIETARY AND STATE PAPERS.

1637—1776.

The following documents were delivered to the Maryland Historical Society, in accordance with the 27th Resolution of the Legislature of 1846-7.

BOUND BOOKS—(*Not in Port Folios.*)

No.				
1.	Proprietary Council Book,		. . . .	1637—50.
2.	do.	do.	. . . . . .	1650—69.
3.	do.	do.	. . . . . .	1656—68.
4.	do.	do.	. . . . . .	1669—71.
5.	do.	do.	. . . . . .	1721—28.
6.	Gov. Sharpe's Letter Book,		. . . .	1754—56.
7.	do. do.	do.	. . . .	1767—71.
8.	Journal of the Council of Safety at Annapolis,			1775—76.

Port Folio No. 2.

Contains a number of paper books relating to the following subjects:

1638—1769.

No. 1. Historical Notices of Maryland, in five parts.

2. Account of the Revenue Laws of the Province in two parts.

3. Some Acts of the Assembly of 1638—39.

4. Instructions of Frederick, Lord Baltimore, to Gov. Sharpe. Additional Instructions, March, 1753.

5. Instructions to Frederick, Lord Baltimore, from George II. with regard to Trade and Navigation, May 10, 1753, signed by his Majesty.

6. Record of a Congress of the Provinces at Albany, 1754, relative to the Indians, and for the purpose of entering into Articles of Confederacy for their general defence.

7. Answers to the Queries in the "Morning Chronicle," with regard to the Taxes, Revenues, &c. of the Province of Maryland, Sept. 1758.

Answers to the Queries relative to the Government of Maryland, published in the "Public Ledger." Nov. 1767.

8. Bill-Book of Lord Baltimore, 1766—1769.

9. Catalogue of North American Trees and Shrubs which will thrive in England.

Port Folio No. 3.

Contains ORIGINAL INSTRUCTIONS from the Lord Proprietary to the Governor of Maryland, and Papers and Letters, relating to the REVENUE, TRADE and CIVIL AFFAIRS of the Province.

1684—1775.

No. 1. Instructions of Charles, Third Lord Baltimore, to the Land Council of Maryland, May 5, 1684.

2. Instructions of Charles, Fifth Lord Baltimore, to Gov. Benedict Leonard Calvert, March 14, 1726.

3. Instructions of Frederick, Lord Baltimore, to Edward Lloyd, Agent and Receiver General in Maryland, March 30, 1753.

4. Instructions of the same to Gov. Sharpe, to proclaim his Majesty George III, Oct. 30, 1760.

5. Instructions of the same to the same, Dec. 20 and 27, 1760.

6. Instructions of the same to the same, January 16, 1765.

7. Imperfect Instructions from the same to the same.

8. Copy of an Instruction of the King to all his Governors in America, directing them how to transmit to him accounts of the proceedings in their respective provinces.

9. Printed Instructions to Commanders of H. M's Ships in America.

10. Printed list of H. M's Ships stationed in America.

11. Copy of a Letter of Lord Colvill, Commander-in-Chief of H. M's Ships in America, to the Captain of the Diana, ordering him to proceed to the Chesapeake to convoy a fleet of merchantmen to the Downs, Nov. 7, 1761.

12. Memoranda concerning the annual charge of maintaining the establishment of Maryland; account of the mode pursued in granting lands in the Province; and of the Quit Rents.

13. Copies of two Proclamations by Governors Charles Calvert and Ogle, in 1725 and 1732, concerning the landed property in the Province.

14. Copy of Letters from President Tasker to the Judges of the Land Office, 1749–51.

15. Account of Lord Baltimore's annual Quit Rents for the Eastern Shore in 1759.

16. Account of Jonathan Hall with Lord Baltimore, 1767.

17. Petition of Samuel Beall of Frederick County to Governor Sharpe, 1756.

18. His Account with Lord Baltimore, 1762.

19. Statement of the Sales of Lord Baltimore's Manors, &c., signed by Horatio Sharpe and Daniel Dulany, 1766—1768.

20. Account how the money granted in February, 1756, for ranging parties, was expended.

21. Account how the money granted in July, 1764, for H. M's Service, was expended.

22. Account of Disbursements made by Gov. Sharpe for the Western Expedition, by desire of Gen. Forbes, &c. 1758.

23. Two Letters from the Commissioners of the Customs, London, 1764.

24. Certificate from Officers of the Customs, London, 1775.

25. Certificate from the Collector and Comptroller of the Port of Annapolis, 1766.

26. Copy of Report of Attorney and Solicitor Generals to Commissioners for Trade and Plantations, 1767.

27. Copy of a Report to the Privy Council on a petition from the inhabitants of Pennsylvania, shewing their defenceless condition, 1742.

28. Memoranda concerning the Fighting Parson, Bennet Allen, a *protegé* of Lord Baltimore and Gov. Sharpe.

29. Papers concerning the passage in Parliament of a Bill allowing the importation of Salt into the Province, 1754–55.

30. List of the Civil Officers of Maryland, in 1754, with their respective salaries.

31. Bond with special condition for the due execution of the office of Secretary of State of Maryland, from George Plater to the Honorable Cecilius Calvert.

Port Folio, No. 4.

Contains a large collection of letters addressed to the Governor of Maryland, and relating, chiefly, to the French War and American Revolution.

1751—1778.

32. Twenty-one letters from Frederick, Ld Baltimore, 1751–68.

33. Fifteen from Cecilius Calvert, secretary of Maryland, 1751—62.

34. Twenty-eight from Sir John St. Clair, 1755—60.

35. Fourteen from Gen. Amherst, 1759—62.

36. Thirteen from Gen. Forbes, April—October, 1758.

37. Two from Gen. Gage, 1764—65.

38. One from Col. Wm. Howe, 1758.

39. One from Col. Haldimand, in French, "

40. One from Major Halkett, "

41. One from Capt. James Sinclair, "

42. Letter from Gen. Shirley, concerning the dispute between Col. Washington and Capt. Dagworthy, with regard to the right of supreme command at Fort Cumberland, in Maryland, enclosing an extract of a letter to him from Gov. Dinwiddie, of Virginia, on the same subject, March 5, 1756.

Another letter from Gen. Shirley, relative to a proposed expedition against the French and Indians, on the Ohio;—speaks of Col. Washington as one to whom he would rather give the second command in the expedition, than any other provincial officer in America, May 16, 1756.

43. Deposition of an Indian Trader, concerning the French upon the Ohio.

44. Paper showing the number of Provincial troops to be raised for the year, 1756.

45. Letter from William Denny, announcing to Gov. Sharpe, his appointment as Governor of Pennsylvania, August 23, 1756.

46. Seven letters from Sir Thomas Robinson, to the Governor of Maryland, 1754—55.

47. Four from Wm. Pitt, 1756—57.

48. Four from Gen. Conway, 1765—66.

49. Two from Lord Shelburne, 1766.

50. Letter from Lord Hillsborough, with two letters from Edward Stanley, of the Custom House, London, to Thomas Bradshaw enclosing two depositions with regard to the murder of one Wm. Odgers, whose assassin had escaped to America. Also, a letter from Thomas Bradshaw to Richard Phelps. One from Gov. Sharpe, on the same subject, 1768. Two letters from Lord Hillsborough, 1768.

51. Two from Christopher Kilby, 1758—60.

52. Letter from Thomas Stephens, 1757.

53. Four letters from Stephen Bordley to Gov. Sharpe, and two to him from the Governor, 1756—60.

54. Letter from Gov. Sharpe to Philip Sharpe, 1760.

55. Letter of W. Sharpe enclosing an extract of a letter from Thomas Penn to Lord Shelburne, 1767.

56. Letter of Edmund Jennings, 1754.

57. Copy of a letter from Admiral Boscawen to Gov. Phipps, Oct. 1, 1755.

58. Copy of a letter from the Lords Commissioners for Trade and Plantations to Sir William Johnson, July 10, 1764.

59. Petition from the Council and Burgesses of Virginia to the King's most excellent Majesty, Memorial to the House of Lords and Remonstrance to the House of Commons, concerning the right of the People not to be taxed without their own consent.

60. Ten letters from Gov. Johnson of Maryland, to the General Assembly, enclosing letters to him from Washington, Pulaski, Luther Martin, Patrick Henry, Secretary Charles Thomson, Cols. Samuel Smith, Beatty, Hollingsworth, &c., written during the months of March and April, 1778.

61. Thirty-five letters from members of the Maryland Legislature and other public men, March, April, 1778.

END OF PAPERS RECEIVED FROM THE STATE OF MARYLAND.

THE GILMOR MARYLAND PAPERS.

This Collection of Manuscripts was presented to the Maryland Historical Society, by the late Mr. Robert Gilmor, of Baltimore. It embraces documents relating to Maryland, and the other Provinces, principally during the administration of Horatio Sharpe, as governor, from about 1753 to about 1770. The greater part of the papers of this period, were given to Mr. Gilmor by Mr. Ridout, whose father was Gov. Sharpe's secretary.

The remainder of the collection consists of papers and letters; a few relating to the early history of Maryland, but the chief portion to Revolutionary times.

Vol. I.

Contains documents referring to the Civil Affairs of the Province.

DIVISION, No. 1.

Contains the following:

1689—1770.

No. 1. Ordinance of the Convention, September 4, 1689, for regulating the civil and military officers of Maryland.

2. Ancient Plat of land in Maryland, 1690.

3. Land warrant, 1714, signed by Charles Carroll, keeper of the seals of Maryland.

4. Deed dated in 1734, signed by Samuel Ogle, governor of Maryland.

5. Deed dated 1735.

6. Instructions from Frederick, Lord Baltimore, to Gov. Sharpe, 1754.

7. Lord Baltimore's announcement to the Governor of Maryland, of the death of George II, and accession of George III, giving instructions to proclaim the latter, October 13, 1760.

8. Instructions from Lord Baltimore to Gov. Sharpe, Jan'y 16, 1765.

9. Instructions to the same, dated May 15, 1765.

10. Letter of condolence from Cæcilius Calvert on the death of George II, to Gov. Sharpe, October 30, 1760.

11. Power of Attorney from Cæcilius Calvert to Gov. Sharpe, with regard to the deputation of George Plater to the office of Secretary of the Province, 1754.

12. Letter from John Morton Jordan, Secretary of Lord Baltimore to Gov. Sharpe, August 16, 1768.

13. Two letters from Hugh Hamersley, Secretary of Lord Baltimore, to Gov. Sharpe, 1768–70.

14. Two proclamations by Gov. Sharpe, 1756–60.

15. Instructions from Gov. Sharpe to Capt. Ferguson, 1759.

16. Two letters from Edmund Jenings, 1743–54.

17. Bond with the signature of Thomas Bacon, (Digester of the Laws of Maryland,) 1754.

18 Two land certificates of Benedict Calvert, 1755–59.

19. Two Receipts for money, 1758–68.

20. Lease to Jos. Warford of the Fort Frederick Land, drawn up and signed, as a witness, by Gen. O. H. Williams, then a clerk in the Clerk's Office of Frederick County, 1765.

21. Letter from David Ross, to Gov. Sharpe, 1758.

22. Address to Gov. Sharpe, of the Lower House of Assembly, 1761.

23. Answers to the Queries, respecting the inhabitants, products, commerce, revenue, &c. of the province, sent to the Governor of Maryland by the Lords of Trade and Plantations in 1761, pp. 8, folio.

24. Petition of James Maccubbin to Gov. Sharpe, 1763.

25. Letter to Gov. Sharpe from Col. Thomas Cresap, father of the celebrated Capt. Michael Cresap, dated Old-Town, July 15, 1763. Published in Mr. Brantz Mayer's "Logan and Capt. Michael Cresap."

26. Letter from Robert Jenckins Henry, 1768.

27. Assessment for Worcester County, 1766, pp. 12.

28. Letter from Robert Heron, Collector of Somerset County, respecting the encroachments made by the Pennsylvanians on the trade of Nanticoke River, 1763.

29. Genealogy of the Brooke and Plunkett family, descended from Lord Baltimore.

DIVISION, No. 2.

1753—1782.

Contains many interesting papers relating to the dissensions in the parishes of Maryland; but more particularly to the conduct of a profligate parson, named Bennet Allen, a *protegé* of Lord Baltimore and Gov. Sharpe; who after a series of quarrels and disputes, killed Lloyd Dulany in a duel in London, in 1782, was tried for his life and acquitted.

DIVISION, No. 3.

1768—1769.

Contains addresses from the clergy, magistracy and legislature of Maryland to Gov. Sharpe, on his retirement from office, and his answers to some of them.

DIVISION, No. 4.

Contains the following Printed Documents:

1737—1768.

No. 1. Votes and Proceedings of the Lower House of Assembly, 1753, pp. 82, 12mo.

2. "The Case of the Province of Maryland touching the outrageous Riots which have been committed in the Borders of that Province by the inhabitants of Pensylvania," 1737.

3. "The Case of the Proprietors and Province of Pensilvania, and the three lower Counties of *New Castle, Kent* and *Sussex,* on Delaware," 1737.

4. His Majesty's Speech to the Parliament, Nov. 9, 1768.

5. "The Humble Address of the House of Commons to the King," 1768.

6. Several Maryland and Virginia "Gazettes," of the same period.

Vol. II.

Contains a large collection of papers and letters relating, for the most part, to the French War. There is also, in this volume, a number of papers, relating to Mason and Dixon's Line.

DIVISION, No. 1.

Contains the following Letters addressed to Gov. Sharpe, of Maryland:

1755—1776.

No. 1. Two letters from Gen. Braddock, one dated at Fort Cumberland, May 22, 1755.

2. Letter from Capt. Orme, aid to Gen. Braddock, giving Gov. Sharpe, an account of the battle of the Monongahela, fought July 9, 1755;—he mentions the gallantry of Col. Washington, dated at Fort Cumberland, July 18, 1755.

3. One from Capt. Bradstreet, dated Oswego, May 29, 1755.

4. One from Gov. Lawrence, dated Halifax, July 1, 1756.

5. One from Sir Charles Hardy, Fort George, April 30, 1757.

6. One from Col. Stanwix, 1757.

7. Four from Col. Bouquet, 1758—64, with a copy of Gov. Sharpe's answer to one of them.

8. Two from Major Halkett, 1758.

9. One from Sir John St. Clair, 1758.

10. One from Gen. Abercromby, 1758.

11. One from Daniel Clark, 1758.

12. Two from Capt. W. Morris, Crown Point, 1759.

13. Two from Gen. Amherst, 1759—60.

14. Two from Gen. Monckton, 1760.

15. Two from Gen. Gage, 1765.

16. Three from Sir William Johnson, 1767—68.

17. Letter from Admiral Boscawen to the Governor of Maryland, 1755.

18. One from Admiral Spry, with a list of the ships and vessels stationed in America, 1755.

19. One from Admiral Lord Colvill, 1757.

20. One from Capt. Adams, R. N., 1762.

21. Order of Sir James Douglas, Commander of H. M's ships and vessels stationed at the Barbadoes, 1760.

22. Letter to Gov. Sharpe from Sir Thomas Robinson, Secretary of State, 1755.

23. Four from J. Pownall, Secretary to the Board of Trade, 1755—76.

24. Five from the Commissioners of the Customs, 1753—61.

25. One from the Lords of Trade, 1764.

26. Two from Henry Fox, (afterwards Lord Holland,) 1756.

27. Two from William Pitt, (afterwards Earl of Chatham,) 1757—60.

28. One from the Earl of Holdernesse, 1757.

29. One from Lord Egremont, 1762.

30. Letter from Capt. Bosomworth to Lord Loudon, 1757.

31. Copy of The Report of the Earl of Loudon and Generals Abercromby and Stanwix, to the Lords Commissioners of His Majesty's Treasury, 1761.

32. Rules for settling rank and precedence in North America. Rank of Provincial, General and Field Officers in North America, 1756.

Letters to Gov. Sharpe from the following Governors.

33. One from Robt. H. Morris, of Pa., 1754.

34. Two from Wm. Denny, of Pa., 1756—59.

35. Two from James Hamilton, of Pa., 1760—62.

36. One from John Penn, of Pa., 1767.

37. One from J. Belcher, of N. J., 1754.

38. One from Henry Moore, of N. Y., 1765.

39. One from Robert Dinwiddie, of Va., 1757.

40. One from George Mercer, of Va., 1765.

41. Two from Gen. Shirley, 1755—56.

42. Account of the expenses of Richard Peters, and Govrs. Shirley and Morris on a journey from Philadelphia to Annapolis, 1755.

43. Letters written by Richard Peters, (Grandfather of the Reporter of the Supreme Court,) 1761.

44. Designs by Judge Peters, for a Medal intended for the Captors of Major André.

DIVISION, No. 2.

Contains a number of miscellaneous papers, relating chiefly to the FRENCH WAR.

1675—1770.

No. 1. Patent of land, signed Nov. 1, 1675, by Sir Edmund Andross.

2. Report of a Committee of the Assembly of New Hampshire, dated Portsmouth, May 13, 1711.

3. Several printed documents relating to the dispute between Gov. Belcher and the House of Representatives, of New Hampshire, 1739.

4. Act of the province of Rhode Island, appointing commissioners to meet Gen. Shirley and the commissioners from the northern Colonies, 1755.

5. List of the Captains, Lieutenants and Ensigns of the Virginia Forces, April, 1755.

6. Minutes of the Council held at Alexandria, April 14, 1755, over which Gen. Braddock presided.

7. Instructions to Sir Wm. Johnson from James De Lancey, Governor of New York, with regard to the attack upon Crown Point, dated April 16, 1755.

8. Message of an Oneida Sachem to Sir Wm. Johnson, 1756.

9. Extract of a "talk" from Conoquieson to the same, at a Congress of the Indians in July, 1770.

10. Letter from Sir Guy Carleton to the same, 1766.

11. Extract of a letter from Sir Wm. Johnson to the Earl of Hillsborough, 1770.

12. Copy of the Articles of Capitulation of St. John's, Sept. 18, 1762.

13. Copy of Col. Bradstreet's Treaty with the Indians, Aug. 12, 1764.

14. Proclamation by Gov. Fauquier, of Virginia, 1766.

15. Journal of Lieut. James Gorrell, commencing at Detroit, Sept. 8, 1761, and ending at Montreal, Aug. 13, 1763, containing an account of several councils held with the Indians;—also, showing the villany used by the Canadians to corrupt the Indians, and excite them against the English, together with a short account of the expedition conducted in the fall of 1763, by Major Wilkins, from Niagara to Detroit, pp. 26, 8vo.

DIVISION No. 3.

1751—1766.

Contains the following original documents, relating entirely, with the exception of the last, to the Boundary Line between Pennsylvania and Maryland, commonly called Mason and Dixon's Line.

No. 1. Field notes of the Surveyors employed to run the Transpeninsular Line in 1751, pp. 40, 18mo.

2. Letter from the Commissioners appointed by Richard Penn, to the Maryland Commissioners, Oct. 20, 1760.

3. Letter to Gov. Sharpe from Thomas Garnett and Jonathan Hall, Maryland Surveyors, Sept. 5, 1761.

4. Mr. Garnett's account of expenditures, 1761.

5. Letter from John Emory, one of the Surveyors, with a sketch of the Tangent Line, Dec. 10, 1761.

6. Letter from the Pennsylvania to the Maryland Commissioners, Nov. 18, 1762.

7. Letter from Chas. Mason and Jere. Dixon to Mr. Ridout, Secretary to Gov. Sharpe, April 14, 1766.

8. Letter of the same to Gov. Sharpe, June 10.

9. Letter of the same to the same, Aug. 12.

10. Letter of the same to the same, Oct. 1.

11. Letter from the Pennsylvania to the Maryland Commissioners, March, 15, 1768.

12. Col. Cresap's original MS. Map of the course of the Potomac, and a copy of the same.

"This was the *first* map ever made to show the course and fountains of the north and south branches of the Potomac river."

Vol. III.

Contains documents relating to Maryland at the epoch of the REVOLUTION and a number of miscellaneous letters, &c. written at the same period.

DIVISION, No. 1.

Papers and Letters of the "Homony Club," a convivial association of Annapolis, which flourished just before the Revolution, and of which Governors Eden and Johnson, Judge Samuel Chase, Daniel Dulany, John Hall and other distinguished citizens of Annapolis, were members.

DIVISION, No. 2.

Contains letters relating to the STAMP ACT and the other measures of the British ministry for taxing America.

1764—1771.

1. Two letters from Dunk, Lord Halifax, 1764–65.
2. Two from Gen. H. S. Conway, Secretary of State, 1766.
3. Letter from the Duke of Richmond. Duplicate of the same, 1766.
4. One from Sir Grey Cooper, 1766.
5. One from Lord Shelburne, 1766.
6. One from Lachlin Macleane, Secretary to Lord Shelburne, 1767.
7. One from the Earl of Hillsborough, 1771, to Gov. Eden.
8. Letter to Gov. Sharpe from Zachariah Hood, Commissioner of Stamps for Maryland, dated November 11, 1765, New York, whither he had been obliged to flee for safety.
9. One from Capt. James Hawker, R. N. with regard to the delivery of Stamps on board his ship, Oct. 22, 1765.
10. One from Capt. John Brown, R. N. as to what he shall do with a collection of Stamps on board his vessel, June 16, 1766. The Stamp Act was repealed, March 18, 1766.
11. Printed Resolutions of the inhabitants of Maryland not to import certain articles into the province, Annapolis, June 22, 1769.

DIVISION, No. 3.

Contains Papers relating to Maryland during and since the REVOLUTION:

1774—1791.

No. 1. Package of Continental Money.

2. Proceedings of the Committee of the Legislature of Maryland, June 22, 1774.

3. Resolves of Congress to raise ten companies of Riflemen, two of them in Maryland, two in Virginia and six in Pennsylvania, June 14, 1775.

4. Letter from Benjamin Rumsey, 1776.

5. One from Stephen West, 1776.

6. One from Judge Samuel Chase to Gov. Johnson, 1777.

7. One from Josias Polk and Edward Lloyd, to Thomas S. Lee, 1777.

8. One from Wm. Paca to Gov. Johnson, 1778.

9. One from Daniel of St. Thos. Jenifer, 1779.

10. Address to Gov. Johnson, by the Maryland Line, in the handwriting of Gen. Smallwood.

11. Arrangement of the officers of the four Maryland Companies of Riflemen, 1781, in the handwriting of the same.

12. Two letters from John Hanson, 1782.

13. Letter of Wm. Le Conte, 1783.

14. One from Elias Boudinot, President of Congress, to Gov. Paca, 1783.

15. Address of the General Assembly of Maryland, to Major Gen. Greene, January 15, 1783. Duplicate of the same.

16. Resolutions of the Officers of the Southern Army, signed by Generals Daniel Morgan and O. H. Williams, in the handwriting of the latter.

17. Address of the Officers of the Continental Army to Congress, dated White Plains, Sept. 13, 1778, in the handwriting of Gen. O. H. Williams.

18. Address of the Officers of the Maryland Line, to the Governor and General Assembly of Maryland, in 1779, in the handwriting of the same.

19. Address of the same to the General Assembly, in 1783, in the handwriting of the same.

20. Letter to Gen. Washington from D. Plunket and Gen. Williams, written by the latter, April 21, 1789.

21. Return of the Hospital, from Dr. Brown to Gen. Williams, 1781.

22. Letter from Col. Scammell to the same, 1780.

23. Letter from James McHenry and R. H. Harrison, dated at head-quarters, Orangetown, Augt. 12, 1780, to the same.

24. Two Letters from Major Giles to the same, 1780–81.

25. One from Gen. Gist to the same, 1783.

26. One from Gen. Smallwood to the same, 1784.

27. Seven letters from Wm. Smith to his son-in-law, Gen. Williams, 1789—91.

DIVISION No. 4.

Contains the following papers relating to BALTIMORE-TOWN.

1773—1794.

No. 1. Papers concerning Robert Moreton, preventive officer at Baltimore, 1773.

2. Warrant of election to represent Baltimore-Town in the General Assembly, in 1773.

3. Correspondence of the Committee of Safety of Baltimore with other Committees and persons elsewhere; together with the proceedings of the Committee, 1775—76.

4. Articles of Association of the Independent Company, commanded by Capt. John Stricker with the signatures of the members.

DIVISION No. 5.

With the following miscellaneous papers and letters of Revolutionaıy date, the collection of Manuscripts presented to the Society, by Mr. Gilmor, closes:

1770—1789.

No. 1. Letter from Daniel Chamier, of Baltimore, dated Boston, June 18, 1770, giving an account of the affray between the citizens and the soldiery. He takes the part of the latter.

2. Commission to James Otis, Nov. 15, 1775, from George III, signed by James Otis, Benjamin Lincoln and others.

3. Letter from Col. Josiah Bartlett, signer of the Declaration of Independence, January 20, 1776.

4. Letter from Robert Morris, signer of the Declaration of Independence, to William Whipple, of New Hampshire, also a signer, 1777.

5. One from Col. Henry Laurens, to the same, 1779.

6. Bill of Exchange drawn by Robert Morris, as minister of Finance, 1783.

7. Letter written by Gen. Thomas Conway, 1778.

8. Letter from Patrick Henry to Richard Henry Lee, 1779.

9. One from Dr. Witherspoon, signer of the Declaration of Independence, to the same, 1781.

10. One from John Adams, dated Amsterdam, September 4, 1780, to Samuel Huntington, President of Congress.

11. One from Ralph Izard, 1783.

12. Warrant for money, signed by Sir Guy Carleton, 1778.

13. Order for money to be paid, from Lord Dorchester, (formerly Sir Guy Carleton,) 1789.

14. Warrant of money to be paid to Col. Goreham, signed by Gen. Massey, commandant in Nova Scotia, 1778.

15. Subsistence Warrant, signed by Sir Henry Clinton, 1781.

16. Memorial of Capt. McKinnon to Col. Balfour, Commandant at Charleston, S. C. and two warrants to the former, one signed by Gen. Leslie, 1781.

17. Printed "Account of Receipts and Expenditures by the Superintendent of Finance, to December 31, 1781."

18. Philadelphia Evening Post of November 2, 1782.

THE PEABODY INDEX

TO

MARYLAND DOCUMENTS IN THE STATE PAPER OFFICE, LONDON.

THIS elaborate MANUSCRIPT was prepared by Mr. Henry Stevens, at the cost and under the direction of Mr. GEORGE PEABODY, who presented it to the Maryland Historical Society as a testimonial of his regard for the State in which he formerly dwelt. The collection is contained in eleven volumes or, solander cases, bound in blue morocco, under lock. There are abstracts and descriptions of *one thousand seven hundred and twenty-nine* documents extending from the year 1626 to 1780, exhibiting a chronological reference to the complete COLONIAL HISTORY OF MARYLAND.

The gentleman who prepared this work states, that he believes it contains an account of every thing at present accessible on this subject in the STATE PAPER OFFICE, though there are still papers in that depository which are unarranged and may contain references to Maryland. There are, also, valuable MANUSCRIPTS relating to our Province in the British Museum, the Badleian Library, the Society for the propagation of the Gospel in Foreign Parts, and elsewhere in England, none of which are described in the present Index.

It may be proper to remark, for the benefit and guidance of those who wish to consult this index for the purpose of obtaining *full* copies of documents referred to, that every paper is described and its length *in folios* accurately given. A *folio* is reckoned in the State Paper Office, as consisting of *seventy-two words*, and the price of copying is regulated by law, at *four pence per folio.*

Vol. I.

1626—1685.

Contains an Index to the Documents in the State Paper Office, relating to Sir George Calvert's Colony of Avalon and the Proprietary history of Maryland from 1626 to 1685, among which are many referring to the religion, laws, trade, productions, &c. of Maryland; the wars with the Indians; the disputes of Lord Baltimore with William Claiborne, William Penn, and the Officers of the Customs, Rousby and Badcock; Bacon's Rebellion in Virginia, and the proceedings of the Dutch and Swedes, on Delaware Bay.

Vol. II.

1685—1691.

Contains an index to numerous letters and papers written by persons of both factions concerning the Revolution of 1689 in the province. Also papers concerning the appointment of Sir Lionel Copley, the first Royal Governor after the Revolution.

Vol. III.

1691—1697.

Contains an index to documents regarding the administration of Governors Copley, Andros and Nicholson; the disputes of the first mentioned with the Secretary of the province, and also with the Surveyor General of North America; the establishment of Protestant ministers in Maryland; the trade of the province, and the Quota demanded from Maryland, for the defence of the frontiers of New York against the French and Indians.

Vol. IV.

1697—1699.

Contains an index to papers concerning the proceedings of the Board of Trade; the laws of the province; the piracies in the American seas; addresses from the people of Maryland to the King, and the administration of Governor Blackistone.

Vol. V.

1699—1702.

Contains an index to similar subjects as the preceding.

Vol. VI.

1702—1706.

Contains an index to documents relating to the condition of Maryland during the government of John Seymour; the war with France and Spain; value of foreign coins in America; salaries of the provincial governors, and religion in the province.

Vol. VII.

1706—1711.

Contains an index to papers respecting the population, laws, trade, &c. of Maryland; perquisites of the Secretary's office; boundary line of Maryland, and appointment of Col. Corbet as governor.

Vol. VIII.

1711—1720.

Contains an index to documents concerning the proceedings of President Lloyd; the appointment and administration of Governor Hart; the appointment of Charles Calvert, proprietary governor, and the trade, &c. of the province.

Vol. IX.

1720—1736.

Contains an index to papers referring to the appointment and administrations of Governors Benedict Leonard Calvert and Samuel Ogle; trade, &c. of the province, and the outrages committed against Col. Thomas Cresap and family, by the Sheriff of Lancaster County, Pennsylvania.

Vol. X.

1736—1754.

Contains an index to papers regarding the foreign coins and paper currency in America, boundary line of Maryland; the appointment and administrations of Governors Bladen and Ogle, President Tasker, Governor Sharpe, and the occurrences of the French War.

Vol. XI.

1754—1780.

Contains an interesting compendium of documents relating to the administrations of Governors Sharpe and Eden; the boundary line; the proceedings of the people of Maryland upon the passing and repeal of the Stamp Act and the various other taxes imposed by the British Ministry; communications between the Governor and General Assembly concerning the Acts of Parliament; addresses and petitions of the people to the King; proceedings of the delegates appointed to the Continental Congress; resolutions of the people; proceedings of the Convention of Maryland; the movements in the other colonies, and the battles fought with the British.

MISCELLANEOUS MARYLAND MANUSCRIPTS.

BOUND BOOKS—(*Not in Port Folios.*)

1745—1810.

No. 1. Rent-Roll of Lord Baltimore, 1749–53.

2. Proceedings of the Maryland Convention, from June 22, 1774, to November 11, 1776, 2 vols.

3. Journal of the Committee of Observation of the Middle District of Frederick County, Maryland, 1775—1776, presented by the City of Frederick to the Maryland Historical Society.

4. Contents, Dedication and Preface to a History of the "Ancient and Honorable Tuesday Club," of Annapolis, 1754.

"Record of the Tuesday Club, containing the first decade of the Transactions of that Society, comprehended in 239 *sederunts*, viz: from May, 1745 to May, 1755, inclusive, with heads of the honorable the President, and the principal officers and members, and figures of the most material transactions of the Club." Vol. 1, pp. 550, 4to.

5. Lectures on Maryland History, by the late Mr. Thomas W. Griffith, presented by Mr. Brantz Mayer, 8vo.

6. Index to the Laws of Maryland, from 1800 to 1810, pp. 263, 4to.

7. The Original Rolls of the Cincinnati Society of Maryland, containing its Constitution, and the Signatures of its Members, deposited with the Historical Society, by the Members. In a tin box.

The list of original members is published in Mr. McSherry's History of Maryland.

Port Folio No. 5.

Contains the following documents found among the Revolutionary Papers of GEN. MORDECAI GIST, and presented to the Society, by Dr. J. Paul Cockey, of Baltimore.

1774—1781.

No. 1. Orderly Book containing the General Division and Brigade orders in Camp, at Morristown, from March 5, to April 15, 1780. Also those issued during the march of the Maryland Troops, from Morristown to join the Southern Army, from April 15 to July 14, 1780, 1 vol.

2. Orderly Book, containing Regulations for the service of the Seige of York. The General Orders from the commencement of the Seige to its close. The correspondence between Gen. Washington and Lord Cornwallis, with regard to the Surrender of Yorktown, &c. General Orders on the march of the Troops from Williamsburg, Nov. 5, 1781, 1 vol.

3. Arrangement of the Maryland Line after its re-organization in 1781, in the handwriting of Gen. Smallwood. Published in Mr. McSherry's History of Maryland.

4. Articles of Association and Signatures of Members of the Baltimore Independent Cadets, Dec. 3, 1774.

5. List of the Officers of the Third Maryland Regiment, April 19, 1777.

6. Proceedings of a Court Martial, held at Wilmington, April 6, 1778, written on British *stamped paper*.

Port Folio No. 6.

Contains documents, manuscript and printed, relating, principally, to the History of Maryland, at the period of the REVOLUTION, presented to the Society by MR. B. U. CAMPBELL.

1659—1786.

No. 1. Original Manuscript Records of Courts Baron and Courts Leet, held in St. Clement's Manor, at several times, from 1659 to 1672, folio.

2. Three Deeds dated 1659, 1663 and 1664, the first signed by Josias Fendall, and the two last, by Charles Calvert, Gov. of Maryland, and afterwards, third Lord Baltimore.

3. Patent of the Baltimore Company, 1732.

4. Printed Scheme of the Maryland Liberty Lottery, Annapolis, 1767.

5. Printed Resolutions of the Inhabitants of Maryland, not to import certain articles into the Colony, June 22, 1769.

6. Handbill addressed to the Inhabitants of Anne Arundel Co., Md., January, 1775.

7. Another to the Citizens of Annapolis, January, 1775.

8. Paper containing the appointment of a Committee of Observation for Anne Arundel Co., January, 1775.

9. MS. invective against the Civil Rulers of Maryland, addressed to the people of Maryland, exhorting them to avenge themselves upon their domestic enemies, and act more vigorously against the common foe of their country, 1777.

10. Letter from Rev. John Carroll, dated Philadelphia, June 2, 1776, to Charles Carroll, Sr., father of Charles Carroll of Carrollton.

11. Letters to Charles Carroll of Carrollton, from James Sterett, James Fitzgerald and Mr. Pliarne, 1777.

12. Arrears of taxes due in Maryland, 1784.

13. Report of Daniel of St. Thomas Jenifer, Intendant of the Revenue, to the General Assembly, 1784, printed.

14. Report of the same for 1785.

15. Three printed papers containing the controversy between D. of St. Thos. Jenifer and Judge Hanson, concerning plans of finance and the revenues and funds of the State, Dec. 1784.

16. Printed address to the General Assembly, tending to show the justice of making specie bonds, "by one of the debtors for *black* money," 1786.

17. Printed account of the value of land in the several counties of Maryland, 1781, with views of the assessments of lands in the same counties in 1781–2–3.

18. Printed proceedings of the General Assembly, 1785, relating to Henry Harford, the last proprietary of Maryland.

19. MS. of Strictures on the Counter Protest to the Protest against the passage of a bill in April Session of the General Assembly, 1783, entitled an "Act concerning the admission and qualification of solicitors and attornies," arguments in support of the protest, signed by Charles Carroll of Carrollton.

Duplicate of the same, without signature.

20. Instructions and Letters from Gov. Smallwood, Thos. Johnson and Charles Carroll of Carrollton, to Judge Chase, respecting the Stock of the Bank of England belonging to Maryland, 1787, appointing him Agent, and letters from Judge Chase on the same subject.

21. Memoranda and journal of Augustine Herman, of Bohemia Manor, with numerous documents relative to the estate.

22. Printed extracts from private letters, dated London, April, 1774, relative to the oppressive measures of the British Ministry.

23. Printed copy of the King's Address to Parliament, October 27, 1775.

24. Printed Address of the Continental Congress to the inhabitants of the United States, May 9, 1778.

25. General Account of Receipts and Expenditures of United States, from 1 November, 1784 to 1 November, 1785.

26. Report of the Grand Committee of Congress respecting the foreign and domestic debts of the United States and the quotas of the several states, signed by Charles Thomson, Secretary of Congress, 1785.

27. Printed Resolves of Congress respecting the laying off of lands to the westward, 1785.

28. Handbill of news from England respecting a proposed peace with the United States.

29. Printed remarks on Lord Sheffield's observations on the commerce of the United States.

30. Inscription for a monument which might appropriately be erected on the Repeal of the Stamp Act.

Port Folio No. 7.

Contains all the remaining Manuscripts relating to the History of Maryland.

1652—1835.

PAPERS WRITTEN BY THE LATE MR. JAMES JOHNSON, SON OF GOV. JOHNSON, OF MARYLAND, AND PRESENTED BY HIM TO THE SOCIETY.

No. 1. Genealogy of the family of Thomas Johnson, the first Republican Governor of Maryland.

2. Biographical Sketch of Thomas Johnson.

3. Revolutionary Worthies of Maryland.

4. Revolutionary Reminiscences.

5. List of the Maryland officers appointed to command the Flying Camp in the campaign in 1776–77.

6. Catalogue of the Professors and Students of St. John's College, Annapolis, 1789–95.

7. Origin, Rise and Progress of Steam Navigation.

MISCELLANEOUS MANUSCRIPTS.

No. 1. Pres. Joseph's address to the General Assembly, Nov. 14, 1688, and two addresses, by Gov. Seymour, 1704, extracted from the Journals of the Upper House of the Maryland Assembly, preserved in the Council Chamber, at Annapolis, pp. 11, folio.

2. Copy of H. M's Order in Council, 1738, for preserving peace between the Inhabitants of Pennsylvania and Maryland.

3. Copy of the Agreement, 1760, between the Proprietors of Pennsylvania and Maryland, pp. 55, folio, presented by Mr. J. B. Morris.

(A printed copy of the same, in the Library, presented by Mr. E. D. Ingraham, of Philadelphia.)

4. Orders and Instructions for Robert Eden, Governor of Maryland, from George III, 1769, copied from the original

Records in the Council Office, Whitehall, London, presented to the Society by Jared Sparks, LL. D.

5. Letter from General Samuel Smith, written in 1821, giving an account of the plan by which the Committee of Safety at Baltimore, intended making Governor Eden prisoner, in 1776.

6. Journal of Charles Carroll of Carrollton, during his visit to Canada in 1776, as one of the Commissioners from Congress, pp. 41, presented by Mrs. J. McTavish. Published by the Society, with a memoir and notes by Mr. Brantz Mayer.

7. Journal of Capt. William Beatty of the Maryland Line, from 1776 to 1781. Also five letters of the same; with his memoir, written by Judge Beatty, of Kentucky, presented by the same.

8. Copy of the Journal of Lieut. Anderson of the Delaware Regiment, in the Southern Campaign, 1780–81, pp. 19.

9. Manuscript of Mr. O. Tiffany's Sketch of the Life and Services of General O. H. Williams, of the Maryland Line, a discourse delivered by him before the Society, and published, pp. 36, folio.

10. An account of Occurrences in Somerset County, 1781, in letters chiefly addressed to Matthew Tilghman, copied from the originals on file in the Council Chamber, Annapolis, pp. 20.

11. Transcripts from the Records of Kent County Court, 1652, made by Mr. George L. L. Davis, and presented by him to the Society.

12. Scale of Depreciation by the Maryland Legislature, for the Payment of Officers, &c. 177–81.

13. Fac-simile of a letter of Charles, third Lord Baltimore, 1687.

14. Letter of Charles, fifth Lord Baltimore, 1742.

15. Three letters from Governor Eden, 1775.

16. Note to him from John Montgomery, in Latin.

17. Letter from Daniel Dulany, 1787.

18. One from Col. J. E. Howard, 1826.

19. One from Col. Paul Bentalou, 1826.

20. One from Gen. Samuel Smith, 1835.

21. Letter concerning John Hicks, a Chief of the Cherokee nation, showing him to have been born of white parents in Maryland; and another letter from the same person concerning Fort Frederick.

DOCUMENTS RELATING TO THE HISTORY OF BALTIMORE.

BOUND BOOKS—(*Not in Port Folios.*)

1774—1838.

No. 1. The Manuscript of Mr. Robert Purviance's "Narrative of Events which occurred in Baltimore-Town, during the Revolutionary War."

2. Orderly Book of the Baltimore Independent Company, commanded by Samuel Sterett, and attached to the 5th Regiment M. M. Aug.—November, 1814, presented by Mr. John S. Sumner.

3. Record of Visitors to the top of Washington Monument, from 1835 to 1838.

Port Folio, No. 8.

Contains all the Manuscripts in this section.

1748—1846.

No. 1. The *original* letters published in Mr. Purviance's "Narrative of Events which occurred in Baltimore-Town during the Revolution," presented to the Society by Mr. Purviance.

2. List of subscribers for keeping the Fence around Baltimore Town in repair, 1748.

3. Do. for building a Town Hall, and Market House, 1751.

4. Census of Deptford Hundred, or Fell's Point, made by order of Congress, 1776.

The above were presented by Mr. Randolph B. Latimer. They were found among the papers of the late Mr. Thos. W. Griffith.

5. History of the Baltimore City and County Alms House; found among the papers of Mr. Thos. W. Griffith.

6. List of subscribers for opening Calvert Street, by underpinning and under-arching the Court House, 1784—presented by Mr. Ramsay McHenry.

7. Paper read before the Society by Mr. Robert Gilmor, relative to certain buildings which once existed in Baltimore.

8. Member book of the Baltimore Lodge of Masons, No. 16, from 1773 to 1780, presented by Mr. Geo. F. R. Waesche.

9. Paper book of descriptions of designs for the Washington Monument, written in 1813. Also, tickets in the "Washington Monument Lottery," 1813.

10. Orderly Book of the 3d Brigade, Maryland Militia, John Stricker, Brig. Gen. Baltimore, Aug.—Nov. 1814—presented by Mr. Hugh Jenkins.

11. Papers concerning the presentation of a sword by the citizens of Baltimore, to Lieut. R. Ridgely, for his gallantry at Palo Alto, and Resaca de la Palma, 1846.

DOCUMENTS RELATING TO THE HISTORY OF AMERICA, ILLUMINATED MANUSCRIPTS, MISCELLANEOUS AUTOGRAPH LETTERS, FAC-SIMILES, &c.

BOUND BOOKS—(*Not in Port Folios.*)

1312—1813.

No. 1. MANUSCRIPT IN LATIN, *on vellum*, of the XIV. Century, beautifully written and illuminated, of the Gospels of MATTHEW and MARK, with annotations and commentaries. Bound in the original wood and stamped leather, pp. about 250.

2. MANUSCRIPT IN LATIN, *on vellum*, Anno 1312, Aristotle's Physics, pp. about 300.

3. SPANISH MANUSCRIPT, beautifully illuminated, and *bound in crimson velvet, with silver clasps*,—giving an account of the Geography, History, Statistics, &c. &c. of the NORTH OF TERRA FIRMA AND THE PROVINCE OF VERAGUA, in a Report to the KING OF SPAIN, signed by DIEGO DE LA HAYA, 1716, pp. 352.

4. Manuscript History (in Spanish) of the American Revolution, for the years 1776, '77 and '78, pp. 450, presented by Mr. S. T. Wallis.

5. Order Book of the United States Army, under Gen. James Wilkinson, from 1797 to 1813, presented by Mr. John I. Donaldson.

6. Fac-similes of Manuscripts on Papyrus, preserved in the Royal Library, Paris, edited by M. Champollion Figeac, of Paris, presented by the Editor, 1 vol. folio.

7. Mons. Alexandre Vattemare's "ALBUM COSMOPOLITE," containing fac-similes of sketches, &c. by distinguished artists and of autograph signatures and letters, of celebrated men, of past and present time, presented by M. Vattemare, 1 vol. folio.

THE FOLLOWING ARE IN MAP FORM:

1765—1843.

No. 1. Two Fac-similes of the Declaration of Independence.

2. Fac-simile of the signatures of the Merchants and other citizens of Philadelphia, as subscribed to the Non-Importation Resolutions, Oct. 25, 1765.—presented by Mr. R. H. Townsend.

3. Fac-simile of the Acts of Separation of the Free Church of Scotland in 1843, presented by Mr. George Brown.

THE FOLLOWING ARE FRAMED:

1776—1847.

No. 1. Fac-simile of the Declaration of Independence, presented by Congress to Charles Carroll of Carrollton, the surviving signer, signed by him in the year 1826, and given by him to Mr. John McTavish, who presented it to the Society.

2. Fac-simile of a letter to Thomas Jefferson, from Benjamin Banneker, a colored man, of Baltimore County, of considerable mathematical attainments, and of Mr. Jefferson's answer, 1791, presented by Mr. Moses Sheppard. These letters are published in Mr. Latrobe's "Memoir of Benjamin Banneker."

3. Letter, dated Monterey, September 22, 1847, signed by Gen. Z. Taylor.

4. Note written by the Duke of Wellington, 1847, presented by Mr. W. S. Peterkin.

Port Folio No. 9.

Contains Mons. Du Bois Martin's Account of his agency in the EMBARKATION OF LAFAYETTE, for this country in 1776. Also, his private papers, in French.

Mons. Martin was a French officer, who, in the latter part of his life, resided in Baltimore.

Port Folio, No. 10.

Contains all the remaining Manuscripts mentioned in the following pages:

1502—1837.

No. 1. Copy of a letter written by Columbus, and preserved in the Ducal Palace, Genoa, dated Seville, April 2, 1502.

2. Translation of a Treatise by A. Von Humboldt, on the "OLDEST MAPS OF THE NEW CONTINENT," and on the name, "AMERICA," prefixed to a German History of BEHAIM, the Navigator, presented to the Society by Mr. Wm. Rodewald, of Bremen. Also, a translation of the preface to the same work.

3. Letter from WILLIAM PENN, dated May 2, 1698, addressed to his Agents in Pennsylvania, concerning six hundred pounds due to him by the province. This valuable relic was presented to the Society by Mr. Richard H. Townsend, of Baltimore.

4. Fac-simile of the same.

5. Do. of a letter from William Penn, dated 25 April, 1682.

6. Fac-simile of Washington's Accounts with the United States, from June, 1775, to June, 1783,—presented by Mr. Geo. B. Coale.

7. Historical Account of Erie County, Pennsylvania, written for the Society, by Wm. Maxwell Wood, M. D. Surgeon U. S. Army.—pp. 30, 12mo.

8. Correspondence between the United States citizens resident at La Guayra, and Capt. Spence, commanding the U. S. Ship Cyane, 1822.—presented by Mr. P. W. Lowry.

THE FOLLOWING WERE PRESENTED BY MR. BRANTZ MAYER.

9. Note from Col. J. E. Howard.

10. Letter from Gouverneur Morris, 1800.

11. One from Chief Justice Taney, 1831.

12. One from Chief Justice Marshall, 1830.

13. One from Mathew Carey, 1837.

14. One from Jared Sparks, 1832.

15. Letter written by Benedict Arnold, 1768, presented by Mr. Charles S. Gilmor.

16. One from Aaron Burr, 1793, presented by the same.

17. Letter from Dr. Hugh Williamson, 1774.

18. Fac-simile of a letter from Washington to Francis Hopkinson, 1785, presented by Mr. George B. Coale.

19. Letter from Lafayette, 1827, presented by Mr. R. H. Townsend.

20. Two from David Crockett, 1835, presented by Mr. George H. Hickman.

21. Letter from John Quincy Adams, dated Quincy, Oct. 26, 1841, to Mr. J. A. Grace, concerning the Genealogy of the Adams family and other papers relating to the same subject, pp. 21.

22. Two letters to the President of the Maryland Historical Society, from George W. P. Custis, descriptive of the uniforms worn by the several corps of the Continental army. Published in Mr. McSherry's History of Maryland.

23. French inscription engraved in 1749, upon a leaden plate found at the confluence of the Ohio and Great Kanawha rivers.

24. Fac-simile of two letters from Thomas Jefferson and Andrew Jackson, 1824 and 1833, presented by Mr. John P. Hughes.

25. Deed of the sale of a negro girl in Newport, Rhode Island, 1742.

26. Various English and American Indentures, of the following dates: 1602, 1607, 1656, 1695, 1696, 1752, 1756, 1770.

27. Various specimens of continental and provincial notes of Maryland, &c. issued during the period from 1774 to 1776, presented by Mr. F. B. Mayer.

28. "An Essay towards an English Grammar, in verse," by the Rev. Mr. Chase, father of Judge Samuel Chase, presented by Mr. J. I. Donaldson, pp. 109, 4to.

29. A Course of Law and Literary Study, prepared by Judge Samuel Chase, presented by Hon. J. P. Kennedy, pp. 28, 4to.

30. "The Materials of History," an essay read before the Society, by Mr. Thomas Donaldson.

31. Fac-simile of the Death Warrant of Charles I, presented by Mr. Louis Servary.

32. Handbill containing an account of the trials of William, Earl of Kilmarnock, George, Earl of Cromartie and Arthur, Lord Balmerino, for High Treason, in 1746.

33. Permit with the signatures of Napoleon and some of his ministers, 1813.

34. Fac-simile of a sketch and notes illustrating the battle of Arcola, made by Napoleon, presented by Mr. P. W. Lowry.

35. Fourth Bulletin of the French Army in Russia, dated Wilna, June 30, 1812, printed, presented by Gen. J. S. Smith.

36. Two pieces of birch bark marked with the picture writing and hieroglyphics of the North-Western Indians.

Autograph letters, presented to the society, by Mr. Lyman C. Draper.

No. 1. Letter dated Williamsburg, 1738.

2. Letter from Patrick Henry, 1784.

3. Benjamin Harrison, signer of the Declaration of Independence, 1783.

4. Thomas Jefferson, 1779.

5. James Monroe, 1802.

6. Gen. S. F. Mason, U. S. Senator from Virginia, announcing the election of Mr. Jefferson, as President, 1801.

7. Alexander Martin, of N. C. 1806.

8. Gen. Henry Knox, Secretary of War, 1792.

9. William Blount, 1794.

10. Passport signed by Gen. Henry Lee, Gov. of Virginia, 1791.

11. Autograph signatures of many distinguished Americans.

MAPS, CHARTS AND PLATS.

1695—1853.

No. 1. An exact MS. Plat of Baltimore Town in Baltimore County, 1756,—presented by Mr. Chas. F. Mayer,—framed.

2. A New and Accurate MS. Map of Baltimore Town; dedicated to Thos. Langton, Esq. by G. Goulds. Presbury, S B. C. 1780,—presented by Mr. B. U. Campbell,—framed.

3. MS. Plat of the lands on which Baltimore City is situated, 1786, by G. Goulds. Presbury, S. B. C.

4. Plan of the Town of Baltimore, and its Environs; dedicated to the citizens of Baltimore. Taken upon the spot, by their most humble servant A. P. Folie, French Geographer, 1792,—presented by Mr. John S. Sumner,—framed.

Duplicate of the same.

5. Plan of the City and Environs of Baltimore, 1799, presented by Mr. J. R. Partridge.

6. Plan of the City of Baltimore, 1818, by L. H. Poppleton, Surveyor.

7. Original MS. draft of a Survey of Patapsco River, and part of Chesapeake Bay, made in 1819, by Mr. Lewis Brantz, and presented to the Society by Mr. Brantz Mayer.

Printed copy of the same.

8. MS. copy of Lord Baltimore's own Map, annexed to his Agreement with Penn, in 1732.

9. MS. copy of an Original Map of the Survey of Mason and Dixon's Line, made and presented to the Society, by Mr. F. Lucas, Jr.

10. Map of Maryland, 1794,—presented by Mr. J. R. Partridge.

11. Map of the Stage Routes between the cities of New York and Baltimore; exhibiting also the operations of the British Army from their landing at Elk River, 1777, until their embarkation at Nevesink, 1778,—presented by Mr. Brantz Mayer.

12. Map of the Chesapeake Bay and Susquehanna River, 1799, presented by the same.

Duplicate of the above map.

13. MS. Plat of St. Mary's River,—presented by Gen. J. S. Smith.

14. Map of the country between Washington and Pittsburg, referring to the contemplated Chesapeake and Ohio Canal, 1826.

15. Map of the various routes surveyed for the Baltimore and Ohio Rail Road.

16. Map of Pennsylvania, Maryland, Virginia and North Carolina, 1778.

17. Account of land in Pennsylvania, granted by Wm. Penn, 1681,—presented by Mr. R. H. Townsend.

18. Map of Pennsylvania, New York, New Jersey, and the three Delaware Counties, 1749,—presented by Mr. S. T. Wallis.

THE FOLLOWING WERE PRESENTED BY MR. BRANTZ MAYER:

19. Plat of the Town of Havre de Grace, Md.

20. Old Map of Pennsylvania.

21. German Map of the States, from Maine to Virginia, 1778.

22. Spanish Chart of the Eastern Coast of Mexico.

23. Spanish Map of the port of Vera Cruz, and the Western Coast of the Gulf of Mexico, 1798.

24. Spanish Chart of the Coasts of the Gulf of Mexico, Gulf of Honduras, Islands of Cuba, Saint Domingo, Jamaica and Lucayas, 1813.

25. American Chart of the Spanish Main, 1823.

26. American Chart of the same, from Carthagena to the River Chagres, 1823.

27. Spanish Chart of the Sea of the Antilles, 1809.

28. Do. of the Old Bahama Channel, 1790.

29. Do. of part of the Antilles, of Porto Rico, Saint Domingo, Jamaica and Cuba, 1815.

30. Spanish Plat of Porto, Capital of Porto Rico, 1794.

31. French tables of Longitudes and Latitudes.

32. Map of the Mississippi River, from the Balize to Fort Chartres, in 1765—presented by Mr. J. R. Partridge.

33. Plan of the City and Environs of New York, 1765.

34. Plan of New Orleans, 1803.

35. Map of Florida and Bahama Islands.

36. Map of Florida, Gulf of Mexico, and the Bahama Banks, 1817.

37. Map of Florida, 1829,—presented by Gen. J. S. Smith.

38. Map of Florida, 1846.

39. French Map of the United States, 1802.

40. A collection of French Maps and Plates, illustrating the Works of Internal Improvement in the United States, from 1824 to 1831.

41. Maps of the Rail Roads in the United States, published by the United States Government.

42. Map of the Western Rail Roads, tributary to Philadelphia.

43. Spanish Map of the Rail Roads in Cuba, 1846,—presented by Gen. Geo. H. Steuart.

44. Chart of the Coast of North America from New York to Cape Hatteras, 1794.

45. Collection of the Maps published by the United States Coast Survey.

46. Various Maps and Charts published by the United States Government.

47. French Atlas of the World, for the use of the Dauphin, published in 1695, presented by Mr. Samuel W. Smith, 3 vols. folio.

48. Atlas attached to a work published in 1808, by order of the Emperor Napoleon, containing an account of the Voyage, in 1791–92–93, of Dentrecasteaux in search of La Perouse, all presented to the Society by the Minister of Marine, of France. Atlas, 1 vol. folio.

49. Directory of the East Indies, 1787, presented by Mr. F. B. Mayer, 1 vol. folio.

50. Complete East Indies Pilot, 1800, from the same, 3 vols. folio.

51. English Pilot of Northern Navigation, 1775, from the same, 1 vol. folio.

52. Chart of the Mediterranean sea, dedicated to Lord Nelson, from the same.

53. Geo-hydrographic Survey of Madeira, 1788, from the same.

54. Chart of the Maritime Flags of all Nations, from the same.

55. French Map of the Internal Navigation of France, presented by Mons. A. Vattemare, of Paris, 1820.

56. French Map of the Republic of France, divided into 103 Departments, 1799, presented by Gen. J. S. Smith.

57. Map of the Southern part of Sweden and Norway, 1792, from the same.

58. Map of the Theatre of War between Russia and France, in 1812, from the same.

59. Pictorial Map of the Rhine from Basle to the Sea, presented by Mr. Alexander B. Gordon.

60. Plat of Trieste.

61. Map of the Seat of War in North America, in 1813.

62. Plans of the Battles fought in the Mexican War, 1846–48.

63. Chinese Map of the World, presented by Capt. Hugh Purviance.

64. Stream of Time, or Chart of Universal History, from the original German of Strass. Duplicate of the same.

65. Ecclesiastical Chart of the Catholic Church, in Spanish presented by Mr. John Murphy.

COINS AND MEDALS.

1776—1815.

Bronze Medals, struck at various times, by order of Congress, in commemoration of military events, purchased and presented to the Society by the following named gentlemen: John Spear Smith, George Tiffany, J. McHenry Boyd, James H. McHenry, R. Cary Long and J. I. Donaldson.

No. 1. Medal for George Washington, on the evacuation of Boston, March 17, 1776.

2. Gen. Horatio Gates, for the battle of Saratoga, Oct. 17, 1777.

3. Gen. Nath. Greene, in commemoration of his Southern Campaign, victory of Eutaw, Sept. 8, 1781.

4. Gen. Daniel Morgan, for the victory of Cowpens, Jan. 17, 1781.

5. Col. W. Washington, for the victory of Cowpens, Jan. 17, 1781.

6. Col. J. E. Howard, for the victory of Cowpens, Jan. 17, 1781.

7. Electrotype duplicate of the same.

8. Gen. William H. Harrison, for the battle of the Thames, October 5, 1813.

9. Governor Isaac Shelby, for the battle of the Thames, October 5, 1813.

10. Col. George Croghan, Sandusky, August 2, 1813.

11. Gen. Jacob Brown, for the battles of Chippewa, July 5, Niagara, July 25, and Erie, September 17, 1814.

12. Gen. Eleazer W. Ripley, for the battles of Chippewa, July 5, Niagara, July 25, and Erie, September 17, 1814.

13. James Miller, for the battles of Chippewa, July 5, Niagara, July 25, and Erie, September 17, 1814.

14. Gen. Peter B. Porter, for the battles of Chippewa, July 5, Niagara, July 25, and Erie, September 17, 1814.

15. Gen. Winfield Scott, for the battles of Chippewa, July 5, Niagara, July 25, and Erie, September 17, 1814.

16. Gen. Edmund P. Gaines, for the battle of Erie, August 15, 1814.

17. Gen. Alexander Macomb, battle of Plattsburg, September 11, 1814.

18. Gen. Andrew Jackson, for the battle of New Orleans, January 8, 1815.

MISCELLANEOUS COINS AND MEDALS.

1652—1852.

No. 1. Silver Shilling and six pence of Cæcilius, Lord Baltimore, 1660, presented to the Society by Mr. George Peabody, of London.

2. Three silver Shillings of Annapolis, 1783.

3. Medal of President Cole, of the Tuesday Club, at Annapolis, May, 1746, presented by Capt. W. H. Fitzhugh.

4. Impression of the seal of Thomas J. Clagett, D. D., Bishop of the Protestant Episcopal Church, in Maryland, 1792.

5. Silver Medal in honor of Charles Carroll of Carrollton, struck by his family, September 20, 1826, on his entering his 90th year; the surviving signer of the Declaration of Independence, after the 50th Anniversary. Presented to the Society by Mrs. John McTavish.

6. Massachusetts Pine-tree Shilling, 1652, presented by Mr. S. T. Wallis.

7. A French Medal to Defleury, a French soldier, who first scaled the walls of Stony-Point, 15 July, 1779.

8. Electrotype copy of the obverse and reverse of a medal, struck during the second presidency of Washington, 1796.

9. Bronze commemorative medal of Henry Clay, struck in 1852, by his friends and presented by them to the Society.

10. Bronze Medal of Daniel Webster.

11. Private medal struck in honor of J. Fennimore Cooper, by Commodore Jesse D. Elliott, silver, presented by Com. Elliott.
12. Medal of Gen. Z. Taylor, cast in Iron.
13. Bronze Genoese Medal, commemorative of Columbus.
14. Cast of a very fine medal struck in France, in honor of Benjamin Franklin.
15. Cast of the gold Coronation Medal of Charles X.
16. French Medal in bronze, commemorative of Louis Philip, as Lieut. General of the kingdom, presented by M. Vattemare, of Paris.
17. Mexican medal, commemorative of the outbreak of the Revolution in Mexico, in 1821.
18. Copper medal in honor of the building of the new Market in Mexico, by Santa Anna, in 1842.
19. Electrotype copy of an ancient Russian medal of St. Nicholas.
20. Thirty-five Grecian and Roman bronze coins.
21. Several hundred miscellaneous copper and silver coins.

THE TOWSON CABINET OF MEDALS AND COINS.

300 B. C.—A. D. 1851.

This fine numismatic collection is comprised in 19 volumes, numbering in all 251 specimens, the larger portion being silver, in fine preservation. The Medals and Coins are firmly set in strong boards, so as to exhibit the obverse and reverse of each through the glasses which cover both sides of the case, and protect the specimens from touch or injury.

The collection was chiefly formed in Europe, by Joel Barlow, minister to France, and author of our American epic, "the Columbiad." At his death it passed to his brother-in-law, the late Col. Bomford, U. S. A., upon whose decease, General Towson, U. S. A. became its owner.

General Towson immediately proceeded, with the assistance of Mr. D. E. Groux, of Washington, who is said to be a very competent Numismatist, to classify and arrange the entire collection, as well as to prepare an ample *catalogue raisonné* of the whole, which he caused to be printed and presented with the Coins and Medals to the Maryland Historical Society, in March, 1852.

The collection presented by General Towson, is valuable for many separate specimens of great rarity, as well as beauty, It is in truth, a numismatic gallery of many nations and various ages. We may especially notice the very fine medal of Gustavus Adolphus, as an admirable specimen of minute and elegant art. But for historical purposes, the unbroken series of silver medals of French sovereigns and illustrious men, from the Merovingian kings in 420, to the Bourbons in 1793, is, if we may be allowed to discriminate, the most valuable portion of the collection.

Vol. 1.

4 Greek Medals from 300 B. C. to 400 B. C.; 2 Medals of the Roman Republic; 12 Coins of the Roman Empire from A. D. 14 to 235.

Vol. 2.

16 Roman Medals from A. D. 260 to 428.

Vol. 3.

4 Roman Medals of the lower empire from A. D. 518 to 685; 5 Miscellaneous English Coins, 1760 to 1788; 1 Portuguese, 1714.

Vol. 4.

2 French Coins, 1715 to 1774; 2 Spanish Coins, 1502 to 1665; 2 Burgundian Coins, 1665 to 1788; 1 Swedish Coin, 1719; 2 U. S. of America, 1792, 1851.

Vol. 5.

4 Mahometan Coins, Circassian Dynasty, 1356; 2 Mogul Empire, 1681 to 1723; 2 Empire of Morocco, 1786 to 1788; 6 Turkish Empire, 1772 to 1803.

Vol. 6.

1 Papal Coin 1559; 2 Austrian Empire 1705 to 1780; 5 Portuguese, 1706 to 1808; 5 Danish, 1670 to 1721; 2 Danish American Colonies, 1746 to 1808.

Vol. 7.

17 English Silver Coins from Edward 2nd, 1350 to James 2nd, 1686.

Vol. 8.

16 English Silver Coins from William and Mary, 1695 to George 4th, 1822.

Vol. 9.

7 French Silver Coins, 1715 to 1742; 1 Holland, 1738; 1 Doventer, 1689; 2 West Friesland, 1632 to 1664; 1 Zealand, 1760.

Vol. 10.

3 Prussian Silver Coins, 1786 to 1800; 1 Sardinian, 1727; 1 Burgundy under Spain, 1611; 1 Schleswig Holstein, 1682; 1 Florence, 1797; 2 Dukedom of Monaca, 1655; 1 Republic of Mexico, 1824; 2 Republic of Peru, 1828.

Vol. 11.

2 American Washington medals, 1796, silver; 1 American silver Jefferson medal, 1801; 1 American silver Gen. H. Gates, 1777; 1 U. S. 3 cent coin of 1851; 2 Massachusetts shillings of 1652.

Vol. 12.

2 French silver medals, (personal,) 1783, 1712, to the brothers Mongolfier, and J. J. Rousseau; 1 English silver battle of Culloden,1746; 1 Swedish commemorative of Gustavus Adolphus, a splendid specimen, 1632, silver; 1 French Republic, An. VI; 1 Louis XVI. 1779; 1 Republic of Chili, 1818.

Vols. 13 and 14.

22 Silver medals of the French Kings, in a complete series from Pharamond, A. D. 428, to Childeric, 752; 11 silver medals of French Kings, in series, from Pepin 752, to Louis IV. 954.

Vols. 15 and 16.

16 Silver French medals, in series, from Lothaire 954, to 1322; 19 silver French medals from Charles IV. 1322, to Louis XVI. 1793.

Vols. 17 and 18.

24 Silver medals of eminent Frenchmen, from 1617 to 1723.

Vol. 19.

1 Spanish bronze medal, 1788; 3 English bronze medals, 1727, 1789; 2 French bronze medals, 1792; 1 King of Etruria medal, 1801.

SCULPTURE.

Casts from the originals of the Dying Gladiator and Apollo Belvidere, presented by the Art Association.

Cast of Canova's Venus, deposited by Mr. Brantz Mayer.

Original Bust of Napoleon, by Canova; Bust in marble, of Eloïse, by Greenough.

Bust in marble of Augustus, and a collection of Medallion casts from the Antique, in 7 vols., all deposited by Mr. David Hoffman.

Collection of Casts from the Antique, in 1 vol.

A Cast of the statue of Venus of Milo, reduced.

A Cast of a statue of Polhymnia, reduced.

Two Bas Reliefs, casts from the Frieze of the Parthenon at Athens, presented by M. Vattemare.

Two Marble Busts of Voltaire and Rousseau, deposited by Mr. James H. McHenry.

Medallion Bust of Washington, by Chevalier, presented by Mr. Johns Hopkins.

Bust of Henry Clay, by Hart.

Bust of the Rev. Dr. J. G. Morris, of Baltimore.

Cast in iron of Thorwaldsen's Swiss Lion.

PORTRAITS AND PICTURES.

Portrait of George Calvert, Lord Baltimore, eng.

Portrait of Cecilius Calvert, Lord Baltimore, eng.

Portrait of Frederick Calvert, Lord Baltimore, eng.

A frame containing portraits of General Oglethorpe and Pocahontas, eng. all presented by Mr. Brantz Mayer.

Full length portrait, in oil, of Charles, fifth Lord Baltimore, copied by Mr. Thomas Sully, of Philadelphia, from the original of Sir Godfrey Kneller, and presented by him to the Society in 1853.

Portrait in oil of Gen. O. H. Williams, presented by Mrs. Williams and family.

Portrait in oil of Col. J. E. Howard, presented by Messrs. James and Charles Howard.

Portrait in oil of Gen. Samuel Smith, presented by Gen. J. Spear Smith.

Portrait in oil of Charles Carroll of Carrollton, presented by Mrs. John McTavish.

Portrait of Archbishop Carroll, eng., presented by Mr. J. S. Sumner.

Portrait in oil of Gen. Mordecai Gist, presented by Gen. J. S. Smith and Dr. J. P. Cockey.

Portrait in oil of Gen. Wm. Smallwood—purchased.

Portrait in oil of Gen. John Stricker, deposited by Mr. C. B. Tiernan.

Portrait in oil of Christopher Hughes, by SIR MARTIN A. SHEE, devised to the Society by Mr. Hughes,

Portrait of Christopher Columbus from an original in the Royal Library, Paris, eng. presented by Gen. J. S. Smith.

Engraving after the Portrait of Wm. Penn, belonging to the Pennsylvania Historical Society, presented by Mr. E. D. Ingraham, of Philadelphia.

Portrait of Mr. George Peabody, presented by Mr. William E. Mayhew.

Original sketch by John Moale of BALTIMORE-TOWN in 1752, presented by Col. Samuel Moale.

View of Baltimore in 1800.

View of Baltimore from Fairmount, 1853.

Portraits of Washington, Rochambeau, Lafayette, Greene, &c. on Yorktown heights, after the Seige, by C. W. Peale, presented by Mr. Robert Gilmor.

Copy in oil of the NOTTE OF CORREGIO, size of original, by V. C. Rothe, Dresden, 1834.

Copy in oil of RAPHAEL'S MADONNA of ST. SIXTUS, by C. Vogel, 1833.

Copy in oil of PAUL VERONESE'S MARRIAGE AT CANA, by Powell.

Potiphar's Wife and Joseph, copied from Cignani, presented by Mr. O. C. Tiffany.

A Copy by T. C. Ruckle, a Baltimore artist, of Murillo's Infant Saviour, presented by Mr. W. J. Tiffany.

A Collection of valuable engravings, among which are many representing memorable scenes in history.

A print published at Boston just before the Revolution representing "The Bloody Massacre perpetrated in King Street, Boston, in March 5th, 1770, by a party of the 29th Regt."

Caricature of the first fight in Congress between two of the members, 1798.

Plate of a View of the Court House and Powder Magazine of Baltimore, 1789.

The *original* Banner presented to COUNT PULASKI in 1778, by the Moravian Sisters of Bethlehem, in Pennsylvania. When Count Pulaski fell at Savannah in 1779, the banner was saved by his first lieutenant and afterwards delivered to Col. Bentalou, of Baltimore, then a captain in Pulaski's Legion. It was used in the procession which welcomed Lafayette to this city in 1824, and then deposited in Peale's Museum. In 1844, Mr. Edmund Peale presented it to the Maryland Historical Society.

A number of Indian, Mexican, Chinese and other curiosities and relics; together with various specimens of minerals, shells, and other natural productions.

ESTIMATE OF THE

NUMBER OF BOUND VOLUMES IN THE LIBRARY

OF THE

MARYLAND HISTORICAL SOCIETY.

The Library of the Maryland Historical Society contains 2128 bound volumes,—of which 390 are purchases by the Society, and the residue, 1738, donations from U. S. Government, States, associations, and individuals, in this state and elsewhere, who, imbued with the true idea of the end of historical institutions, and believing that they are depositories for every thing that may contribute to the elucidation of past or present events, have done all in their power to increase the collections of the Society.

Of Histories of the States, of Local Histories, of Biographies and Memoirs of distinguished Americans, and of General Histories of the United States and the Americas, there are 730 volumes. Among these are almost all the standard works on American History and Biography, and several very rare and valuable books.

Of Public Documents and Publications by the United States Government there are 605 volumes.

Of Newspapers there are 307 bound volumes, comprising some of the earliest published in Maryland.

There are 56 bound volumes containing 703 Pamphlets, *all accurately indexed and catalogued.* These pamphlets relate principally to the history of Maryland and the United States, and to political, scientific and literary subjects generally. Among them are some of great rarity and historical importance.

Of works on Universal and European History, Travels and Voyages in the Old World, and Biographies of distinguished English and French, there are 195 volumes.

Of Miscellaneous Works on the Fine Arts, Science, Theology, Law, Literature, &c. there are 230 volumes.

NOTICE

TO MEMBERS OF THE SOCIETY, AND TO HISTORICAL STUDENTS GENERALLY.

I. The Assistant Librarian, who is constantly in the Society's Rooms during hours of study, has charge of this Collection under the Library Committee, and is strictly responsible for every article contained in it, as well as for the preservation of its systematic order. He will keep the Manuscripts under lock, in the fire-proof safes.

II. No Manuscript, Medal, Coin, Map, &c. of any character or value, shall be taken, by any one's authority, or for any purpose, from this Society's Hall.

III. To preserve order in the custody and use of the articles comprised in this catalogue, and those which may, hereafter, be added to it, the Assistant Librarian, alone, will find and exhibit any document, work, or matter of interest desired for examination.

IV. The Assistant Librarian is expressly inhibited from allowing any one to inspect or use this Collection, in any other way, or out of his presence.

V. These fundamental rules are not adopted to prevent the legitimate use of the Society's Collection by all who require its aid in the spirit and for the purposes that originated the Institution. The experience of other Societies, in Europe as well as America, has demonstrated the necessity of strict *rules and accountability* in the guardianship of *literary or scientific rarities;* and it is for this reason alone, that the Maryland Historical Society offers its pledge to the public and to students, that whatever may be entrusted to its care will be watchfully *preserved,* at the same time that it is made accessible.

BRANTZ MAYER, *Chairman.*
GEO. WM. BROWN,
M. COURTNEY JENKINS,
Library Committee, M. H. S.

BALTIMORE, 1 *July*, 1854.

AFRICAN SLAVE TRADE

IN JAMAICA,

AND

COMPARATIVE TREATMENT OF SLAVES.

READ BEFORE THE

MARYLAND HISTORICAL SOCIETY,

OCTOBER, 1854.

PRINTED FOR THE MARYLAND HISTORICAL SOCIETY,
BY JOHN D. TOY.

AFRICAN SLAVE TRADE

IN JAMAICA,

AND

COMPARATIVE TREATMENT OF SLAVES.

The cruelty of the Spaniards towards the Aborigines of the Island of Jamaica, has ever been the theme of just and strong indignation by Historians:—but the cruelties inflicted by British subjects upon the Africans in the same Island, as will be evidenced by the statistics hereafter shown, have never met with the reprehension they deserve.

It is true, Parliament has abolished Slavery, but how much of this measure was due to humanity, and how much to policy, is uncertain. The fact, that England for one hundred and seventy-nine years, tolerated the Slave trade, a system so cruel, and so destructive to the lives of its unfortunate victims, should forever silence all reproach on the part of British subjects against the United States, so far as Slavery in connection with the treatment of those held in bondage is concerned.

In the march of humanity, different motives may combine to impel the mass forward:—sympathy and policy may unite to effect a common object; policy in the government, philanthropy in the people.

Formerly, English manufactures, to an immense amount, were introduced into the Spanish possessions in America, through Jamaica. The dismemberment of these possessions from Spain, opened the ports of Spanish America to the direct trade of England; and Jamaica ceased to be profitable to her; hence the reduction in the differential duties; and what were those duties but a premium on slave labor?—

Before the emancipation of the slaves in Jamaica, many of the owners of the Estates were deeply involved in debt, notwithstanding the premium in the form of protection; and emancipation only hastened their ruin.

England, therefore did not abolish Slavery in the West Indies, until it had become *unprofitable.*

The Slavery in disguise now being introduced into the Island of Jamaica, called Apprenticeship, will be more profitable:—nearly the whole amount of capital heretofore employed in the purchase of slaves, will be saved. It is obviously more economical than the former system, and may enable the planters to retrieve their circumstances.

English writers tell us with exultation, that the British drum and fife may be heard successively, until the music goes round the world;—but they omit to tell us, that the groans of oppressed humanity, the cries of infant innocence, and the shrieks of virgin purity, mingle with the sounds that herald the dominion of the British Isles.

There is another aspect of the subject, which it would be well for the Parliament of "Exeter Hall" to consider, whenever American Slavery becomes a matter for anathema. *Slavery in this country had its origin in the commercial policy of England.* Under the fostering protection of the British Government, the trade in African slaves which supplied all her Colonies, America included, was begun and continued;—and continued too, in many instances, against the earnest and repeated remonstances of the Colonists.

Here is the origin of American Slavery;—and it exhibits an effrontery unparalleled, for England, with all her severities in the East Indies; with the toleration of Slavery in Jamaica, for one hundred and seventy-nine years; and the enormous sacrifice of life it entailed upon its miserable victims, and with the continuance of the Slave Trade, with all its horrors, for so many years, forcing its evils upon unwilling Colonies, to be uttering reproaches against the citizens of the United States, for the existence of a system fastened upon them, by her own arbitrary acts.

That Slavery here, is not what English Abolitionists profess to believe, nor what in reality it has been in their own Colonies, is clearly proved by the following statistics, collected from their own writers.

The number of slaves in the United States,

In 1850, was	3,204,089
In 1790, ...	697,897
Increase in sixty years, ...	2,506,192

(Two millions five hundred six thousand one hundred and ninety-two;—)

The number of free colored people

In 1850, was	428,661
In 1790, ...	59,466
Increase in sixty years, ...	369,195

(Three hundred and sixty-nine thousand one hundred and ninety-five.)

It is estimated that one-half of this increase of the free colored population was from emancipation of slaves:—and of course so far, it lessened the increase of the latter, and added to the increase of the former.

The number of slaves brought into Jamaica by the Spaniards during their possession of the Island, from 1509 to 1655, say in one hundred and forty-six years, was 40,000, (forty thousand.)

Of these, there were found by Penn and Venables, at the time of their conquest of the Island in 1655, only 1,500, (fifteen hundred.)

Now if 697,897 persons in sixty years amount to 3,204,089,—1,500 persons, in one hundred and seventy-nine years, by the same ratio, would amount to, ... 20,544

Add the number imported into Jamaica in one hundred and seventy-nine years, say from 1655 to 1834, (eight hundred and fifty thousand,) 850,000

And the amount will be, ... 870,544

The number of slaves found on the Island, at the time of the Emancipation in

Amount brought over, .	870,544
1834, was (three hundred twenty-two thousand four hundred and twenty-one,)	322,421
Showing a waste of human life under British rule, as contrasted with the ratio of increase in the United States, of .	548,123

(Five hundred forty-eight thousand one hundred and twenty-three,) exclusive of any estimated increase upon the eight hundred and fifty thousand (850,000) who were imported, that would have accrued under a humane system of treatment.

In submitting these comparative results of British Colonial slavery, with slavery in the United States, it must not be supposed that the compiler of this Exhibit is an advocate or friend of slavery. He is not. The question we are considering, is not slavery, but the comparative treatment of slaves.

His object is to show, that the odium of its introduction here, and the evils that it has inflicted or may inflict upon the United States, are chargeable to England:—and that the iniquity of the institution may be aggravated or lessened, according to the manner in which the slaves are treated.

Under their treatment in the United States, upon an original stock of 697,897, (six hundred ninety-seven thousand eight hundred and ninety-seven,) they have increased to 3,204,089, (three millions two hundred and four thousand and eighty-nine,) while by their treatment in Jamaica, they were reduced in one hundred and seventy-nine years, upon a stock of 851,500, (eight hundred fifty-one thousand five hundred) to 322,421, (three hundred twenty-two thousand four hundred and twenty-one.)

This statement needs no comment. It exhibits Slavery in the British Colony of Jamaica, tolerated by the Parliament of Great Britain for one hundred and seventy-nine years sufficiently revolting, without dramatic skill to render the picture still more repulsive.

Again; we may assume, that allowing the 850,000 (eight hundred and fifty thousand) imported, and the 1,500 (fifteen hundred) Spanish slaves, making 851,500; forty-five years of the one hundred and seventy-nine, of equal productiveness with the American slaves, would give an increase of 2,931,450, (two millions nine hundred thirty-one thousand four hundred and fifty.)

Here we have a loss of 2,931,450 lives destroyed in embryo, infancy, and maturity, in the time intervening between the capture of the Island by Admiral Penn and General Venables, in 1655, and the period of Emancipation in 1834;—a number nearly equaling the population of the United States, at the period of its dismemberment from the British Empire.

Further;—in the capture of the slaves, the march of the Koffle to the coast, and on the middle passage, the smallest estimate is ten per cent. loss, until the slaves are landed in the West Indies. We must therefore add 85,000 (eighty-five thousand) to the 850,000, (eight hundred and fifty thousand,) making 935,000, (nine hundred and thirty-five thousand,) requisite, during the whole period of slave importations, to land 850,000 in Jamaica.

This gives a grand total of 3,016,450 (three millions and sixteen thousand four hundred and fifty) that perished in one hundred and seventy-nine years; or in round numbers, 17,000 (seventeen thousand) annually.

It results from these facts and deductions, that the evils and fatal effects of Slavery, consist as much in the *manner* in which the slaves are treated, as in the *fact* of their being held in servitude.

The importation of slaves into the United States was not prohibited until the year 1808:—but very few were introduced; there were no sugar lands in the country; cotton was unknown as an article of commerce, and slaves were not wanted. The low estimate of ten per cent. loss on the importation of them into Jamaica, and the assumption that they were productive but forty-five years of the one hundred and seventy-nine, will more than balance the small number that were brought into the country.

A very important question presents itself here:—what is to be the future situation of the black man?—

The colored race have possessed a luxuriant soil, and balmy climate for unknown ages:—to these are added, now, the offer of civilization and its attainments, which they have never acquired. The capacity of the race for progress, will now be determined. The African family will decide for itself its position in the great family of mankind:—I say, decide for itself:—for it is not the acknowledgment of the independence of Liberia, by one nation, or another nation, or by *all* nations, that will elevate the people of that Republic to the desired point;—*that* must be achieved by intellect and labor.

The division of the human race, called Caucasian, or Anglo-Saxon, and its numerous subdivisions, will not dispense with the luxury of Tropical productions;—they cannot produce them—therefore, if the black man will not furnish them voluntarily, it is to be feared, compulsory means will be adopted to compel him.

It is then apparent, that the black can render the white race tributary to them—this is *now* to be decided, and *forever*, in Liberia. Colonization in Africa, therefore, is an experiment far more important than the mere question of manumission.

It is an auxiliary in the elevation of the colored race, by transferring to them the knowledge possessed by a race that has preceded them in the march of civilization and its concomitant arts and sciences. If the colored race adopt them, and join in their onward progress, they will then be placed on an equality. Emancipation alone will not effect it; it is but a minor object, the gift of others; and can only have conferred upon its beneficiaries, the opportunity of their ascending to equality. The colored man in his own domicil, and by his own energies must ascend to it. The facility is presented him, of emerging from the long and dark night of time in which he has been enveloped.

I have said, the crime of slavery consists as much in the manner, as the fact:—it is equally true of manumission. The merit of conferring it, and its value, depend upon the previous preparation for it. This is abundantly proved in the Island of Jamaica. It would be absurd, to suppose a person capable of understanding Algebra, who was ignorant of Arithmetic.

The Colonization Society, is in fact, an auxiliary to the elevation of the colored man. If it succeeds, it will guarantee the freedom of the colored race in North and South America, by deciding the long mooted question of the cheapness of free compared with slave labor; and thus rendering slaves valueless.

The psychological question that presents itself here, belongs to another department:—I will therefore, only add a sentence.

The native Africans have a plurality of local Gods; powerful, and as malignant as they are powerful. What then must be their sensations, when a knowledge of the true God is unfolded to their minds?—when they are made acquainted with a Deity, not confined to lakes or chained to rocks; and are taught that he is the friend of all?

The doctrine of equal civil and religious liberty after its rise, spread rapidly through wider regions than the "Roman Eagle overshadowed." It could not be arrested by fleets or armies, for it pervaded *them;* it was not stopped by seas or mountains, it passed over *them.* Like the magnetic influence, it spread from meridian to meridian; and like that subtle fluid, it promises to wrap the globe from pole to pole. But the zones of the earth give character to their inhabitants; and in the highest point of attainment to which the human family may progress, there will doubtless be a difference in the destiny of nations.

www.ingramcontent.com/pod-product-compliance
Lightning Source LLC
LaVergne TN
LVHW010152110826
845151LV00002B/492

* 9 7 8 1 4 2 5 5 3 7 8 3 8 *